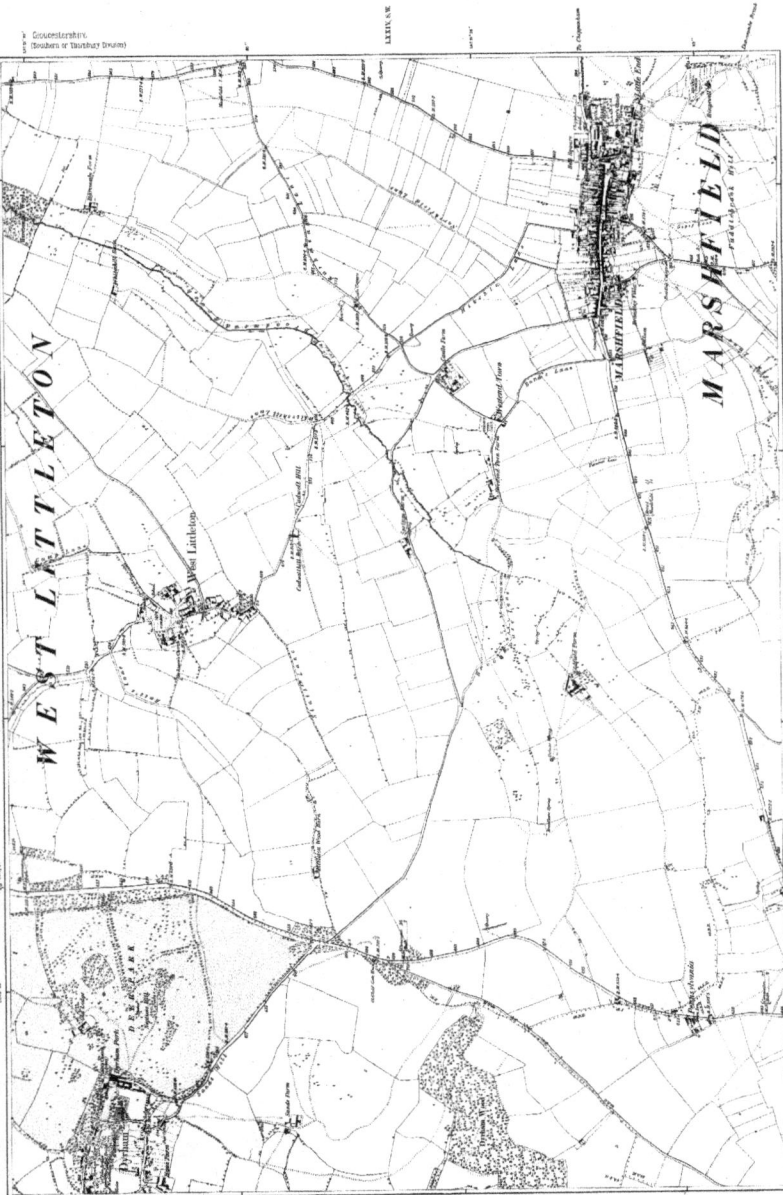

MARSHFIELD

WEST LITTLETON

West Littleton

Gloucestershire.
(Southern or Thornbury Division)

First published in the United Kingdom in 2025 by

The Choir Press

ISBN 978-1-78963-567-6

# THE GIRL FROM WEST LITTLETON

—

A Wartime Birth, Village Childhood,
and the Seasons of a Life

Cynthia Anne Smith

To the late Maggie Oxland for inspiring me to write.

Painswick Beacon and Turning Pages where I found Rowland Oxland who has led me on this journey.

Finally The Choir Press for all their help.

# PROLOGUE

—

This is the story of a young girl called Cynthia, born on the day in 1941 when one of Hitler's pilots, having discovered he still had a bomb left after their bombing raid on Bristol, got lucky finding Parnall's munitions factory in Chipping Sodbury. A huge disaster for those working in Parnall's that day, opposite the cottage hospital where Cynthia's mother gave birth to her.

The cottage hospital is now obsolete and turned into prestigious apartments. But what happened to Cynthia?

She was raised in a sleepy hamlet called West Littleton. 'Where?' did I hear you say? Just one mile from the highway of frantic life leading to Bath and Bristol, the A46. This was in the ideal, naive days when children were seen and not heard, lost in time, while Britain was still involved in the Second World War.

A move to Marshfield, just two miles away, was a time of awakening. The main road to London from Bristol went through the village, until they laid a bypass and the village returned to its delightful self again. The coaching house, where stagecoaches stopped to change horses in the days before buses and trains, returned to being just a pub. Otherwise not a lot changed. Everything moved with the seasons, winter being the best for us children, as compacted snow on Tog Hill rendered it impassable for the school bus!

As time passed boys seemed to disappear to do something called conscription. Two years later, they returned walking upright, with respect and good company. Girls grew swellings on their chests. Mothers and fathers became even more protective as these erstwhile unnoticed girls flowered into women. When they walked up the street gentlemen would doff their caps and say 'good morning'. It was an amazing feeling.

1

Now Cynthia found herself singing in the church choir for her friends' weddings. Friends who mostly left the village with their new husbands on a new adventure together.

So would you like to discover what life gave to Cynthia? If so, turn the page, sit comfortably, and I will begin.

# CHAPTER 1

—

There was a huge rumble, and panic set in. I was grabbed by the arm and rushed to the little house under the stairs, where my mother had put a mattress and blankets and pillows, some books and a torch. When a wailing sound occurred we would dive in for shelter. Not sure what was making the wailing sound, but it was enough to send everyone into their little houses to hide.

Mum realised she had not brought her handbag – shot to the kitchen to get it. On the way back the front door crashed open, and a man shouted for us to grab a blanket and jump in the lorry!

We rushed out into the street, where men were throwing us children into the lorry and giving the mums a hand to get in. With a great deal of revving of the engine we flew through the streets of Bristol and out into the countryside.

The poor lorry was tired and found it difficult to climb the steep slope I now know as Tog Hill. When we got to the top, the lorry's driver pulled off the road to give it a chance to get its breath back. We leaned over the side of the lorry and could see nothing but fire and smoke: the results of the German pilots' work. Bristol had been badly bombed again.

Eventually, the lorry dropped us off at my grandmother's house in Old Sodbury, then Mum took a deep breath. Aunt Rene, who lived with Nan (as I knew her), made a cup of tea, and we settled down in front of the big old open fire to try and get some sleep.

Early next morning, Dad came rushing in with a huge sigh of relief to see we had arrived safely. He was still in uniform and looked very tired, but a cup of tea seemed to help, and off he went to help build aeroplanes at Filton. 'They haven't found us yet' was his passing shot.

A lot of toing and froing went on while I stayed with Nan and Aunt Rene, who made it quite clear she did not like children. 'Messy things,' she could be heard to mumble as she cleared the table.

# CHAPTER 2

—

One day, I found myself wrapped up in a warm blanket and back in a lorry, this time with all our furniture and bedding and, best of all, a lovely big black dog. He was so warm and cuddly and gave an awful lot of kisses. I just loved cuddling his lovely warm body. His name was Bruce, and he was being trained to work with my father. I was not quite sure how that fitted in with making aeroplanes, but I was not going to make a nuisance of myself asking silly questions, as Mum and Dad didn't seem too happy.

We turned off the main road onto a lane. I whispered to Bruce, but he just licked my nose as if to say we were okay. We passed a farm with tractors in the yard, and I was glad we would not be meeting one of those. We passed open fields with cows in one; we went round a sharp bend, with the furniture readjusting itself in the back. We plunged down into a dip, rounded a corner and went up a slight hill, and there it was, all set out before us: West Littleton.

There were some cottages, but we drove past those. The village green was in the middle, with another farm and the village hall on the right, along with a church and village pond. Another farm up ahead, but Dad turned down a lane that bordered the green, then he stopped at the first house on the left and switched off the engine. Bruce and I sat very close, but I could feel he was wagging his tail.

Dad jumped out, and Mum got out and picked me up; Bruce jumped out after me. We all walked over to the door in the wall, which Dad opened to reveal a lovely big garden with a huge tree in the middle. We walked up to the front door, which was sheltered by a large canopy. Dad put the key in the lock and opened it.

There was a wide hall leading to the kitchen with two doors opening off it, one on either side. In the one on the left was a big room with a grand fireplace. 'We'll have this as the sitting room, only to be used on Sundays, high days and holidays,' Mum said. 'No shoes on the furniture, and you must sit still! And this is the dining room,' she added, crossing the hallway and opening the door.

The kitchen was a big room, quite dark, with only one window at the front. It had a huge fireplace with a range in it.

'We'll soon get that lit,' Dad said, opening a door to the right of the fireplace. Inside were two steps which led to a washing boiler and a brown sink, and a door to the garden. Another door in the kitchen led to the pantry.

A blanket was put on the flagstone floor by the window for me and Bruce, as well as some toys, while they started to unload the lorry. Somehow we just knew to stay put and not cause a problem.

A big surprise for me was the dining room, where we were sitting now. It didn't have a wall dividing it from the kitchen, so it was all open, and the window had a seat in it. If I pulled myself up on Bruce I thought I could just reach it. But that was for another day.

Dad had found a door in the middle of the back wall that opened at bedroom level, so it was easy to take in the bedding. Mum had brought groceries, and Dad had brought wood and coal. The lady who owned our house had left us a jug of milk, a bucket of water and some lovely brown eggs. 'That was nice of her,' said Mum.

So before too long everything was in place, the fire lit to boil a saucepan of water and a cup of tea made. Aunt Rene had made some sandwiches and a lovely sponge cake.

Hey presto! We had moved into the Old School House, West Littleton.

Dad jumped up and said he was taking the lorry back and he would be back before you could look round. He lifted me high to the ceiling with a big kiss for being a good girl, and a pat on the back for Bruce, who was to stay and look after us!

Mum set about unpacking boxes, and before Dad got back the plates and cups and saucers were all back on the dresser. The big scrub top table had been dusted off and a clean cloth put on, the dining chairs tidy around it and my highchair placed at the table. It looked just like home, just in another house.

The fire was going well. Mum decided to put the pie she had made in the oven in the hope it would be ready for supper. Groceries had been put away in the pantry, and the two old Windsor chairs placed either side of the fireplace, with two cushions all plumped up.

'There,' Mum said, picking me up. 'Welcome to our new home in the country. Let's hope Mr Hitler's pilots don't find us here.' She took off my hat and coat and jogged me up and down on her knee. 'You have been such a good girl today – thank you.'

She carried me upstairs, plonked me on the floor again and set about making the beds. 'This is your new room,' she said, glad to see Dad had put my cot together.

As she busied herself making up the cot, I realised it was a big room with two large windows. I managed to pull myself up as the windows had seats like downstairs, but I just couldn't see out of the window even standing on tiptoes.

My cot ready, Mum placed it against the wall between the two windows. She hung the picture I liked on the wall where there was already a hook, threaded some curtains on to the rings and hung the poles over the windows, then looked at the big bed in my room and pulled the counterpane over it. 'There,' she said, as she scooped me up, 'looks like home already. Let's go and make Mummy and Daddy's bed now.'

We crossed the landing, which now had a table with a lamp, and Mum set about making their bed. She hung the clothes in the wardrobe, found her book and placed it on the bedside table, and put the clock on Dad's side of the bed.

We had just got downstairs when we heard Dad's motorbike.

'How's that for timing?' Mum said, giving Dad a big kiss to welcome him home.

'Some good news,' Dad said cheerfully. 'I have been given two days' leave to move house,' and so life started in the Old School House, West Littleton.

The next day we explored the garden, with me in my pram. My parents parked the pram and looked around to discover there were still a few apples on the big old tree, and quite a lot of fallers surrounding it. Dad picked one, took out his pocket knife and cut a slice. It looked very green, as if it would be sour, but on eating his first slice he declared, 'It is delicious, try it,' so we all munched slices in turn and agreed it was indeed a lovely apple.

'I wonder if they make a good pie,' said Mum, gathering some in her apron. 'I will try later.'

The lawn, with a path down the middle from the front door, ran down a slight slope to a stone wall at the bottom. There was a gate in it to go out onto the village green. 'Do you suppose we have commoners' rights?' asked Dad.

There were goats tethered on the common, all four clean and very white, greeting us as they saw us in the garden. Bruce looked quite keen to say hello, but Dad gave a warning sound, and Bruce slinked away.

In the corner of the stone wall was a little house; this was our toilet and garden shed, where Dad had stored the wood and coal. It was quite pretty, with ivy climbing up the stone walls, and the slate roof shone in the autumn sunshine.

To the left of the sitting room window was a high bushy hedge boundary between us and what looked like the rest of our house, where the Robinson sisters lived with their brother Albert. Halfway down was a kind of gap where we could see through into their garden. Bruce was about to go exploring when Dad told him to stay; he obediently sat and peered into the garden instead.

'Looks to me as if I'm going to have to dig some of this lawn up and make a vegetable garden,' announced Dad, 'so that we can grow some vegetables. Perhaps if I do it now, roughly, the frost will break the soil down and make it easier to plant in the spring. What do you think?'

'Good idea,' said Mum. 'But could it just be half, so that Bruce and Cynthia have somewhere to play? And a clothes line, please, dear, maybe a priority.'

Birds were singing. The church bell tolled to call us to church, but not today.

# CHAPTER 3

—

Life at the Old School House felt happy and good. We found the nearest source of water was at Knight's Farm, across the lane and up the field to the dairy, where the pump was kept in its own little house and had a big handle to pump the water into our buckets. It was lovely cool water.

There it came again: a heavy rumble and lorries going past our house, heading to who-knows-where on down the lane. The lorries were carrying semicircular pieces of shiny metal, and a big digger and tractor were travelling with them. Whatever was happening, we would have to investigate, so when the lorries went back home I was put in my pram and off we all went.

The bottom of the lane was closed off by a gate, but Mum and Dad could see over the gate, and I could look through the bars. There were rows of sheds made from the shiny metal, and the stream had been dammed to make a big pond. We stared at the site, wondering what it could be. Was Farmer Knight going in for some kind of mass production?

On our arrival home a lady was coming down the lane towards us. She introduced herself as Mrs Blake, the owner of our house; she had brought us some eggs.

Mrs Blake came in for a cup of tea, and Mum and Dad told her how happy they were with the house. She was concerned by the lack of water supply, but Mum reassured her we were managing quite well and were getting used to grumpy Farmer Knight.

'We were wondering what was happening at the end of the lane,' said Dad. 'It all looks very mysterious.'

'Well,' said Mrs Blake, 'we have heard that Italian prisoners of war are being brought here. We're hoping they can help us on the farms in the village, now all the young men have gone to fight in the war.'

Mrs Blake said her goodbyes and pinched my chubby cheeks. 'Is Cynthia walking yet?' she asked.

'Oh, goodness, yes!' said Mum. 'She really is quite steady on her feet.'

Next day the rumbling noise came again while we were in the garden, and the lorries came again. This time, over the top of the garden door, we could see lots of men sitting in the lorries, all singing happy songs and wearing the same blue clothes.

\*\*\*

Mum wasn't at all happy being left in the house now Dad's leave was up, which meant another month on her own with me; even Bruce was going with Dad this time. The days were all right, but she didn't like the long dark nights. She got the oil lamps out, filled them with paraffin and trimmed the wicks, and fiddled with the radio, which made funny sounds before she tuned it to find something of interest. She made sure all the doors were locked and curtains drawn. Now we were safe!

The farmers and farm workers had been trained to guard us should the Germans land nearby. They had big sticks and pitchforks as weapons and marched up and down the lane. They turned the little turnpike house into a first aid centre and painted a big red cross on the roof. Being so far from Bristol and Bath, the probability of a fire engine getting to us in time was pretty slim, so all the farms and houses were supplied with a stirrup pump to put out a fire should one arise.

The ladies of the village got very enthusiastic in the spring, and used the stirrup pumps to spring clean their houses, cowsheds, dairies et cetera with whiting, making all the rooms bright and fresh-smelling. If you touched it, though, it would come off on your hands and clothes, so we made sure we stood upright.

# CHAPTER 4

—

The sound of marching feet and happy singing woke us to a lovely sunny day. Both of us still sleepy, Mum and I had a cuddle on the spare bed. We make a plan to make the best use of the day, not that I had much input.

With me holding Mum's hand, we went to the window. The marching feet had all gone, but a happy feeling hung in the room.

'Shall we go to see Mrs Blake?' Mum asked. 'She did ask us to call and collect milk on a regular basis, plus some more eggs.'

She got dressed and dressed me, and we went down to breakfast. The fire still had life from last night; it just needed some kindling and coal and it would burst into life, said Mum.

Suddenly there was a knock on the front door, so loud it made me jump. Standing there was a tall man all in black uniform, with a tall helmet, a shiny badge and a silver chain going into his top pocket. He asked Mum to identify who she was. He came in, pulled out a chair for Mum and himself, and told her her husband Leon Driver had been involved in a fatal accident.

He had had a surprise weekend off, and in his rush to get home on his motorbike in the darkness he had run into the back of a stationary lorry. A fixing on the lorry had pierced Dad's skull, and he was killed instantly.

Time just stood still. The policeman took his hat off and put it on the table. He made Mum a pot of tea, and asked if there was anything he could do; people to notify, perhaps? And did she have family nearby?

I looked at Mum. She was just staring at the wall. Whatever he had said did not make Mum happy.

Eventually Mum looked up at the policeman and asked which station he had come from.

'Chipping Sodbury' was his reply.

'Would it be possible for you to call on Mrs Tudor at the cottage on the Dog Hill, Old Sodbury, to give her the news, and to ask if I could come and stay to sort myself out? She's my mother. If my sister, who lives with her, could go to the public telephone box and telephone Mrs Blake – she has the number – with the answer, she can organise our transport.'

'Of course,' said the policeman. 'The army will be writing to you to give you more information, and maybe send someone to see you. I will notify them of your possible change of address for the moment.'

He picked up his hat and told me, 'What a good girl you are,' and took his leave of Mum, reassuring her he would call at Nan's. She closed the front door behind him, came back into the kitchen, picked me up, and gave me a big hug and cried and cried.

Eventually she sat down. She sat me on the table in front of her with my legs dangling down, wiped her tears, then held my hands and asked, 'What do we do now, with no Daddy, no transport, no money, and stuck out here in the sticks?' She gave me another big hug, and declared, 'We had better go and see Mrs Blake to get the answer from Nan.'

Realising we had not had breakfast, she went to the biscuit barrel and gave me a biscuit, and had one herself. She put our coats on and the guard round the fire, and we set off walking in silence; she held my hand.

Up the slight incline to the door into the farmyard, where we would usually walk through to the dairy to collect some milk and eggs. Mum picked me up to save me from the geese we knew would be waiting for us and would come rushing at us, necks stretched out, hissing. 'I think we had better go to the back door today.' So we followed the high garden wall past the barn door and the big bay window of the house, and walked down the short drive to the back door.

Mum gave a knock, and the familiar smiling face of Mrs Blake greeted us. 'Hello, good to see you, come on in.' She took my hand to help me over the threshold, and led us into a room looking out onto the courtyard and the farmyard behind. A fire blazed in the fireplace. She pulled out chairs for Mum and herself, sat down and plonked me on her knee.

Mum looked Mrs Blake in the eye and said, 'I have just received some devastating news.' She took a deep breath. 'Leon has been killed in a road accident.'

The shocked silence hung in the room as if forever.

'Oh! My dear soul, I am so sorry. When did it happen?' Mrs Blake asked, reaching out for Mum's hand. 'Is there anything we can do?'

'The policeman said he would call in to home to tell Mum, and I have asked if I can go to stay, as I don't think I can cope with this on my own. I also asked my sister to telephone you with their reply; I hope you do not mind.'

'Not at all; I will open the hall door so that we can hear the phone when it rings.'

Mrs Blake hitched me onto her hip and opened the hall door. 'Now, my dear,' she said, 'I will put the kettle on and call Barry. I am sure he will be able to take you home,' and she handed me over to Mum.

'Oh, I don't want to be a nuisance,' my mother said, panicking. 'I'll ring Mr Hendy from the kiosk.'

'It is the least we can do,' said Mrs Blake. 'Please keep in touch; we will be pleased to help.' She called for her husband.

'What's the emergency?' Mr Blake asked, striding into the kitchen. As he passed the doorway to the room we were in, he stopped. 'Hello, Mrs Driver, how are you? All settled in?'

Mrs Blake guided him into the room and told him the news.

'Oh! My dear soul, what happened?'

Mum related what the policeman had told her, trying so very hard not to cry.

The telephone rang and Mrs Blake rushed to answer it. 'Hello, Marshfield 231?' A pause, then 'Certainly, I will tell her,' and she replaced the phone. 'They are so shocked and want you to get there as soon as possible.'

Mrs Blake went into the kitchen and brought through the tea, poured three mugs and joined everyone at the table. 'I told Barbara you would take her down to Old Sodbury,' she told Mr Blake.

'Of course, no problem. What time would you like to go?'

'In about an hour, if that is all right for you. I'll just pack some clothes for us both. Bruce is still at the barracks, so he is safe. Perhaps you wouldn't mind checking the fire goes out, as I just banked it up.'

'No problem,' said Mrs Blake.

We walked home in silence, went upstairs. Mum plonked me on the bed and proceeded to put clothes in bags.

When we returned to the stairs Mum said, 'We're going to learn a new trick of getting up and down stairs.' She turned me around and placed me on the top step and showed me how to find the step behind me, with my hands across the step until my feet were firmly on the next step down. I soon got the hang of it and was pleased I was able to help Mum.

Once I was safely at the bottom, Mum went back up, gathered the bags and took them to the front door. She picked up her shopping basket and put food in from the pantry, then checked her handbag, wondering what she could need in the days ahead.

Mr Blake arrived at the front door and collected the bags; he put them in his big black car. Mum picked me up, gathered her handbag and gave Mr Blake the basket of food. She locked the door, then we got in the car and drove off to stay with Nan and Aunt Rene.

# CHAPTER 5

—

I cannot relate how the time passed. There were a great many days when Nan's house would be full of people who all seemed to know Nan and Mum and Aunt Rene, and at other times it would be full of strangers and men in uniform. The one thing that was constant was Nan and her comforting lap and the way her arm wrapped around me, keeping me safe.

I was aware something awful had happened to Dad, as he didn't come home any more, and people spoke of him in hushed voices. A sadness came over me every now and then as I missed him and Bruce, but I didn't know how to voice it.

My relationship with Aunt Rene was not a happy one. I realised quite early on she did not like children. My stay with them meant she had to look after me as well as Nan, and, even worse, I had to share Aunt Rene's bed. It was a large feather bed that looked huge with just me in it. I would make a dip in the feathers and try to lie still. My aunt was tall and slim, but I still managed to touch her and wake her. She would moan, say something about sodding kids and go back to sleep.

Nan came to the rescue and suggested that the camp bed in the box room may be the answer. The box room did indeed have a lot of boxes, which seemed to form another wall in the room. The little bed was very cosy, and if I left the door open a little I could hear my nan sleeping. In the mornings I would hear Aunt Rene go downstairs, then I could creep into Nan's bed for a cuddle.

My hair grew long, and at bedtime Nan would take bunches of hair and wrap them up in cloths: rags, she called them. Then in the morning I would have lovely curly hair that would bounce up and down as I walked.

On sunny days Nan and I would go and explore the garden, smell the flowers, pull out the weeds and ease the soil around some plants that had become compacted. Nan loved her garden, and I loved being with her.

She gave me a little fork, and a patch of garden that was for me. So started my love of gardening, but I was not too keen on some of the things that lived in the garden. The stinging wasps and bees would only hurt me if I went to hurt them, said Nan, and the beetles and earwigs helped keep the garden clean; ladybirds ate all the greenfly that would suck the life out of her flowers, but there seemed to be no good reason for the slugs and snails that would eat holes in new leaves.

But the things that frightened me more than anything were worms. The first time I saw one I went running to Nan, screaming. 'Is it a snake?' I remember asking.

'No, my love, that is a worm. They make little tunnels as they move through the earth, aerating the soil.' She picked me up and gave me a tickle. 'You are a funny one,' she said, laughing, but my dread of snakes is with me to this day.

Nan's house rose straight from the main road, and up steps too deep for me to walk up as yet. I remembered Dad would put me on his shoulders and dash across the road, making me laugh, if one of Mr Febry's fire-eating lorries came down the road. On rainy days I would watch for Mr Febry's lorries as they chugged their way up Dog Hill, with fire and smoke belching out of the little chimney in the middle of the roof.

Now Daddy no longer came to see us. There was no expeditions to let us explore.

# CHAPTER 6

—

**M**um had gone back to West Littleton by now, but I was still living at Nan's. I got used to the new way of life there.

Once you got up the steep steps from the road to the path at the top, it led you around to two big doors. The first one I never saw open; the second opened into the kitchen, which was always quite dim, as the tree opposite the door stole the light from the only window in this room. Behind the open door were a sink and draining board, then some wall and floor cupboards, and a table on the other wall. Opposite the door were the stairs, and a small window giving very little light as the garden outside wandered diagonally over half of it.

On the other wall was a dresser with all the china arranged on it, and the big door into the sitting room, a quite generous room with a huge fireplace that took almost the whole wall. The mantel shelf above it housed candlesticks, a clock, a selection of jars, tapers for the fire, and a large biscuit barrel. Above all this hung a large mirror.

On the two opposite walls were two big windows, one looking on to the road. The other seemed to rise out of the garden, with flowers growing right up to the window, and bumblebees bumped into the glass as they made their way between the flowers.

Flanking the fireplace were two big Windsor chairs with comfy cushions, one for Nan and one for Aunt Rene. Behind Nan's chair was a large oil painting of men in kilts fighting, and wounded men propped up. This had a big golden frame around it.

On the wall behind Aunt Rene's chair was a big window and the other door leading outside. Hanging on this door were two brass instruments, one of which my uncle Vin would come and take to church to play, then hang back on the door for another year. The other just stayed where it had been since my uncle Perce had died. His army hat hung next to it.

Nan sat me on her lap after supper and said Aunty Rene was going to be very busy this evening and we were going to watch her get ready.

'Is it another play she is in, Nan?' I asked.

'No, dear, this is for real.'

When Aunt Rene came in from the kitchen she was carrying a long bag and a box. The bag she put on the floor, and the box on the table. Out of the box she took brass cleaning materials; out of the bag she took a hat, a pair of gloves, a big piece of brass, white cleaning cloths, a bottle of white liquid, a tin of not-very-nice-smelling liquid, and an old but white towel.

The towel was laid on the table and everything else arranged on it. Aunt Rene proceeded to clean the gloves and the hat and the shiny piece of brass until you could see your face in them, and the white was so bright! She slid the towel to the other side of the table, with a warning for me not to go touching anything with my grubby hands. I instinctively sat on my hands, daring them to come out.

Aunt Rene took out a long pole, on which was a big golden piece of material with beautifully embroidered motifs. She laid this flat on the table, then, with a white-bristled brush that she had sprayed with a liquid, she carefully brushed the gold material. She left it to dry as she sank into her chair.

'That's a good job jobbed,' said Nan. 'It will do you proud tomorrow.'

While I had watched, Nan had put her rags in my hair. The milk that had sat warming on the hob was just right for making the Ovaltine, then it was off to bed for me and Nan. We slowly climbed the stairs and knelt by Nan's bed to say our prayers, then a big hug and kiss from Nan and a slide into my lovely cosy bed.

'Night night,' we both called.

'God bless,' said Nan.

# CHAPTER 7

—

Sunday morning broke with a cold but clear blue sky, and sunshine gave a dappled effect out of the sitting-room window. We had been woken early by Aunt Rene to get breakfast over and cleared away, vegetables prepared for lunch and the leg of lamb ready to go in the oven, all before ten o'clock so that Aunt Rene could prepare for the Remembrance Day service at Old Sodbury church. Everyone was to be assembled at the beginning of School Lane to begin the procession at 10.30.

The Old Sodbury brass band turned out in their best uniforms, and lots of people started to gather on the corner opposite Nan's house. A tall man rushed in, gave Nan a kiss and turned around to see a resplendent Aunt Rene all dressed up in the uniform she took such care cleaning the night before. 'You scrub up well, gal,' said the man, grabbing his brass cornet from the back of the door.

Aunt Rene wound the golden cloth round the pole and collected another pole from the long bag. With a 'bye' in unison they were gone, and silence fell on the room.

'Go and stand in the window, Cynth, and you will be able to see them march to church.'

Aunt Rene had joined the two poles together and had unfurled the golden cloth, which made a beautiful flag; she caught one corner of it between her fingers to stop it flying. The band struck up and they all marched to the church.

Nan was explaining what they were all remembering when the door opened, and in came Mum!

'What a lovely surprise,' Nan said as I ran to greet her.

'Lovely to see you,' Mum said as she came and gave Nan a kiss. She enquired of me whether I had been a good girl.

'Good as gold,' said Nan.

'I hope I have got a job helping Mr and Mrs Blake on the farm,' Mum said. 'It's picking up stones off the potato fields. Doesn't do a lot for your fingers,' which looked all sore and cracked, 'but they pay well: enough for me to buy a bicycle, which is how I got here today.' By now she was sitting on the floor with me on her lap. 'Mr Hendy, from the garage where I bought the bicycle, hopes to find me a seat for my bike, then I can take Cynthia with me. What do you think?'

'It sounds as if you are finally getting things sorted out, my dear,' Nan said. 'I am so proud of you. Give yourself a little more time, and get yourself some gloves for those poor old fingers and for riding your bicycle; winter is coming.'

Mum made up the fire and went to lay the table. 'Will Vin be staying for lunch?' she called from the kitchen.'

'Not sure, dear, so lay in case.'

I showed Mum the little book Nan had given me with my latest drawings of Bruce, and how I was coming on with my alphabet and numbers.

'That's the next thing, I suppose, getting her to school,' Mum said.

'Let's save that for another day, dear. I am sure it will all fall into place,' said Nan, with a lovely smile and a pat of her hand.

Aunt Rene and the tall man, who I now knew as Vin, returned from the parade very cold. We all budged up to give them space by the fire. Aunt Rene thanked Mum for getting lunch going; it smelt so good.

Vin announced he must get home to his girls, and with kisses all round he was gone. Aunt Rene went to change her clothes and put everything back in its home for next time.

Nan and Aunt Rene agreed that I should remain with them through the winter and see what the spring brought, and that Mum should come down as often as she needed.

# CHAPTER 8

—

F riday dawned, a wintry sunny day, and at breakfast Aunt Rene announced that if I was a good girl she would take me for a walk to collect Nan's homemade butter from Farmer Webb's farm. 'There will be no crying to be carried!' It all sounded so good, and I didn't usually cry to be carried, so I looked forward to our trip out.

Coats and gloves on we set off, my hair blowing in the breeze under the bobble hat Nan had knitted for me. Aunt Rene held my hand going down the steep steps and listened at the bottom for any traffic. The road clear, we ran across and up the footpath to some steps which were shallow and easy for me to climb. At the top was a wide path between high hedges; the leaves all falling off for winter allowed the sun to shine through.

After a while there appeared on the skyline a castle turret on a mound. 'Is that a castle?' I asked.

'No, love, that is the ventilation shaft for the Severn tunnel. It's where the trains go under the river Severn.'

We walked on in silence until suddenly there was a rumble, and a quick look of concern must have crossed my face.

'Well, there goes a train; fancy that. Look at the top of the castle and you may see smoke in a minute. Of all the years I have walked up here, that is the first time I have heard that.'

Then, sure enough, there was the smoke coming out. Well, that deserved a hop, skip and dance, and Aunt Rene joined in. Aunt Rene loved acting on the stage and had just begun rehearsals for the Christmas pantomime, so we used to test her on her lines. Sometimes she would get them all muddled up and give us a good laugh.

The hedgerows were covered in berries of all kinds, and little birds tweeted in their excitement at such a feast.

Then in the distance could be heard road traffic. Aunt Rene asked me to come and hold her hand as we were going to cross the road. We had to watch traffic from all ways, then the lights changed and suddenly a gap for us to cross. We ran as if there was a ghost behind us and got to the grass verge just in time.

Wades Farm was a low redbrick building set off the main road in the middle of the farmyard. Aunt Rene opened the gate into the farmyard, and I was waiting for the geese to come rushing at us, but thankfully there seemed to be no geese on this farm.

Aunt Rene opened the back door and called, 'Coo-ee!'

'Coming!' said a voice a good way off, then there she was: Mrs James, a cuddly lady in a white apron, holding some blocks of butter.

'I guessed it would be you,' she said, with a big smile. She looked at me curiously. 'And who might this be?'

'This is Cynthia, Barb's daughter.'

'Ah, yes, how are things going for her? Tough, I bet?'

Aunt Rene agreed.

'And how is Mum this week?'

The chat went on as I did my twirls to see if my skirt would come out, then stumbled because I was getting giddy. The look my aunt gave me was enough to say *stand still*.

The butter bought, the goodbyes said, we were back on the road again to go home. The traffic lights went red, and we dashed across the road to the safety of our lane and an uneventful return to Nan. I blurted out all that we had seen and heard, and Nan agreed it had been quite an adventure.

# CHAPTER 9

—

The topic of conversation this morning seemed to be planning for something called Christmas.

'Cynthia will understand all about Christmas this year,' said Nan, 'so maybe we could go to town a bit and make Christmas happen for her. I could make Christmas chains with her, and we still have the big bell, and maybe a small tree in a pot in the window. What do you think?'

'Okay,' said Aunt Rene, not too enthusiastically. She started to get into the swing of things while she cleared the breakfast table, though. 'You won't be able to have Christmas pudding this year, Mum, with your diabetes, or Christmas cake, so maybe I'll have a look in those Christmas magazines and see if there are alternatives when I go for the pensions on Thursday. We could order a bigger chicken and some of those newfangled sausages, chipo-something-or-other; would be fun.'

Aunt Rene left the room, and when she returned she was carrying a small tray. She put it down at the end of the table. It had a little lamp with a wick coming out of it, like the nightlights we used when we go to bed, along with a little jug with pale yellow fluid in, a glass tube about as big as your finger, and a box of matches. She lit the lamp, put the yellow fluid in the tube, then carefully held the tube in the flame of the lamp. After wiggling it about in the flame she declared, 'No change, Mum, so we must be getting something right.' She blew the light out, poured the yellow liquid back in the little jug, and left the house.

I sat by Nan and asked what Aunt Rene was doing.

'She was testing Nan's wee to see if it contained too much sugar,' Nan said, 'because Nan has something called diabetes, and if there is too much sugar we have to change what she eats.'

22

'Oh!' said I, none the wiser, really. I moved on swiftly. 'What is Christmas? It sounds quite fun.'

'Well, Christmas is a time we celebrate the birth of Jesus. You know when you say your prayers you say, "Gentle Jesus, meek and mild, look upon this little child"? Well, Jesus has a birthday on the twenty-fifth of December where people all over the world celebrate. We give each other presents, and families come together. It's a happy time for us all.' She put my hands together and kissed them.

'How long it is before Christmas?' I asked.

'Just ten days, so we'll be busy. It's Thursday today, so we must wait to see what Aunt Rene finds in the shop.'

I raced over to the window to watch for her return.

Suddenly there she was with arms full of bags. She came in and collapsed in her chair, bags falling to the floor, legs outstretched and arms flopping over the sides. 'Golly, that hill doesn't get any shorter,' she puffed, 'but I think I have done quite well.' She unbuttoned her coat. 'I have ordered logs and coal, and a large chicken, or small turkey. I found some recipes for puddings you could have. Packs of strips of coloured paper to make chains, and Mr Philips, who came into the shop, said he had a small Christmas tree he could put in a pot and bring with the accumulators in the week. I found some cards as well; Cynth could do her best colouring in for the aunts.' Then she firmly closed two bags: 'to be opened later', she said with a wink to Nan.

'Well, you have done well, dear,' Nan said, with a big thank-you!

\*\*\*

The next day, breakfast cleared and the testing done, in came Aunt Rene with a big tray which she unloaded onto the table, having put down a waterproof cloth first. There was a big bowl, butter, a bag of flour, a little jug of water, a rolling pin and small brush, and a jar of something black. She propped the tray up against the table leg and went to the kitchen, returning with two metal trays with sort of cups in them and a big oblong piece of thin wood, which was also propped against the table leg.

Nan put some coal on the fire and sat me on her knee.

'What is Aunty going to do?' I whispered, trying not to break Aunt Rene's concentration.

'She is going to make some mince pies,' Nan whispered back.

A tablespoon and knife were taken from the table drawer. Aunt Rene proceeded to count spoonfuls of flour into the bowl, then cut a block of butter into small pieces, added a pinch of salt and began playing with the mixture with her fingers until the butter had all disappeared. There were just crumbs in the bowl. She then measured spoons of water into the mix and played with it again until it formed a ball.

She set the bowl to one side and brought the board up onto the table. She scattered some flour all over the board, plonked the ball on the board, and started to roll the rolling pin all over it until the ball was reduced to a big sheet. Nan whispered that this was the pastry.

Aunt Rene took two cutters, and Nan whispered, 'Now, you count quietly how many rounds she cuts with the biggest cutter.'

'Twenty-four,' I declared when she stopped.

She placed the rounds one at a time into each of the cups in the trays. She then squeezed all the bits left over into a ball and rolled this out very thinly, and cut twenty-four smaller rounds.

Into the trays she added a spoonful of the black stuff Nan said was the mincemeat, then she put her little brush in the water and brushed it over the little rounds, pressing them tightly over the ones in the trays to seal them. She brushed them all over with some milk and turned to Nan to ask if she thought the oven would be hot enough.

'I think so, dear,' said Nan.

So she opened the big black door and slid the trays into the oven, then looked at the clock. 'I'll give them about thirty minutes,' she declared.

She pushed the remaining bits of pastry into a much smaller ball, put all the items she had brought in back on the tray and disappeared to the kitchen, to return with a round metal plate. She rolled out the pastry into a small round which she placed on the plate, emptied the remaining mincemeat into the middle of the pastry, gathered the pastry around it and set it to one side.

After a while there was the most delicious smell coming from the oven. A glance at the clock told Aunt Rene that she could look in the oven now, and out came two trays of golden mince pies. She put the tin plate in the oven, told us to remind her it was in there, and lifted the mince pies onto the cooling rack she had just brought in. This way of making mince pies has stayed with me to this day.

Sausages in a tray were popped into the oven, and the tin plate removed. The mince pies were stored in a big round tin when they were cold. 'Ready for Christmas,' Aunt Rene declared.

The sausages were cooked; we enjoyed them with mashed potato, peas and a delicious gravy. That cleared away, Aunt Rene brought in Nan's egg custard from the new refrigerator, and the tin plate with the leftovers of the mince pies. 'None for you, I'm afraid, Mum,' she said as she served the pie, because of the diabetes, 'but just enough for me and Cynth to try.'

My legs wriggling in anticipation, my spoon sank into the pie. How lovely was that? 'Thank you, Aunty Rene,' I said, licking the crumbs from the corners of my mouth.

'Time for a little nap now, I think; just forty winks,' said Nan. So I got up on the settee, took my slippers off, pulled the cushion down for a pillow and cuddled into my comfy blanket. Aunt Rene came to join us, and we all fell asleep replete.

Nap over, Aunt Rene brought in some crayons and some cards. 'Now I would like you to show us your very best colouring. Inside the lines if you can,' she said, opening the packet.

The cards were pictures of a jolly-looking man with a sack with toys spilling out. Aunt Rene suggested his big coat and trousers should be bright red and passed me the red crayon.

'I think I would like a go at this' she said, picking up a crayon and settling down to colour. 'These will be happy Christmas cards to give to your aunts, and my sisters.'

The light soon faded, so Aunt Rene lit the oil lamp, and we continued with our task.

\*\*\*

The next day was a cooking day again. This time butter and sugar were placed in the big mixing bowl, and Aunt Rene seemed to get very cross and beat the butter and sugar until they changed colour to pale cream. She then added eggs, one at a time, and proceeded to beat the living daylights out of that. She counted spoons of flour into a sieve and shook it by banging it against her hand until all the flour had gone through, then, with a metal spoon, she gently folded the flour into the cream mixture.

Next she greased a medium-sized basin and two sandwich tins and divided the mixture between them, then with a knife she spread the mixture until they were all level. Nan having made sure the oven would be hot by banking up the fire. Aunt Rene put the two tins in the oven, then took some paper from the cereal box and wrapped it around the basin. She tied some string around it and put the basin in a pan of hot water Nan had waiting on the hob.

A cup of tea later, the two tins came out of the oven and were turned upside down onto the cooling rack. Aunt Rene took the basin out of the steamy water and declared, 'There, that is the cake and pudding done, much quicker than normal. Hopefully that will do the trick, instead of the fruit-laden pudding and cake we usually have.' The two sponges had been stored in a big round tin.

'When is Christmas?' I asked.

'In two days' time,' came the reply, 'so lots to do!'

After lunch and our naps, Mr Philips came with the new accumulators, a Christmas tree in a pot, groceries, and meat from the butcher. 'I said I'd be calling here, so I helped with the deliveries.' He loaded the accumulators onto the table. 'Be able to listen to the King now,' he said jovially. 'Where would you like the Christmas tree?'

'On the table in the window, please,' said my aunt, while I stood close to Nan, trying not to be in the way. 'That is so helpful, thank you. Will you have a cup of tea? Kettle's on the boil.'

'No, thank you; better be on my way to get home before dark. Happy Christmas!' he called as he left the house.

Aunt Rene flopped into her chair. 'Where am I going to put all this?' she asked, spreading her arms.

'Well,' said Nan, 'the new fridge should take a lot of it, and the fruit could go in the silver punch bowl. That should look Christmassy, as we won't be making punch this year. Swap the accumulators around in the radio already for carols from King's College.'

I did feel sorry for Aunt Rene, who had to do all the work.

After tea we sat at the table and Aunt Rene brought in the packs of paper to make chains. That was good fun as soon as I got the hang of how to link them and not to lick all the glue off them.

When the chains were done Aunt Rene hung them on hooks on the beams across the room, and put the big bell in the middle, which was fun as she had to crawl on the table. She brought in another box that jiggled as she walked. 'Now, Cynthia, if you could hand me things from the box I will hang them on the tree while I balance on this stool.'

This sounded good fun, thought I.

'There,' declared Aunt Rene, as she put the angel on the top of the tree. 'Christmas has arrived!'

Nan and I clapped our hands, and she took a bow.

\*\*\*

Next morning, when I crept into Nan's bed, she told me today was Christmas Eve. She said that Aunty Rene would be very busy today, and that my mother would be coming to stay for Christmas Day tomorrow. It all sounded very exciting. I cuddled down and we both had another little sleep.

When we finally woke up and got dressed, Aunt Rene could already be heard busy downstairs. She was making up the fire and cleaning the fireplace, and taking out the ashes, which she would put on the path to the privy so that we wouldn't slip on the frosty surface.

'Thought you two would never come down. I have made boiled eggs for breakfast as a treat; they'll be good for your diabetes,' she said as she held bread on the toasting fork in front of the fire. The smell was lovely.

Nan put some butter on a slice for me and cut it into strips, which she called 'soldiers' for dipping in your egg. I watched as she ate hers and followed her. It was delicious, and I was sorry when it was all finished, as it was a fun thing to do.

The table cleared, testing done, washing-up done, Nan made up the fire. 'Your mummy will be cold when she comes in after riding her bicycle,' she said.

I, not knowing what to do, hopped on one leg, then the other.

'That's enough hopping around,' declared Aunt Rene, carrying a loaded tray. I quickly sat on the settee, out of the way.

Nan moved the kettle over to heat up, and Mum arrived all hot and cold, with a drip on the end of her nose. I put my arms out for a hug, but Mum said she would take her coat off first.

'Oh, that's good timing,' said Aunt Rene. 'Just in time to do the sprouts.'

'Oh, good, I hoped I would be of some use,' said Mum.

A cup of tea was made. Mum warmed her hands round the cup, and talked to Nan and Aunt Rene about all her news while she sat on the floor in front of the fire. I stood close to Nan and listened, but nothing made very much sense to me. Then Mum turned to me and asked, 'Have you been a good girl for Nan and Aunty Rene?'

I nodded, and Nan pulled me closer and said, 'Good as gold.'

I pointed to the tree and the chains.

'It all looks very Christmassy,' said Mum.

'Well, the stuffing and sprouts aren't going to get done if we sit doing nothing,' said Aunt Rene, pushing the bag of sprouts in Mum's direction.

Nan brought a bag up from beside her chair. 'Now, we must find you a black stocking to hang up for Father Christmas.'

'Why would Father Christmas need a black stocking?' I asked.

'Because if we have been good he will leave us little gifts to say Happy Christmas.' She brought out her darning mushroom, a book of darning needles, and three dark lisle stockings which all had a hole in the toe. So Nan darned the holes, and delved in the bag again until she found a black stocking for me. Then she took a peg and hung the stockings on the little line under the mantelpiece, to the side of the fireplace. I jigged my knees in excitement, not knowing really what was going to happen, but it sounded fun.

Stuffing, sprouts and potatoes all prepared, Aunt Rene took them back to the kitchen and returned with soup bowls, crusty bread and butter. She put the soup on to heat through, and cut thick slices of crusty bread. Nan put some butter on my slice, and we all laughed and joked with each other as we ate.

'Time for that nap,' said Nan, so I got on the settee with my blanket and made room for Mum, and we all had a nap.

When we woke up Aunt Rene pulled the curtain to stop the light shining out, as war was still happening. Then she lit the lamp, and it was all cosy and warm with the tree ornaments twinkling in the light from the fire.

'Now I had better see if I can make a Christmas cake appear,' said Aunt Rene.

She came back from the kitchen with the big round tin, and some packets on a tray. She put some butter and white powder in a bowl, and began beating it as if very cross.

'Shall I have a go?' asked Mum, taking over the bowl and beating like mad. She held up the spoon and let the creamy mixture drop into the bowl. 'How's that?'

'Looks good,' said Aunt Rene, picking up a jar of her strawberry jam and rolling back the greaseproof paper on top. She lifted out a spoonful and spread it over one layer of sponge, then she put a big spoonful of the cream mixture on top of the jam and put the other sponge on top. The whole cake was placed on a shiny cake board.

The remaining cream Aunt Rene spread over the top of the cake. She took a fork and made little peaks all over the top. Then she put a cake frill around the outside, and fastened it with a scraping of cream from the bowl.

From a tin she took out a tiny Christmas tree, which she placed on the cake. Next came a little house she placed under the tree, then a little Father Christmas with a sledge loaded with pretend parcels.

'That looks fantastic,' said Mum.

'Good enough to eat,' said Nan.

Aunt Rene turned the cake tin upside down over the cake and returned all the things to the kitchen.

'Shall we invite Nora to join us?' asked Nan, when Aunt Rene had come back. 'She is all on her own.'

'Good idea,' said Aunt Rene, who went off with a torch.

When she came back with Aunt Rene, 'Aunt' Nora from next door was pleased to see that I was still up. She said how she missed seeing me and Nan in the garden; we looked such friends.

Nan said she didn't think the carol singers would be around this year.

'Well,' said Mum, 'we could sing carols together. What shall we sing?'

Mum loved singing, and started the ball rolling with 'Once in Royal David's City'. They all seemed to remember the words, and even I was getting the hang of the tune.

Aunt Rene poured three glasses of sherry, and Nan made our Horlicks. Mum struck up 'O Little Town of Bethlehem'. Then after a while it was 'Away in a Manger', which I remembered as Nan had been teaching it to me.

Nan and I climbed the stairs hand in hand and changed into our nightclothes. We knelt by Nan's bed and said our prayers. It still felt funny not to pray for Daddy anymore. We gave each other a kiss goodnight and I slid into my cosy bed. Mum came up to say goodnight, and that tomorrow would be Christmas Day; she was all excited. We went to sleep to the sound of carols being sung quietly, and the rustle of paper.

*\*\**

Next morning I woke to feel something heavy on my bed. I rubbed my eyes and struggled to sit up.

I looked across at Nan, who was peeping over her bedclothes to see me. I saw the black stocking on my bed, and a lisle stocking on Nan's bed. I waited for her to put a finger to her lips for me to be quiet, but she didn't.

'I think Aunt Rene is up already,' said Nan. 'Would you like to come into bed with me? Can you manage your stocking?'

I got out of bed and struggled with my stocking as it slid along the floor behind me, then hopped under the covers with Nan, who pulled the stocking up onto her bed. Sticking out of the top was a black and white panda, which I gave a big hug.

Nan opened one of her parcels to see a paperback book. 'Oh! That looks interesting,' she said, putting it on the bed and delving for another. Out came a small box of chocolates, especially for diabetics, said Nan.

'Your turn,' she said as I delved into my stocking and pulled out a small parcel.

I ripped the paper off quickly to find a brand new box of crayons. 'Oh, look, Father Christmas has brought me some new crayons. My others were nearly all worn away.'

Nan rummaged in her stocking again and came out with an orange. 'Where did he find one of those in wartime?'

Now my turn. I came out with a long rolled-up parcel. When undone, it was a new colouring book.

'That is the end of my stocking,' said Nan, 'but you still have lumps in yours.'

I put my arm in and found an orange like Nan's and a pink sugar mouse. I would save the mouse and orange until later, as I could smell that Aunt Rene and Mum had breakfast on the go.

We have special clothes to wear today. There on the bed was a lovely red dress for me, and a black velvet skirt for Nan with a pretty red jumper. We got dressed and brushed our hair, I picked up my new panda and we went downstairs.

'Happy Christmas,' said Nan as we entered the sitting room.

'Happy Christmas!' came the reply in unison from Aunt Rene and Mum. There was a lovely smell of cooking, and under the tree were presents all wrapped in Christmas paper.

'Father Christmas came,' said I, all excited.

'He came to us as well,' said Mum and Aunt Rene, holding up their half-empty stockings.

We had a jolly breakfast with everyone seeming happy. Except I felt a change in Mum, no hugs and kisses now; perhaps she was tired.

We all sat around the table after breakfast had been cleared away, and Aunt Rene handed Nan a parcel. She read the label on the parcel and handed it to me. Then other parcels were handed out until we all had a parcel in front of us. 'Ready, get set, go!' said Nan, and we all started to open our parcels.

Mine revealed a fine tweed jacket and trousers from Mum. She excitedly held the coat up and measured it across my shoulders. 'I think that is going to fit fine, and with room for a warm jumper underneath.'

The next parcel was a warm hat that covered my ears and buttoned under my chin, from Aunt Rene. Mum tried it on me. 'That fits perfectly,' she said to Aunt Rene. A nudge from Mum reminded me to say thank you.

The next parcel for me was a warm scarf from Nan to match my pompom hat. I gave her a big hug and a thank you.

Then one last present, again from Mum, was a lovely little pair of warm leather gloves. She pulled one onto my hand. 'Lovely,' she said, with a big smile. 'Now you are all set up to travel with Mum on her bicycle.'

The presents all opened, the table was cleared of paper, and presents were left in tidy heaps on the settee. The wireless was turned on for carols. Attention once again returned to the preparation of the Christmas lunch. Mum and Aunt Rene were busy round the fire, with things going in and out of the oven.

'Better come and sit on Nan's knee with all this activity going on,' Nan said, hoisting me up onto her knee. 'Weren't those lovely presents? Clever old Father Christmas.'

Eventually the toiling stopped. The table was laid and looking very festive with sprigs of holly, napkins folded into pyramids, silver shining. Nora from next door had joined us, and we were invited to sit. The smell of all the different foods steaming from the dishes was very inviting.

Aunt Rene took a big knife and sliced thin slices of meat from the chicken, then added roast potatoes, roast parsnips, Brussels sprouts, buttered carrots, bread sauce and gravy. My little plate was piled high.

Everyone served, Nan said a little prayer, raised her glass of water and wished everyone a happy Christmas.

'Happy Christmas!' we all replied.

Silence then filled the air as everyone tucked into their Christmas lunch.

Eventually Mum said, 'There were no crackers to be found anywhere this year, thanks to Mr Hitler.' So everyone started telling jokes that would have been in the crackers, and we all had a good laugh.

Main course finished, the table was cleared. Aunt Rene returned with the sponge in a basin she had steamed earlier. She turned the pudding out and stuck a piece of holly in the top. When she cut a slice through it, out came ice cream from the middle.

'How did you do that?' asked Mum, all of us surprised.

'Well, that's my secret,' said Aunt Rene. 'Mum not being able to have rich fruit pudding, I looked through the magazines in the shop, and this was an alternative. I hope it's okay.'

Everyone tucked in and agreed it was a lovely surprise.

Replete from our meal, we all sat round the fire and told stories of past Christmases and the fun my mum used to have with her brothers and sisters, all six of them growing up at the Old Mill.

# CHAPTER 10

—

It was sad to see Mum leave after all the fun and games of
Christmas. I watched as she wheeled her bicycle down the steps
to the road, listened for traffic, crossed the road and started to
walk up the hill. She looked so lonely and sad that I wanted to give
her a big hug.

'This is a new year,' said Nan, 'and soon you will be going to
school, so we had better make sure you know your ABCs and get
you reading properly.'

I had mixed feelings about school. The idea of having children
to play with sounded fun, but all these things we had to learn and
remember were quite a challenge for me. I would often slip off into
a daydream about something or other and not concentrate on what
Nan was saying.

The outings to Wades Farm seemed to be regular now, which
was lovely, except my hair, now quite long, would get knotty bobbing
up and down as I walked and skipped my way along the path. Aunt
Rene, having taken over the brushing, was not as gentle as Nan. So
there was a lot of complaining, which seemed to give Aunt Rene a
lot of pleasure, until the job was done.

Mum came down again the next weekend and thought maybe
I could cope with helping her at home while she went out to work
at the farm. She had made enquiries about me starting school, but
they seemed very reluctant to put on transport for the three-mile
journey to and from Marshfield, where the school was. If the school
changed its mind about transport, though, it would make sense to
have me at home with Mum.

Nan seemed reluctant to let me go, but she understood what
Mum was trying to do. So it was decided to have a test run to see
whether I would be a good girl in the new seat on Mum's bike.

I was all dressed up in my new outfit, with my warm hat and leather gloves, and we prepared to set off for somewhere I had heard my family talk about: the Old Mill. 'If I can get up the hill there to Doddington crossroads, it will save me wobbling about on the main road up to Cross Hands,' said Mum.

They all seemed to agree this was a good idea, so off we went, me in my little seat and Mum up front pedalling. She braked gently as we were going down Dog Hill. At the bottom Mum took a sharp left into Chapel Lane, past some houses, then it was hedges both sides of the road.

Suddenly Mum took a sharp right down a lane. She came to a stop outside a black and white, timber-framed house. It looked very cosy snuggled into the land with its white-painted brick buttresses gently holding it upright, a warm glow coming from the windows.

'This is the Old Mill,' said Mum, with a nostalgic smile on her face. 'This is where Mummy grew up with my two brothers and three sisters. We were very happy here, paddling in the stream.' The stream still meandered through the orchard with its gnarled fruit trees, then flowed under the bridge to who knew where.

She stood daydreaming for a while, with the bike and me balanced between her legs. Then with a sigh she was back on the bike and heading back up the road, which was now becoming steeper. Eventually Mum got off the bike and pushed it and me up the hill, until we came to some cottages, where Mum stopped and surveyed the scene.

Deciding that was far enough for one day, she turned the bike around, got back on and freewheeled back down the lane with her feet off the pedals. 'Whee!' she called, with the wind blowing in her hair.

We were soon back to Dog Hill and a walk up to Nan's house. Mum lifted me off the bike and held my hand, then we ran across the road together. My legs were now able to get up the steps.

Nan was pleased to see us back with our rosy cheeks, and to hear I had been a good girl on our visit to the Old Mill.

'Those were some happy days, Mum, weren't they?' said Mum.

'Thankfully they were for you all,' Nan said, 'but there were bittersweet memories for me, your father being killed in the war. Then brother Perce, who had lived with us. Then happiness meeting and marrying Frank Tudor, only for the war to take him as well. Thank goodness we had the joy of Rene before he left us.'

'But we had the great joy of Marie's wedding, and all the fun and laughter we had at that. Happy memories.'

'Sadly I just could not make the farm pay, and, no men left to help, I had no option but to sell. It's a good thing Nora took pity on us and gave us half her house, so we were still able to be together.'

We had a cup of tea and a slice of Aunt Rene's sponge, with the family still reminiscing round the warm fire.

'Well,' Mum said eventually, 'what do you think of Cynth coming home with me? She is a good girl, thanks to you both, and I think we will manage at home. She is very helpful, and she'd be able to come up to Mrs Blake if she got into difficulty or just wanted some company.'

The look on Nan's face was one of sadness. She hugged me close and said how she would miss me, and told Mum to take great care of me; I was a very precious soul. 'Stay tonight and have Sunday lunch with us, then you will have the energy to do the journey.'

Mum agreed and said she would pack up her clothes in the morning, and so it was decided.

# CHAPTER 11

—

The clothes packed and strapped to the bike, a food parcel loaded on the front, my lovely new suit on with my hat and gloves, the inevitable moment came. A big kiss and hug from Nan with a promise from me to be a good girl, and we were off with waves goodbye. 'See you soon' rang in my ears.

Poor Mum seemed to have to pedal hard to move us along the road, up the hills and down again, this time keeping her feet on the pedals. It was beginning to get dark when we turned down the lane and came to our home.

Mum wheeled the bike right into the hall and closed the door quickly behind us to keep out the cold. She lifted me out of the seat, undid both the parcels and went into the kitchen. 'Now to get the fire going,' she said, 'before we freeze to death.'

She put the bags on the table and went into the little oven of the range to bring out some kindling wood. She scrunched up some paper and put it in the grate, followed by the kindling, then a small log and some coal from the coal hod. She struck a match and, hey presto, the fire leapt alive. 'There; we shall soon be nice and cosy,' she said, taking off my hat and gloves and unbuttoning my jacket, with the advice to keep it on until the room had warmed up.

I remembered the day we had moved in and the warmth of Bruce. I walked over to the window and was surprised I could now look out of it.

There was still some water in the big water bucket. Mum ladled some into the small saucepan and put it on the trivet over the fire, then came to the table to unpack the food parcel Aunt Rene had prepared for us. She put most of the food away in the larder, after leaving the sandwiches and sponge on the table to have for our tea when the saucepan boiled.

Mum trimmed the oil lamp, lit it and went up to check the lamp on the landing. She came down with two hot water bottles. 'I think we are going to need these tonight.'

Tea made and more water put on to make hot water bottles, we sat down to eat. Mum must have been tired after all that pedalling, but she didn't say anything, She pulled the two Windsor chairs near the fire and opened the stairs door a little to see if the heat would warm the bedrooms at all, then she put the radio on and twiddled the knobs until she found the programme she was looking for.

'In the morning,' said Mum, 'I will have to go to work helping Mrs Blake, so I am going to bank the fire in to keep you warm, and you must promise Mummy you will not touch it. I will put the fire guard round to keep you safe. I'll leave you a sandwich and a glass of milk for your lunch, and I will be home by 3pm.'

***

The sun was shining when we woke up to the familiar sound of the singing soldiers, but there was a white frost on the garden.

'Looks as if it could be a sunny day, but cold, so please stay in the warm,' Mum said. 'I have got the books for you to do your colouring, and maybe some number work, like Nan did for you.'

I was all bundled up in my long woollen socks, warm skirt and two jumpers, so I felt nice and warm. Mum busied herself preparing to go out and leave me safe.

'When you need the toilet, use the gazunder upstairs, okay?' Mum squeezed my cheeks. 'It's so nice to have you home with me,' she said, putting on her coat, then a close of the door and she was gone.

I stood looking at the door for I don't know how long. I blinked and realised I was feeling cold, so I hurried to the kitchen and the warm fire, well banked up with potato peelings. All I could hear was the ticking of the clock on the mantelpiece. Nan had been teaching me to tell the time, so I tried to remember what she had said. When the little hand is on the number, the big hand goes all the way round. Luckily this clock struck the hour and half-hours, so if I wasn't watching it still told me the time.

I cuddled up in the big old chair and watched the shapes the flames made, and came to with the clock chiming; I had nodded off. I tried to count the chimes. The little hand was on the 12; had I really slept that long? I wished Bruce was here.

I slid out of the chair and climbed up to the table. Time for my sandwich and glass of milk, I thought. Next was some colouring, trying to keep inside the lines, but it didn't seem to go so well without Nan by my side.

I made my way up to my bedroom to use the gazunder, and remembered I had slept in the big bed last night, as my cot was now too small. It had been really warm and cosy with the lovely warm eiderdown on top. I climbed back into the bed and cuddled under the covers, and wondered what Nan was doing now. Probably nap time.

Next thing I knew, Mum was gently pulling the bedclothes back. 'Golly, you gave me a scare,' said Mum, 'when I couldn't find you downstairs.' She took my hand and we went down.

'I have to collect some water from the farm; would you like to come with me?' she asked, getting my hat and coat.

Off we went across the lane, through the gate and up the field to the little house where the pump lived. It had a big handle, which Mum pumped up and down to fill the buckets, not quite full so as not to spill any on the way back.

We were just leaving when a big man with a florid face showed up, on his way to the little house. 'Well, who is this?' he asked. 'Not little Cynthia, is it? My, she has grown; she'll soon be able to fetch the water for you.' He chuckled, turned his back and went on his way.

'That is Farmer Knight,' said Mum. 'He isn't usually as jolly as that; you must have cheered him up.'

With our buckets of water, we walked carefully back to our house, closed the door quickly behind us to keep out the cold, took our coats off, and Mum lit the lamp. 'Apparently they forecast snow,' said Mum, 'so I hope I can get a lift with Mr and Mrs Blake tomorrow to get some groceries in.'

Mum got busy stoking up the fire and preparing our evening meal. I knelt on the chair that she had turned round for me and watched her.

***

We heard the marching soldiers singing, and so the day began. 'Can't have snowed overnight,' said Mum, 'as we can hear the soldiers' boots, so I must take my purse in case I can get to Marshfield.'

Sandwiches made and glass of milk poured, Mum gave me a big hug and, with a promise from me to be a good girl, she was gone running out of the door.

I stood wondering what to do and thought of how I had helped Nan and Aunt Rene. Mum had cleared our cereal bowls from breakfast, so I put my sandwiches and milk on my chair, took the tablecloth outside and shook the living daylights out of it like Aunt Rene did, then closed the door behind me and put it back on the table.

I thought I would do some colouring, so I got my books and crayons and busied myself for a while. I then remembered how Aunt Rene used to give me a duster and ask me to dust the rungs of the chairs and table legs, as I was nearer the floor! So I found a duster and did the dusting.

Now what could I do? Have my sandwich, I thought. Taking my sandwich, I climbed onto the window seat. Sitting on the big cushion, I could see out into the garden and over the wall to where the goats were having their lunch on the village green. The sun was shining but made long shadows from our house, and the frost still glistened.

I took my plate to the scullery, as Mum called it, and saw that the little bucket of water was empty. I could go and get some water for her; that would help her. So I put on my hat and coat and new welly boots and, with the bucket, set off to get some water. I crossed the lane and, carefully closing the field gate behind me, walked up the slope to the pump house.

I pumped the handle as Mum had done, but no water came out. I kept pumping, but no joy. I was just wondering what to do when Farmer Knight put his head round the door. 'The pump has packed up for some reason; you will have to go to the well in the village pond,' he said.

I picked up my bucket and went back down to the lane. I looked in the direction of the village pond and thought I would have a go.

When I got to the pond I could see the stone sides of the well, but to my horror it was covered in a green weed, and, what was more, a frog was very definitely guarding it. I stood fixed to the spot for quite a while, wondering what to do, and then a voice came over my shoulder to ask if he could help.

A tall man with a moustache and wavy hair knelt down beside me as I explained my dilemma.

'Well, now,' he said, standing up, 'we had better find a stick, then we can scrape off the weed and persuade Mr Frog that we mean him no harm. Then we can dip the bucket in the water and fill it for you. How is that?'

I just looked at his smiling face, said, 'Thank you,' and went in pursuit of a stick.

Stick found, weed cleared, Mr Frog hopped off and we were able to fill the bucket with water.

'Now, where are you taking this bucket of water, as I think it is going to be just too heavy for you?'

So I showed him the house, and we walked off together to the back door. Inside he put the bucket down and thought for a moment, then he said, 'Is Daddy not at home?'

'No,' said I, 'he has died.'

'Well,' said he, 'I think Mummy is going to want this water boiled before she can use it, so how about we put this good water in the big bucket into saucepans and the kettle and this big bowl?'

I nodded my head, as it made sense.

'Then we can fill the big copper with the pond water so that Mummy can boil it and make it safe for you to use. They forecast snow, so that would help her, wouldn't it?'

I nodded again vigorously, pleased I would be helping Mum.

So we set off for the well again, now with two buckets. 'Mummy will be surprised when she comes home,' the man said.

After three trips the boiler was full.

'Now, where does Mummy keep her firewood?' the man asked.

'In the shed down the garden,' I said enthusiastically.

Off he went, returning with his arms full of wood. He put some ready for the boiler, then asked where Mum kept her kindling, so I showed him the small oven in the range. He noticed the coal hod and the log box were quite low, and said, 'I think I will just fill these for Mum; that will help, won't it?' Off he went again, and he quickly returned with the wood and coal.

I was just shaking his hand, and thanking him very much for all his help, when Mum came in.

She looked very cross and pulled me to her, enquiring of the man what he thought he was doing.

'I am so sorry to give you alarm,' he said. 'I was just trying to help your daughter.'

'What were you doing, going out? I told you to stay in' she said, shaking me. I was very frightened, and wanted to run away to my Nan and her safe lap, but Mum's hand was very firmly on my shoulder, and I was going nowhere.

After what seemed ages Mum calmed down and the man asked if he could make her a cup of tea.

'I am very sorry,' she said. 'It was such a shock seeing a strange man in the house and my daughter on her own, I forgot my manners. Thank you so much for all your help. Having the pump not working is a real pain; let's hope it will soon be mended. I can make the tea; would you like a cup?'

So we all went into the kitchen, made the tea and warmed ourselves by the fire.

'I had hoped to get to Marshfield today to get some stores in, as they forecast snow, so we will have to do a quick trip on the bike before the shops close,' she said, looking at me.

The man, who I now knew as Harold, offered to take her as he had a car parked in the village, and he had to get one or two things for his mother, with whom he had been living since his wife had died. Mum thanked him very much and asked if he was sure, while putting our hats and coats on once more. We walked to the car, and were soon on our way.

Shopping done, we were back home in no time. With the groceries unpacked, Harold took his leave of us, but not without asking if he could come again. Mum looked at me and asked if I would like that, to which I nodded my head vigorously. 'Well, that's agreed,' she said, and she thanked him once again for all his help and kindness.

Mum sank into her chair, legs outstretched, like Aunt Rene after a tiring day. 'Whatever made you think you could carry buckets of water, my girl? My heart misses a beat every time I think about it.'

'I just wanted to help,' I said.

'I think if you feel you are able to carry buckets of water, we had better see if we can get you to school.'

\*\*\*

Next morning we heard the soldiers singing but didn't hear their feet. Mum came in and drew the curtains, and there was snow. When she opened the curtains behind my bed the snow was all over the window; you couldn't see out.

'Well, no going out for you today, young lady,' Mum said, dressing me with purpose. 'Do you hear me? It is so important you do as I ask so that I can keep you safe.'

I took in her concern.

The usual morning preparation was taking place, as Mum prepared to go to work, when we heard shovelling coming from outside the landing door. Mum ran upstairs to my bedroom window to see Harold scraping snow off the steps.

'I think it's probably easier if you come out this way,' he said. 'The front door and porch are filled in with snow.'

Mum put the lamp in the window and moved the table into my room, then he was able to come in. He closed the door quickly, as it was still snowing, and ran down to the fire to thaw out.

'However did you get here?' Mum asked.

'Well, they've got snow ploughs trying to keep the A46 and the Marshfield–Bristol road open, so I came that way, as I guessed the little road to Marshfield would be well and truly blocked. I left my car in the farmyard and walked from there.' Mum had made him a cup of tea. His hands firmly around the warm cup, he gradually warmed up his fingers.

Mum busied herself putting out bread, cheese and chutney for our lunch, along with a jug of milk and the tea tin for making a hot drink. She took a deep breath and thanked Harold for coming. She said how much she appreciated his offer to look after me, and, as much as she wanted to trust him, she felt the need to say she hoped she wasn't making a big mistake. He understood and reassured her that he only wanted to help, if it was wanted.

All that said, Mum put her hat and coat on, pulled on a pair of Dad's woolly socks, left Harold a pair to use as gloves, and said she would be back soon. She gave me one of her looks to say *be a good girl*, and she was off up the stairs. 'Thank you,' she called from the bedroom door.

It was really quite dark in the kitchen, with snow all over the window.

'Do you like playing in the snow?' Harold asked.

'I don't know,' I replied.

'Well, would you like to try and help me clear a path round to the back door so that you and your mum can get out? I think we can leave the snow by the front door; it will keep the draught out.' He helped me on with my coat and the gloves Nan had knitted me, pulled my hat down over my ears and handed me the coal shovel. 'There, you look well suited for snow clearing.'

He pulled on his big army jacket and the socks Mum gave him, and upstairs we went, heading out into the cold.

Harold picked up his shovel and we started to clear the snow filling the path round to the back door. It was hard going; as soon as we cleared a bit the wind blew the snow back again. 'Let's throw the snow into a pile,' Harold said, 'then the wind will not be able to move it so easily.' This we did, and eventually the path began to clear; after a while we were turning the corner for the back door.

'Now, here we are going to have to make a tunnel for the kitchen window while leaving your bedroom window covered.' So we tunnelled away, making a huge pile of snow on the garden. When we had finished, Harold took my shovel and began patting the snow until It made a shape of a snowman!

We cleared the path to the toilet and patted the snow firm along the path, hoping the wind wouldn't blow it back again.

'There,' Harold said, 'job well done. Now you must be ready for some bread and cheese after all that hard work; well done! But first we need two pieces of coal for the snowman's eyes, and a twig for his mouth.' We were able to find them and give our snowman a face. 'There; we will have to see if Mum can spare us a piece of carrot for his nose.'

Holding hands, with shovels on our shoulders, we marched back into the house. Coats hung up nice and tidy, boots in a neat line, we went into the welcome warm kitchen. We stood by the fire, which Harold brought to life. He put the kettle on the trivet. My cheeks were burning.

'Well, did you enjoy working in the snow?'

'Yes, thank you, it was good fun.'

I had set about laying the table when the back door opened and in came Mum.

'Mrs Blake let me off early, which was kind of her,' she said. 'I see you have been busy at work. Thank you very much; that is a tremendous help.'

'Oh,' said Harold, 'you have to thank my little helper here as well; she did very well!'

'You went out shovelling snow as well, did you?' Mum asked, with a look as if to say *I told you to stay in.*

'Don't be cross, Mum; it was good fun, and Harold took good care of me. Did you see the snowman Harold made?'

'Sounds as if you had fun, and no crying because you are cold,' said Mum, as I laid another place at the table. 'Well, who's for some bread and cheese?'

Harold said he had better be going in daylight, before the roads began to freeze again. He gave Mum a piece of paper with the telephone number of the pub next door to his mother's house. 'They are very kind and will get a message to me if you need help. In the meantime, I hope I can call again; I have enjoyed myself, and I'm glad to be of help.'

Mum walked with him to the door, thanked him and said she was looking forward to seeing him again. She pushed the roly-poly tight to the door and came in, quickly rubbing her hands between her knees. We sat for a while, happy in our thoughts.

Two days later I woke with the most awful sore throat, and I felt very hot. Mum declared I had a temperature and went up to Mrs Blake to say she was sorry she couldn't come in, and could she ring the doctor?

Dr Newton said he would come as soon as possible, and to keep bathing my head with a cool flannel to reduce the temperature. This Mum did, but the sore throat developed into an awful cough; I could hardly catch my breath. Mum propped me up with another pillow in an attempt to help, but nothing was making it better, and now I was coughing until I was sick.

The doctor arrived and declared it was whooping cough. 'Boil some water and put it in a bowl with a few drops of Friars' Balsam to ease the congestion and cough, and I will see her in two days unless her condition worsens.'

Mum searched the medicine chest, but no Friars' Balsam. How was she going to get that? Mr Blake wouldn't want to go out in weather like this.

Then the thought came: should she ring Harold? *Needs must* hung in her thoughts, as she put on her boots and jacket and ran up to the phone box. She gave the message to the lady at his neighbouring pub, who as he had said was very nice, then she ran back to sit with me and wait.

After what seemed like an eternity she heard the back door open and close and running steps up the stairs, and there he was, breathless and with a paper bag in his hands. 'Hope this is the right stuff; how is she?'

Mum said my temperature was still high, and would he stay with me while she got the bowl of hot water?

She came in with the bowl and a towel, and put the measure of Friars' Balsam in the water. Harold helped me to sit up and breathe in the steam with the towel over my head. One sniff and I was violently sick, fortunately into the bowl.

'Was that the reaction expected?' asked Harold.

Mum admitted she had no idea; she had never seen anyone with whooping cough before. The raised pillows seemed to help my breathing.

I seemed to go in and out of knowing where I was, but the doctor said it would take its course and not to use the Friars' Balsam again. All the while Harold stayed and took turns looking after me so that Mum got some sleep. Eventually I turned the corner and gradually got stronger, and the cough lessened.

Even to this day, eighty years later, I still heave at even the words 'Friars' Balsam'!

# CHAPTER 12

—

The big freeze seemed to go on forever. Harold came over most days after I got better, and kept the paths open. The snow plough finally got into the village and cleared the road and lane, so farmers were once again able to move their livestock around.

Mum announced that we were going to have a brother and sister coming to live with us, and their names were Bobby and Maureen. They lived in London, but were in danger because of the bombing, so families in the country were being asked to share their homes with these children.

Mrs Hendy brought them over with their mummy. Mrs Blake had loaned Mum a single bed to put in my room for Bobby, and Maureen was to share my big bed. Their mum Betty shared Mum's bed, and so began a lifetime friendship.

Whenever she could get away from London, Betty would catch the train to Bristol, then a bus to Marshfield, and Mr or Mrs Hendy would bring her to us and a very happy Bobby and Maureen.

The worst part was when Betty went home to London, where she was a nurse. For Bobby and Maureen, the parting was so sad, and the only thing that would pacify them was sitting around the fire and having a spoonful of Virol. The sweetness seemed to calm them down, and we would play a game of I Spy.

One day Betty arrived with a suitcase and said she was coming to work at the home for evacuee babies at Church Farm. Although she would be away some days of the week, she would only be across the road, so in her time off she would pop over and be with her children.

'What a brilliant idea,' said Mum. 'How did you manage that?'

'Well, I saw this advert in the station, so I applied, and as luck would have it I was one of the lucky ones,' said Betty, with a big smile and big hugs for her children.

Bobby and Maureen loved the singing marching soldiers (Italian prisoners of war), and if breakfast was finished they would rush out to wave as they went past. The soldiers seemed to like this as well, and would wave and smile as they went on their way. Bobby and Maureen were older than me, but I did my best to keep up. When Harold had some spare petrol he would take us out for a ride around or down to the stream to wash his car, or take Mum to get groceries from Marshfield. Time passed very happily.

Having the evacuees also gave Mum the chance to fight the case for school transport, and she was delighted to announce that I would be starting school after the Easter holiday.

During the wait to go to school, Mum announced that she was going to be very busy helping with the threshing at the farm, as the threshing machine was doing the rounds in the village. If I was very good and didn't get in the way, I could come and watch. Mrs Blake came out to see the fun and held my hand as the huge traction engine arrived in the threshing yard, where all the sheaves of corn had been made into ricks on top of staddle stones to keep the rats out.

The steam engine itself was painted in bright colours as if from a fairground, with a big chimney with smoke belching out. Small wheels in the front, but huge ones at the back. With its chains and belts and wheels whizzing around, it looked as if it were alive.

Then came the threshing machine pulled by the steam engine. Very bland in comparison, on four wheels, it seemed to be made of planks of wood with lots of belts and trapdoors. Men stood on top, feeding the monster with sheaves of corn; it pushed out straw at one end and filled sacks with the corn on the other end. The dust that resulted turned everyone dark with bits of corn sticking out of their hair.

The dogs seemed to know what was going to happen and took guard at the bottom of the stacks. As the men moved the sheaves of corn, the rats ran out and the dogs would chase them. Absolute mayhem.

At lunchtime all stopped and a lovely lunch of freshly baked bread, farmhouse cheese, pickle and chutney was served in the barn with hop bitters. Then back to work till the job was done.

The threshing machine went from farm to farm, and each farmer helped the other. Some farmers had ladies in a kind of uniform of a green jumper and tie, brownish shirt and jodhpurs, and a farmer's pork pie hat. These ladies, I learnt, were called 'land girls'.

# CHAPTER 13

—

We all budged up to squeeze everyone into Mrs Hendy's car, and off we went to school.

I was the first to be dropped off as I was going to the top school, a big building that looked like the chapel next door. I was standing by the door, not quite sure what to do, when some more children came and we all seemed to tumble into the room: a big oblong room with little tables and chairs making a big letter 'C'.

I hung my hat and coat on the hooks with the other children, then turned round to see what happened next. There, standing in front of me, was a lovely lady with a big smile. 'Hello, my name is Mrs Wilson, and you must be Cynthia,' she said. 'Welcome to our school.'

Taking my hand, she led me to a table and chair halfway round the room. 'This is your desk and chair, Cynthia, and a new book and pencil for your schoolwork.' She gave me a reassuring smile and walked to her table on the opposite side of the room.

There was a big black round thing with a pipe going through the ceiling. Mrs Wilson opened a little door in the round thing, took the coal hod and poured coal into its big red mouth, then quickly closed the door and sat down.

'Good morning, children,' said Mrs Wilson, and everyone replied, 'Good morning, Mrs Wilson.' She then introduced me to the class, and everyone turned round to look at me. I felt like sliding under my desk, but somehow knew that was not a good idea.

Mrs Wilson went on to explain that Nurse Whittard would be coming to school after lunch, so we should all head back to school promptly. She then asked us to get out our reading books and for Robert to start chapter two.

Mrs Wilson came and gave me a book and found chapter two. Robert began reading; I tried to follow, but had not really got the hang of reading while with Nan. I listened to the story while admiring Mrs Wilson, who wore a jumper and cardigan that complemented her warm tweed skirt. While she listened to the reading, she crossed her legs, showing a little line of lace from her petticoat. I liked Mrs Wilson.

All too soon it was time for a break, and everyone collected a little bottle of milk and went out into the playground. I followed.

Milk drunk, there was a great deal of running around playing tag. I looked at the ground, and it was covered in ash from the fire. I made a mental note not to fall over here, as it would hurt.

Mrs Wilson appeared and took me to the building in the corner of the playground. 'This is the toilet block, Cynthia. If ever you need the toilet in class you put up your hand, otherwise you are free to use it when it's break time.'

Children going to the toilet was a constant interruption, and seemed to be something to do when they got bored. I found this necessity so inconvenient, as undoing and doing up all those buttons that fastened my liberty bodice to my knickers always took so long.

After break we did times tables, which I was more familiar with as Nan had been teaching me. Then, all too soon, it was lunchtime.

Mums were waiting at the door for little ones, and the bigger children just ran off. Not sure what I was to do, I stayed at my desk.

'Now,' said Mrs Wilson, 'did Mummy give you a packed lunch?'

'Yes,' said I, 'it's in my bag with my coat.'

'Good, you get your bag and I will get you a glass of water.' Off she went through the door just behind my chair, and she came back with the water as I got back to my seat. 'Enjoy your lunch. If you need the toilet, you know where it is. Be sure to put your coat on, and I will see you soon,' and she vanished through the door.

It was a bit lonely eating my lunch by myself, but not much different from being alone at home. Soon the children started coming back, and went out into the playground with their coats still on as it was still quite chilly in the shade. I stayed where I was until Mrs Wilson came back, then it was time to come in and await the arrival of Nurse Whittard.

Nurse Whittard arrived in a navy blue raincoat, and a navy blue hat she had just rammed on her head. In her hand was a big black doctor's bag. We all sat very quietly.

She took off her coat, let down the corner of her apron that had been tucked into the bib, then delved up to her elbows into the black bag. She brought out a comb, a kidney-shaped dish, and a bottle of cloudy liquid, which she poured some of into the kidney dish. 'Right, Mrs Wilson, shall we do this alphabetically?'

As my surname was Driver, it didn't take long for it to be my turn. When I was behind the screen she had carefully placed, Nurse Whittard first asked me to open my mouth and checked my teeth. Then she turned me round and looked in my hair. She put the comb in the liquid, drew it through my hair, held the comb against the tissue paper, looked in my ears, then said I could go. I felt like a horse at the horse show being judged.

My hair had been all piled on top of my head in two plaits, with several hair pins my mother had positioned carefully to keep it in place all day. When I got home and told Mum about Nurse Whittard, she said that would be the nit nurse, as she was called. 'The reason why I pile your hair on the top of your head is so that you won't catch any,' she said.

Next day, we all piled into the car again, hoping to be in the front. Mrs Hendy explained that we took turns sitting in the front, as the purpose was to look out for Alfie Burcombe, a farm worker from Church Farm who rode his bike to and from work. With the high bank and the wall on top it was not always possible to see someone coming.

Then one day coming home, as we rounded a corner, there was Alfie coming towards us in the middle of the road. Mrs Hendy braked hard, turning the steering wheel hard to try and avoid him. We all had to hang on tight as we were halfway up the bank.

Alfie hit the bonnet of the car and flew over the roof. He slid down the back onto the road.

'Are you all right?' asked Mrs Hendy, giving Alfie a hand to stand up.

Brushing himself down, he put on his hat. 'Think so, though my bike looks a bit twisted.'

Mrs Hendy busied herself getting the current inhabitant of the front seat into the back and getting Alfie into the front. She drove to the farm where he worked and helped him into the kitchen.

'A cup of tea is what you need, Alfie,' said the farmer's wife.

'I will collect him when I have dropped this lot off,' said Mrs Hendy.

Next morning Mrs Hendy collected Alfie and brought him to work, and so it continued until a farm cottage became available.

I didn't see Alfie again until Harvest Festival in our little church. We had all been very busy decorating the church with flowers, fruit and our best vegetables, and Mrs Blake had made a big loaf in the shape of a sheaf of wheat, which was put on the altar.

Just before the service began Alfie came into church, looking a bit unsteady on his feet. Mr Blake helped him into their pew and propped him against the pillar for support. Alfie didn't stand for the hymns or kneel for the prayers, so after the service the doctor was called, who pronounced Alfie had died.

# CHAPTER 14

—

The first week of school passed without too many problems, and the ritual of lunch in the classroom was beginning to feel the norm. The children were preparing to go home for lunch when a lady bustled in and asked Mrs Wilson if I would like to join her mob for lunchtime.

'What do you think?' asked Mrs Wilson. 'Would you like to go with Mrs Fuller and the children for your lunchtime?'

I looked at the lady, then smiled at Mrs Wilson, nodding my head.

'Well, we had better get your coat on,' and off I went with the other children to Mrs Fuller's house down the road, with its warm fire and chairs round the big square table. The chatter was fun and everyone was getting along.

After a while Mrs Fuller came over to me and asked why I never visited my grandma. I was puzzled and said I did as often as my mummy and I could, as we had to go on her bicycle.

'Well,' she said, 'you have another grandma who lives in the almshouses and would very much like to see you. She is your daddy's mother.'

When I told my mother the story, and asked if I could go to see her, the room went silent, and the subject never arose again.

***

The winter was over and spring was showing us her colours. On my arrival back from school Mum had a surprise for me. She was looking very happy and very smart, standing close to Harold. She announced that Harold was my new daddy and would be living with us, and her new name was Mrs Hall.

I was so happy as I had grown very fond of Harold, and loved it when he came to visit. Now he would be with us forever.

'We are going to see your new granny,' announced Mum, 'so a quick change into your Sunday dress, okay?'

We dashed upstairs and I tore off my school clothes, on with my best dress, quick adjustment of my hair and, hey presto, I was ready to meet my new grandma.

Dad, as I could now think of him, had washed and polished his new car – maroon, he said it was – and off we went, with Mum carrying a big bunch of flowers.

It didn't take long to get to Grandma's house in Cold Ashton: the first in a row of cottages next to a public house, with a wall that curved round to the front door, and a gate that squeaked when it was opened. Dad opened the door and we all tumbled in. We went across the hallway into a large sitting room with a lovely big fire.

'Hello, Mum,' said Dad, giving her a big kiss. He smiled. 'Well, we did it.'

Mum gave her a big kiss too, and pushed me forward. 'And this is Cynthia, my daughter.'

Not sure what to do, I took my new grandma's hand and shook it.

'How lucky am I to have a readymade granddaughter as well?' she said, lifting me up onto her knee. This grandma's knee wasn't as big as Nan's knee, but she was rounder and smiley. 'Would you like to come and stay with me for a night while Mum and Dad' – she winked at Dad – 'have a little holiday?'

She was looking at me very closely and obviously willing me to say 'yes, please'. I automatically nodded my head, and looked at Mum for approval. She picked up on my anxiety and, smiling, said it would be like staying with Nan in another house. Dad had poured a glass of sherry for everyone and a glass of lemonade for me, the fizzy bubbles going up my nose.

Granny, as she wanted to be called, took me upstairs to show me where she slept and where I would sleep. It was right next door, so she would hear me if I called. My bed was big and looked very cosy, and there was a big window, so all was well.

So began a routine of staying with Granny Hall.

Granny had a big wireless which she liked very much. Apart from listening to the news, she liked *Henry Hall's Guest Night* and *Dick Barton – Special Agent*. I didn't like the last one very much as the music was scary and I didn't understand what the story was about, but some colouring usually took me to a nicer place in my imagination.

She had to collect water from the pump house in the middle cottage. They had children there, but they were big boys who liked playing football. They sometimes helped Granny with her bucket of water.

One warm summer day a knock came on Granny's door that she was not expecting. There stood a lovely lady and a little girl.

'Hello,' the lady said. 'I am Mrs Austin, and this is my daughter Jennifer; we live at the farm just up the road. We wondered if your little girl would like to come and play with Jennifer in this lovely sunny weather?'

Granny looked at me and asked, 'Well, what do you think?'

I nodded my head, so, cardigan on, off I went to play. 'I'll bring her back after tea,' said Mrs Austin, looking over her shoulder.

Jenny's home was a farm. It was a bit scary when the cows came in for milking, as they all had horns, which was confusing as I thought only bulls had horns. They had brought themselves in for milking as Jen's father was in the next field making hay.

Jen took my hand, and we ran into the field and jumped into a big pile of hay. The grey tractor was coming nearer and nearer, and suddenly we were lifted up and carried to the rick and dropped in the middle. We then slid down the stopped elevator and ran to the next heap until Jenny's mother came out with a tray of tea, glasses of milk and slices of homemade cake. Both her mum and dad had jolly laughs and were delighted to see us having such fun.

Tea over, it was time to milk the cows and feed the pigs and hens and baby calves. The calves loved their bottles; you had to hold on tight.

All too soon it was time for Mrs Austin to walk me down the busy main road. She said she hoped I would like to come and play again when I was staying with Granny. I thanked them very much for a lovely time.

This was the beginning of a lifelong friendship, and now, eighty years later, we sip tea and reminisce.

# CHAPTER 15

—

Mum and Dad were hoping to make plans to move to Marshfield. Mum was considering training for the new Home Help Service when everything had to be put on hold as she was going to have a baby. This was very exciting, and I thought it was coming for Christmas, but no.

Life ebbed and flowed through the daily routines and summer in all her glory, when trips to the ford to wash Dad's car were like going to the seaside. Little did I realise how lucky we were to have a car, let alone fuel to go in it.

We all settled into the darker nights, and suddenly it was time once more to prepare for Christmas.

I liked Christmas. This event always seemed to need a lot of forward planning, which seemed to start with Stir-up Sunday, when the Christmas puddings would be made. Everyone in the household had to make a wish, stirring the pudding mixture before it was put in the basins to be cooked. This mixture was heavy even without all the rich fruit that usually went in them. Mum had found some sultanas and raisins, and added grated carrot, as all the magazines had recommended because of the lack of dried fruit through rationing.

Mum made three puddings, one for us and two smaller ones for Aunt Rene and Granny. They cooked in the basins for a whole day and night, with Mum making sure the fire stayed on; the smell was delicious. Then she used the boiler stick to pull them out of the water by the cloth handle. Once they had cooled, she put clean dry cloths on the puddings and put them in the larder to keep dry.

Next it was time to find my black stocking, which I had kept with me on leaving Nan's, but to my absolute distress I could not find it. Every day I checked and checked again. Christmas Eve was here, but I could not find it. Finally, with tears streaming down my face, I had to tell Mum and Dad I had lost my stocking to hang up for Father Christmas.

Mum disappeared and came back with a brown stocking all full of holes. The hoped-for stop to my howling didn't happen. Dad suggested we pin the holes closed and hang it on the hook at the side of the fireplace. Hot drinks finished, I went to bed still sobbing.

Next morning was Christmas Day, but the excitement didn't come. Dad put his head round the door and wished me a happy Christmas with a big smile.

'Has he been?' I asked, in anticipation of a no, but he said yes.

I slid out of bed and put on my slippers. Dad helped me with my dressing gown, and off we went hand in hand down the stairs. I peered round the door, and there the stocking was, hanging by the fireplace, all the holes mended with string. Happy Christmas.

\*\*\*

My new brother Christopher didn't arrive until April 1946; it seemed like forever. Sadly he cried an awful lot until the doctor concluded he didn't like Mum's milk or cow's milk, so the only thing that could help him was goat's milk.

With two resident goats on the common, Dad asked their owner for her help. She agreed but wanted Dad to get a goat of his own as she used the milk to make cheese. She advised him as to where he could enquire, and so we acquired a goat.

When the goat arrived she was a bit frisky. 'But that's just the drive over,' said the owner; 'she will calm down.' He showed Dad how to milk her and tether her on the common, and instructed him to bring her in at night. The owner had some straw and made a bed for her in the coal shed, and said to let him know if we had any trouble with her.

Our goat was beautifully white all over, with yellow eyes that had a narrow green slit going through the middle. We called her Nanny, which she seemed happy with.

There was just one problem: she had to share the coal shed with our hens. This seemed to be a problem for the hens and caused a great deal of clucking, but eventually they all calmed down and laid us some lovely eggs, and they had the freedom of the garden in the daytime.

Christopher seemed to enjoy the goat's milk and soon began to put on weight and grow.

One day Mum had a visitor and had to deal with him in the sitting room, so I was in charge of baby Christopher. He seemed happily asleep, so I got on with my colouring. After a while he began to grizzle, so I did as Mum did and jiggled the pram to get him to sleep again. Sadly Chris was having none of this and began to cry. I peered into the pram like Mum did to see if he was all right, but Chris slid out of the pram onto the floor and made an even louder cry.

Mum arrived on the scene and rescued Chris, but all hell broke out on me; her hands didn't seem to stop hitting me, as if I did it on purpose. I scrabbled away and hid under the table where she couldn't get to me.

It wasn't until Dad came home that I felt safe enough to come out. He gradually coaxed me out, saying it was an accident and he was sure I hadn't meant to. No harm done, and Chris was enjoying his milk as usual. Dad held me close and stayed with me till bedtime.

Sadly, Mum and I didn't seem to be friends any more. Whenever anything went wrong or upset her she would lash out at me with her big hands, which really hurt when they landed. One day Dad came home and found her laying into me once again; he put himself in between us and told her if she wanted to hit anyone she was to hit him. I sometimes wonder if she had depression after Chris was born, as often I had no idea what I was being beaten for.

# CHAPTER 16

—

News finally came that we were to move to a new house in Marshfield. Mum began her training to become a home help. I was to leave the top school and move to the bottom school, at the bottom of the high street, and Chris would start at the top school; it was all change for all of us.

There were three classrooms at the bottom school. One was a spare room used for lunch, which was delivered to the school and cost half a crown. We had to take the money to school every Monday, and for that we got a hot meal of main and pudding. In the middle classroom was Mrs Edwards's class; she was my new teacher. Beyond the wood and glass sliding screen door was Mr Davis's room. Mr Davis was the headmaster, who from day one put the fear of God into me.

Mrs Edwards was okay, but she spoke with a Welsh accent, so I had to try to concentrate on what she was saying as opposed to how she said it. The best thing was that she taught us crafts. I learnt to knit and went into production making round tea cosies, quickly graduating to two-colour knitting.

The playground was still covered in stove ash, and the loos were now a brick-built row of six toilets, with six little washbasins for us to wash our hands. The roller towel was varying shades of grey and always wet. We were separated from the boys, who we could hear on the other side of the wall, and just as well, judging by their knees.

We were given a skipping rope. Well, a piece of smooth rope that at least four girls could use to skip at once. The rope and ash made an awful dust, so we cleared a space using the sides of our shoes, making our socks filthy, much to our mothers' annoyance.

Life in Mrs Edwards's class continued at a steady pace as I prepared to go into battle in Mr Davis's classroom, where I had heard the shouting and seen the exercise books flying through the air.

The headmaster wasn't a tall man, particularly; more like a rugby player, with receding hair, a bulbous nose and a bit hanging from his lip, as if he had bitten it badly and the swelling hadn't gone down. To top it all he spoke with a Welsh accent as well, with sprays of spit which would fly when he got excited. Both rooms had heaters like Mrs Wilson's, but Mr Davis's stocky build made it difficult for him to stoke up, so he appointed a stoke monitor to go with the ink monitor and paper monitor.

Once a month we had the vicar, the Reverend Moss, come to take assembly. He was tall and slim, with children of his own who didn't come to the village school. But he must have read them stories, as he knew how to tell us a story. It wasn't until much later I realised the stories he told were from the Bible.

I enjoyed most subjects, but maths was a mystery. We had homework every day, and, try as I might, I just couldn't get the hang of how it was all worked out. Sometimes I would just add all the numbers together, and my answer, to my amazement, would sometimes get a tick!

# CHAPTER 17

—

The move to Marshfield was huge: going from small, intimate West Littleton to large, exciting, almost secret Marshfield. Our new house had been newly built with something called 'breeze blocks', with pebbled concrete on the outside. We had a newly fitted kitchen with a white sink and draining board, and space for a modern cooker. There was a larder and a big cupboard where we could hang our dog walking coats, as, yes, we now had a black and white collie dog Dad had thought we would like. We did, but Mum didn't like the hairs he left around, so Dad and I made sure he was groomed outside so that as little as possible came inside. Like our last dog, he was called Bruce.

The living room was very large, with a Rayburn to heat the water, as we now had taps and hot and cold running water; we were in heaven. It also had an oven, which was always ready to go while the fire was kept stoked up, keeping the room warm and cosy.

The room next door had a fireplace, and a telephone point that was going to be needed for Mum's new job. This room was for Sundays, high days and holidays.

The front door had a glass panel down the side. If you looked sort of cross-eyed through the little dimples in the glass, you could just see who was ringing the doorbell. The hall was big enough for us all to stand in line so Mum could give us the once-over before we went out.

From the hall the stairs went straight up to a landing with three bedrooms and, excitingly, a bathroom. It had a bath, a washbasin, and, best of all, an *inside* toilet that had a long chain you pulled to flush everything away. I don't know where to, but it was bliss.

On a very cold February morning, with frost on the inside of the windows in the hall, I froze to the spot. Mum had the radio on in the living room, and as I came down the stairs I heard the announcement that the King had died. What would happen now? Would we have to be at war again? Mum told me that we would now have a queen and to look forward to a coronation.

***

Mum enjoyed singing. She had a voice that was deeper than mine. She had singing lessons from Mrs Kitley, who said she sounded like Kathleen Ferrier, who had a lovely contralto voice.

Mum had managed to get a piano that fitted very well in our new sitting room, and Dad could just pick up a tune without music but just couldn't get the hang of Handel's Largo, so I was set to learn piano. Mr Cook would come to the house on a Tuesday after tea, and so began the torture: the endless playing of scales and a rap over the knuckles with a ruler when I got it wrong. I did get the hang of Handel's Largo but could not play it without mistakes at speed, so it was decided that Mr Cook would play for Mum's rehearsals, and when she gave concerts for the elderly and so on.

This led to my mother and I joining the church choir, and to my absolute distress who was the organist? The very same Mr Cook, and the headmaster stood in for the vicar. Was there no getting away from these people?

As I was new, I couldn't process down the aisle at services or sit in the choir stalls, but had to sit on a chair at the front of the organ so that Mr Cook could keep an eye on us. The fact that my mother was sitting diagonally opposite me didn't seem to count.

I soon learnt what a good seat this was, as I could feel the vibration of the organ as it was played with gusto for all to sing along with. A powerful feeling.

I seemed to do well at singing. One day I plucked up the courage to ask Mr Cook how the organ worked. He seemed to be encouraged by this and brought me round to the side of the organ, pulling the curtain aside so I could see it in all its glory.

He sat at the organ on a long bench, and called to George that he was going to give her an airing. I had seen a man standing by, but now that man began pumping a handle up and down: to 'put air in her lungs', explained Mr Cook. Mr Cook pulled out lots of knobs (stops, I would later learn) and began to play. To my astonishment he was using his feet as well as his fingers on different levels, and the most glorious sound was coming from the very depths of her. So started my love of organ music.

# CHAPTER 18

—

The long-awaited coronation seemed to be gathering pace, and I was excited about the prospect of a party and the fact I had been given bottom space at Mrs Ball's house to watch the ceremony on her new TV.

Mum had made me a sundress, as the event was going to be in June. The dress was white, with pictures of the coronation emblems on it and a pretty border. As luck would have it, it was drizzling on the day, so I had to wear my mac.

At Mrs Ball's house children were already gathering. We were seated on the floor in front of an oblong wooden box about the size of Grandma's wireless, on which was a grey screen that showed us what was happening in London.

The memory of that day is still very strong. The magnificent music and the glittering crowns; the pageantry of it all gave me a fuzzy feeling of something much greater than me, but that I was part of.

The excitement of the coronation over, we all settled back into school and the usual routine. The confirmation service we had all been receiving lessons on was to take place the following Sunday. A new white dress had been made for me, which made the event feel special.

On the Friday before the confirmation we were taken on a trip to Weston-super-Mare as a reward for good attendance. As usual the tide was out, but the donkeys were there, and ice cream, so a good day was had by all.

On return I got off the coach, and, waving to my friends instead of paying attention, I ran straight out into the road to be knocked down by a slow-moving car.

People rushed out from their houses, and I was carried into the nearest. My mother sent for Doctor Eastes. He decided I would live, as I had only badly grazed my knee. 'You caused more damage to the car, I gather!' he said. Some white powder was put in the wound and a bandage applied. Mum, of course, was furious – mostly, I think, because of the shock of the whole thing.

Sunday dawned, and my knee was still too swollen to bend. 'Oh, Mum,' I wailed, 'how can I get confirmed if I can't kneel down?'

'Don't worry yourself,' said Mum. 'I will take you up to the vicarage and explain to the vicar.' This she did.

For the ceremony, the other children and I, in my new white dress, went into the vicarage to have our veils attached. We processed over to the church, holding on to our veils, and entered via the big west door. Here we were lined up in pairs, veils readjusted, and waited for the verger to open the doors and lead us into church.

Eventually the doors opened and we started the procession down the aisle. There before us was the bishop in all his finery, who was as black as black could be. A great deal of nudging went on, as none of us had seen a black man before, let alone a bishop.

Everyone except me knelt before the bishop. I was at the end, standing by a pillar. Hymns were sung, prayers said, then it was time for the confirmation. The bishop laid his hands on each kneeling person's head until it was my turn. He stood up, gave me a big smile, laid his hands on my head and said, 'Bless you, my child.' All done; I was confirmed.

Back at the vicarage, and minus our veils, we enjoyed squash and cake. The bishop came over to speak to us and explained he came from Nigeria, where it was very hot, and that he had been invited to take part in the coronation. He was staying with the bishop of Bristol, who had invited him to do our confirmations, and he said how honoured he was. He then gave us a red prayer and hymn book each as a memento, which I have to this day.

# CHAPTER 19

—

One day I came home and Dad was already there. He gave me a big hug hello and sat me down on the settee.

'Now,' he said, holding my hand, 'when Mum comes home she is going to be very sad, and I want you to be the very best girl you can be, as today your nan has died.'

I looked at him in total disbelief. 'No,' I said, 'she can't have; she is my nan.'

He gave me a big hug as my shoulders shook and the tears just flowed. I don't know how long I cried, but he offered me his handkerchief to wipe away my tears and blow my nose, and got me a glass of water.

I couldn't believe outside the window everyone was going about their usual business when I was never going to see my nan again. It was my saddest day ever; tears still flow as I write this. She had really loved me, and I still feel that love to this day, seventy-five years later.

\*\*\*

That summer I had my first of many holidays with Aunt Mim, Mum's elder sister. She lived in Badminton, another village about four miles away from us, in the house next to the village post office.

Aunt Mim had a daughter, Christine, who was about the same age as Christopher, and a husband, my Uncle Perce, who worked on the Beaufort estate. My aunt also worked for someone called the Duke of Beaufort as his housekeeper, which sounded very important. She would have to be at work from time to time, so I was to keep Christine safe and to have fun playing with her, and not to leave the house. The fire was banked in and not to be touched; it all sounded familiar. Christine quite liked being read to, so we passed the time quite easily in a fantasy world of make-believe.

After lunch one day, having sat quietly for fifteen minutes to *Listen with Mother* on the radio, Aunt Mim said she was going ironing, so if we were good we could go to the swings in the school playground.

Before we were let out we had to be checked over for cleanliness, our hair tidied and our clothes properly adjusted. 'Now,' she said, 'a few rules to be obeyed.'

If we met a tall gentleman walking with one black dog and a black walking stick with a silver knob, that would be the Duke of Beaufort. If he spoke to us, we should address him as 'Your Grace'. If we met a short lady with grey hair and walking with lots of dogs, that would be the Duchess of Beaufort, and if she spoke to you she also was addressed as 'Your Grace'. But if we met an older lady walking upright, wearing a hat and carrying a basket, that was Queen Mary and we were to cross the road.

So, in fear and trembling at the prospect of meeting such folks, I stuck my head round the porch to check the way was clear, grabbed Christine's hand and ran as if the devil was behind us to the school playground, where we enjoyed playing with other children who were there. This information stuck in my memory bank and stood me in good stead in later life while in the employ of the royal family.

My aunt had given us each a penny to get a penny lolly from Mrs Foster's ice cream shop on the way home, which was licked with joy sitting on Aunt Mim's front doorstep.

Some days Aunt Mim would pack a picnic and we would walk out into the great park and find Uncle Perce, who would be making hay. We would sit in a hillock of hay and enjoy our sandwiches, delicious cake and mug of squash. Other days we would go for a walk to find the hermitage or the ice house, or just walk around the great lake in front of Badminton House.

One evening Aunt Mim announced that, if we went and stood by the garden gate, we might see the Queen go by. We looked at each other in astonishment, but she wasn't joking.

She opened the front door for us and stood with us a while. The sun was beginning to set down the middle of the street, the birds were getting ready for bed, when around the top corner of the street came this lovely big black car with a light on inside, and there she was, beautiful and happy, with her prince beside her. It all passed so quickly, but slowly at the same time.

We went indoors full of wonder. I asked why she had come to Badminton, and at this time of day.

'Well, you know how busy the park has been, and the village street? Well, there is going to be something called the Three-Day Event, with competitions for horses, and the royal family have asked if they can come to stay with the Duke and Duchess to watch. How amazing is that? What is even funnier is I have been asked to organise the pee tent, and to charge everyone one penny to go, so if you will be good girls you can come too.'

'Hurrah!' we both shouted, jumping up and down.

There were no grandstands and tiered seating like today, but an arena made of farm trailers with hay bales round the sides; people could sit in the trailers or on the bales for a better view. There was a marquee with open sides and seating where the Queen would be. That was all for the dressage on Friday and the show jumping on Sunday, but on the Saturday it was cross country day, so we could walk around the course, watching the lovely horses jump. Everyone was rooting for Colonel Llewellyn and his horse Foxhunter; they made a dashing sight.

\*\*\*

One Sunday we were told that Aunt Mim wouldn't be coming to church with us as she had to be at Badminton House over lunchtime, so we were to be good girls and go to church without her, Christine in the choir and me in the congregation.

Now, I had helped to clean the church on a Friday afternoon with Aunt Mim many times, so the tall pews didn't bother me. In fact it was like being in a secret place as, once you had sat down, no one could see you. I had also taken a liking to one of the crosses on wooden poles that were in certain seats. It was plain but beautifully mounted and caught the sun if it was shining for the morning service.

So Christine went off to the choir vestry to robe up for the service, and I sat in the pew with my favourite cross. I found the morning service in my prayer book and the first hymn in my hymn book. The organ started to play the first hymn and the choir walked down the aisle to the choir stalls. I was happily singing away when in came three people who sat in *my* pew. There were so many other seats, and I was here first; why did they have to sit in mine?

The service over, the choir all back in the vestry, I waited for the three people to leave the pew before standing to leave as well. The gentleman held the door of the pew open, and the two ladies went into the aisle. He held the door open for me to leave as well. As I approached he asked if I was visiting the village, to which I answered, 'Yes.'

'Can I ask where you're staying?' he asked.

'With my aunt, Mrs Bird.'

'Ah, yes, we know Marie very well. This is my wife, the Duchess of Beaufort, and this is my cousin, the Princess Royal.'

I shook the proffered hands, and everyone went on their way. They left the church through a small door, and I waited for Christine.

On arriving back at my aunt's I reported the event with great glee. The horrified look on her face said everything. 'Of all the pews in the church, why did you have to sit there?'

When I explained she understood, and said she should have told me to avoid that pew as the Duke was a church warden and that was his seat.

'Well,' I said, 'they didn't have any dogs.'

The next day the Duke apparently related the event to my aunt; he complimented her on my good behaviour and very good singing, and asked if I would be joining the choir!

# CHAPTER 20

T he time had come for something called the 11 plus. It didn't mean very much to me except that I had to pass it to go to the next school. I had been doing my homework, but sums were still a mystery to me.

With all the preparation for the exam done, Mum said we were going to the cinema in Chippenham to see *The Wizard of Oz*. Off we went, just Mum and me. We got to our seats, it all went dark and the film began.

It was all so real. I really felt sorry for the scared lion, but, worst of all, the wicked witch comes and takes Dorothy's dog. I just howled and howled so much Mum had to take me outside to calm me down, 'Oh, you,' she said, 'always so easy to tears. Never mind; we had better find our bus.'

Next day there was a visitor in class, so we were supposed to be reading to ourselves, but my ears pricked up on hearing, 'They are all council house kids, so none of them are expected to pass.' What did that mean? I knew the council had built our lovely new home, but I didn't realise it was some kind of second-class citizenship that meant living there got you labelled 'council house kids'. I was shocked and filled with disbelief. I kept it to myself, as I felt sure Mum would not believe what I had heard.

The day of the exam came. We all had to be quiet, concentrate on the paper in front of us and answer the questions as best we possibly could. No talking was allowed, and Mr Davis would tell us when to stop.

I can't recall how much time passed before we had the results, but it felt like forever. Eventually we were handed a slip of paper with our results on. I opened mine, as did all the other children, only to read I had not passed. I was filled with horror and knew my mother would be furious.

I walked the long way home, and saw Mum's bicycle was already home, so I walked on and on until eventually I came to the home of a friend of Mum's who I liked. I knocked on the door and she kindly asked me in. After a while I told her what had happened and said Mum would be so cross I couldn't go home.

She made me a drink, and went to the kitchen to get tea, then to my absolute horror Mum appeared at the door. I hid behind the settee, but she saw me and said she was not cross; she hadn't expected me to pass, and all was well.

We walked home in silence, and nothing more was said about the subject. But inside I was hurt still by the comments I had heard, and vowed to myself one day I would show them what council kids could do.

The good thing was that Jen didn't pass either, so we would be going to Oldland Common School together on the school bus. We both looked immaculate in our new school uniform; I loved it. I brushed my navy blazer, with the school badge on the pocket, every evening, washed my white blouse and hung it over the Rayburn to dry each night, and was very proud as I walked up the road to catch the school bus every morning. The children who had passed their 11 plus went to Kingswood Grammar School, wore a coffee-coloured uniform, and travelled to school on the regular bus service.

Oldland Common School was a collection of what looked like army buildings, all in regimented rows, with the headmaster's office in the middle. Children came from all around the area. So I was no longer at a cosy village school, but many of us wanted to do well and make a better situation for ourselves.

The headmaster was once again Welsh, with thick glasses that made his eyes look a long way back. If you did wrong, you had to stand out on the path for all to see until he called you into his office. Jen and I were really pleased we didn't get in trouble.

We were both in the school choir and enjoyed days out attending competitions, where we actually won a couple of times. We both enjoyed sport; Jen really excelled, but I did well in hurdling, so I got some brownie points for that.

We also joined the Girl Guides, which was great fun, and both aspired to the level of patrol leaders. We were very proud of the uniform, and the badges we achieved.

As Marshfield show day approached, Mrs Farmer, our guide leader, told us we had been allotted a wagon in the parade, and we were going as guiding throughout the world, so all of us should dress up representing a different place.

I thought I would represent Hawaii, and Mum entered into this with great fun. She got lots of raffia and sewed it to a waistband (I had to stand on the table for her to trim it level), found a bikini top at the jumble sale, and I made a wreath of flowers for my hair.

Come the day it was warm and sunny. Mum covered my body in gravy browning to give me a tan, and put a Christmas decoration round my neck for a garland. Jen came in Guide uniform. Dad took me to the top of the street, where the procession was starting from, so that I didn't have to walk up the street as I was.

The band marched up the street and fell into place at the head of the parade. The vicar blessed the parade, and off we all set, waving as we went.

Just when we were about halfway down the street, the heavens opened. All the gravy browning went streaky, the raffia went soggy and stuck to my legs, and by the time we reached the village hall the colour had run out of the garland, making coloured streaks all down my body; I felt like something from outer space. A quick run home and a change into play clothes, and I ran back to the village hall, which all the fun and games had moved into.

Around this time, I had my tonsils out. It was not a pleasant procedure, although the ice cream afterwards was very soothing. For being a good girl, Mum said she would buy me a bicycle. True to her word, when Dad brought me home from Cosham Hospital, there it was: a brand new Hercules, all black and shiny. I was so thrilled.

Mum said that she would be using it while I was at school, and I could have it to go to Jen's at weekends. Mum's area for caring had widened, and, as she had not been able to learn to drive, she would have to cycle to her patients. I often think back to that time and wonder how on earth she did it, as her area now went outside Marshfield to Wick, Doynton, Pucklechurch and all the little hamlets in between, all up and down steep hills and in all weathers.

In the fullness of time Mum was awarded Best Home Help, and went to Norway to represent Great Britain. She was so proud and thoroughly enjoyed the whole experience. It also gave her a taste for travel. If she didn't have us blooming kids, she said, she could see the world.

I had started to learn cookery at school, so I tried to help by making tea ready for Mum and Dad when they got home. We had cheese and potato pie a lot, with pilchards or luncheon meat or bacon, but soon my repertoire widened and puddings were introduced. The fun thing was that on school cookery days we had to take the ingredients and bring back the finished product, so trying to resist eating it on the bus was quite a challenge.

Eventually, a new school was built just down the road. It was just for girls, so we made the move to this lovely new school, with a new headmistress and female teachers. Being among the oldest, Jen and I were made prefects and tried to keep the girls under control, which on the whole we did.

# CHAPTER 21

—

At assembly one morning, Miss Nichols announced that the school was organising a visit to Switzerland at the beginning of the summer holidays, and that any interested pupils should put their names down on the list on the noticeboard. Jen and I looked at each other and we knew this would be good fun, so we put our names on the list. The trip would be to Wilderswil, Interlaken, in the Bernese Oberland, and a letter would be sent to parents of interested pupils.

Eventually a letter was handed to us to be given to parents, with all the details for the trip, which I duly handed over when Mum came home.

When the dust settled following the opening of said letter, the 'what?!' and 'where did you think the money was coming from?' still ringing in my ears, the realisation that this was not a school-funded trip hit home, and that awful sinking feeling went straight to my boots. 'We just thought it would be a lovely thing to do. Sorry,' I explained, and I left the room.

When I came down for breakfast in the morning, Mum, getting ready to leave, handed me a letter for Miss Nichols, which I would duly hand in to the school secretary on arrival at school. Jen had a letter also. We sat on the bus, holding our letters, knowing we would not be going.

In the afternoon a list of names was read out in class, including the two of us, and those on the list were told to go to the assembly hall at 3pm. This we did with fear and trembling, as we could not think of what we had done wrong. It was a relief to see rows of chairs arranged in the hall, as without fail at assembly, when we stood in class rows, I would faint and have to be carried out to the nurses' station.

We all stood to attention as Miss Nichols came in. She cheerfully invited us to sit.

'Well, I am pleased to tell you your parents have all agreed for you to go on the school trip to Switzerland, making the trip viable.' We looked at each other in total amazement, as Jen's parents had reacted the same as mine. We had assumed the trip was off. 'Please collect your itineraries as you leave the hall, and be sure to give them to your parents.'

Jen's mother had become good friends with mine. On receipt of the letter, they had made contact, both agreeing it would be a lovely thing for us to do.

The journey was as eventful as the arrival. We had a coach journey to Paris, going on the channel ferry, then a train from Paris to Interlaken, and a walk to Wildersvil.

We were allotted bedrooms, and thankfully Jen and I had to share. When I was investigating the veranda and the view, Jen closed the door, locking me out. No amount of knocking or whisper-calling encouraged her to open the door, and needs were becoming desperate, so I shouted, which brought Miss Nichols to demand what all the racket was about. Severely disciplined, we went down for dinner in sombre mood.

The thing that was intriguing both of us was the big bag of soft something on our beds; what were we to do with it? Eventually I had enough courage to ask what was it for, and whether we were supposed to take it off. Realising this had come up several times, Miss Nichols explained that it was called a duvet and we were to sleep under it, as it got really cold at night.

Great mirth followed as we got into bed with this bag on top. You could not see across the room or your toes, but it was really cosy. Result: we all slept well and were ready for our mountain adventure.

The train stopped the other side of the road from our 'pension', as it was called. We all piled into the train, having noticed three big mountains ahead of us. The view was amazing, with deep valleys and almost vertical mountainsides, and green pastures full of beautiful wild flowers. The one we had to look for was called edelweiss, which was just grey and white in comparison with the bright blues and yellows of the other flowers.

The train went into a tunnel, and our guide explained we were now going through the Eiger: the big mountain next to the one we would be getting out onto, which was called the Jungfrau. There would be trainers there to show us how to ski. We were warned not to rush around too much, as the oxygen levels were low and we could get altitude sickness.

We alighted from the train into bright sunlight, really appreciating the advice to wear sunglasses as the reflection of the sun on the snow was quite powerful. I noticed the sign telling us we were at 11,333 feet, so I tried not to rush about.

The ski instructor showed us how to glide down the slope into the big football net that stretched across the glacier, stopping us from whizzing off down the mountain. To get back up there was a rope to hold on to, which pulled you back up to the top. Great fun.

After some time we were told to go into a hotel that was made out of ice and get a drink and a snack, ready for the journey back to Wilderswil. This we did with great gusto, as we were feeling a bit peckish.

All too soon it was time to get on the train, our faces glowing with fresh air and sunshine.

After a while Jen and I looked at each other and mouthed, *I feel sick.* I had noticed paper bags had been put in the backs of the seats, and now I knew what they were for. Boy, were we poorly, and very glad to see our fluffy sacks when we got back to the pension.

We slept until morning the next day, and a welcome breakfast. But what a day to remember always!

# CHAPTER 22

—

Soon we were being asked what we wanted to do when we left school. I asked Mum if she thought I would make a good nurse, as I liked the uniform. Mum gave me a big smile and said, 'You would be no good at all at being a nurse; you faint at the sight of blood!'

I was heartbroken. 'Well, what am I to do?'

'Well, there are two things,' was her reply. 'People have to eat, and we all die at some point, so cooking or undertaking.'

The latter filled me with horror, so I decided to apply for catering college.

Jen decided she was not going to work on the farm like her father wanted her to, so she got herself a job in a very upmarket ladies' shop in the Corridor in Bath. As the catering college to which I had gained a place was in Bath as well, we were once again travelling together.

We also ventured out to the Saturday night dance held in Cold Ashton, where Jen lived. Jen's parents knew the husband and wife who ran the evenings, who said they needed more ladies, so we got all dressed up and walked up to the village hall with a torch to show us the way. We had to go by the church and churchyard, which always made us run, arriving at the village hall out of breath.

The dancing here was something called 'old time dancing', which looked good fun. We realised there were set dances, always with a partner, so we watched very carefully. Luckily, when we were asked to dance, our partners were very aware we were newbies and showed us the steps in time with the music.

We loved these evenings, soon getting the hang of it. I would stay the night at Jen's afterwards, which added to the fun.

# CHAPTER 23

—

Jen always looked very smart in her slim pencil skirt, white blouse and black cardigan, and wore it like a uniform. I was in mufti – a circular tan skirt and tan high-necked jumper, with just the tips of a green silk scarf showing under the collar – until I got to college, where I wore white wrap-around overalls, a white apron and a round white hat. But, if it was my week for waiting in the college restaurant, I too had to wear a slim black pencil skirt and white blouse.

I was in heaven; I loved the course, and, if I did well, I could go to the top in City & Guilds certificates. Our tutor was Chef Nichol, who had a wicked sense of humour. During a question time, having just learnt about bottled water, I asked if you made Vichy carrots with Vichy water. The answer of 'Well, would you make Bath buns with bath water?' had the class in uproar, but I never made the same mistake again.

We had been asked to cater for a very special event to be held at Longleat House in aid of charity, but also to celebrate the release of a book by Andre Simon, who was the guest of honour. We were to provide the food and wait at table dressed as flunkies, with a champagne reception in the great hall.

The butler showed us where the secret still room was in the great hall, and where the kitchen was in relation to where the meal was to be served. It seemed like miles, and how were we to keep the food hot on such a journey? The butler went off and came back with a couple of tea trolleys and large silver meat covers. 'Hope these help,' he said. 'You will have to run!'

We had brought all the china and cutlery from college, and partially prepared food, which we carried on our laps in the coach. No cling film or foil in those days, just clean tea towels. The trolleys came in handy to unload the coach as well. Mercifully they had glassware.

The event went well, and the coach was loaded again to get back to college. There we were at 2am, trying to get all the cutlery and crockery back into college, so the coach driver could go home.

When we were trying to get a trolley loaded with cutlery back up the steps into college, it ran away from us and straight across the street, crashing into the railings and sending all the cutlery cascading into the healing pool opposite. We all looked in incredulity at the situation. There was nothing we could do until they came to unlock the pool later in the morning, so we all decided to crash out in the common room, still in our flunky outfits, and try to get some sleep.

The caretaker took pity on us, put on his swimming trunks and hauled all the cutlery out of the pool. He hosed it all down and helped us load it all into boxes on the trolleys. 'A job well done' was our chef's remarks, and so went our baptism of fire into the catering industry.

*** 

As part of our ongoing training, when the college was closed for the long summer holidays, we were encouraged to go to hotels that applied for student help.

The first hotel job came for the week of Christmas. Jane and I, along with a couple of the boys, thought it would be fun to do this for a week and get some experience of hotel work and hopefully some pocket money. The hotel was the Madeira in Weston-super-Mare, so not far to go, and Dad volunteered to take us.

We were to arrive two days before the guests to prepare the bedrooms and so on. Luckily it was raining, rather than snowing, but it just didn't stop. Mum had given me a stiletto umbrella as a Christmas present, which was jolly handy.

We got unloaded and were shown to our rooms, the boys not having arrived yet. We set about making up our beds, but it all felt very damp. I put a hot water bottle in my bed, and steam started coming off the blanket! When I looked up there was a steady drip falling from the ceiling onto my bed.

I put up my umbrella and turned it upside down to catch the drips. I went down and reported it to the owners, who said they couldn't change my room, as the hotel was full, but they would try to get someone to fix the leak.

When the boys arrived their room was as bad, so the management suggested we sleep on the settees in the lounge when everyone had gone to bed.

I rang Chef Nichol for advice, and he told us to get out of there first thing in the morning. So I rang Dad, who duly came and collected us. Home for Christmas after all.

The next placement was to Frinton-on-Sea for the summer holidays, at the Frinton Lodge Hotel. This was very upmarket: a lovely black and white timbered building with just a road between it and the sea. We had our own rooms in a staff house, which was very nice.

Here I was to be a commis waiter: the one who did all the fetching and carrying for the station waiter. Boy, was I tired. The only thing that really fuelled me up was the delicious toast we had for breakfast, made in an electric toaster, so no black bits!

After the dinner service I assisted in the drawing room, where I carefully balanced trays of alcoholic drinks in service to the guests. One evening the drawing room waiter was very busy and asked me to serve brandies to four gentlemen playing cards. I could use a service trolley for this, as I had to have a selection of brandies, glasses and the dreaded spirit lamp. I had practiced this procedure, but in kitchen glasses, not the brandy balloons I was going to have to use tonight.

The gentlemen were very cooperative and I think could see my nervousness about lighting the spirit lamp. I rotated the glass gently in the flame, having put my hands around it first so that it wasn't quite as cold, and gently poured the chosen brandy down the side of the glass. Relief; I had managed the first one without it exploding. Eventually all four brandies were served, and no disasters, so my confidence grew.

During the week, a very well-known family moved into the hotel and quickly started to enjoy the facilities, except for an older woman who seemed to spend a lot of time on her own. I got to know her, and she seemed to enjoy my company. I made sure she was comfortable and had all she needed. The head waiter complimented me on being observant and making sure all guests were catered for.

It had been made quite clear to me from the start any tips were given to the head waiter, and were divided out in order of seniority at the end of each week. Being a commis waiter, the lowest of the low, I got a very small portion of the pot. When the elderly lady was leaving, though, she gave me £100 and said, pressing it into my hand, 'This is for you, with many thanks for making my stay so enjoyable. I believe you have a birthday coming up, so enjoy, enjoy.'

Now what did I do? She said it was for me, but I knew the head waiter would want to know what had happened.

Before I parted with my king's ransom, I asked the advice of Major McNally, the owner of the hotel. He thanked me for being honest and took the money. My heart sank to my boots, not so much for losing the money but from wondering what the head waiter was going to say.

Come the end of the week, I was called to the head waiter's office. Afraid and trembling, I stood waiting for him to speak. Eventually he said that Major McNally had told him the story and, in light of my honesty, they had decided I should keep the money!

I was so thrilled and couldn't wait to get home at the end of the six weeks to show Mum all the money I had collected over the weeks away. When I did, she went with me to the post office to open a savings account. Mum didn't say a lot about my adventures, but she was pleased I had enjoyed the experience.

On our return to college, Chef Nichol gave a report on all of our placements during the holiday. Some hadn't been that good, but, lo and behold, Jane and I came out on top. We had represented the college well, and further placements would be going to Frinton-on-Sea.

In the meantime I took weekend jobs serving at Carwardine's, which was a coffee house at the bottom of Milsom Street in Bath. I personally hated coffee, so working in the smell all day was not good, but it paid well.

Then came an opportunity to work for Fortt's, an upmarket restaurant in Milsom Street, but with the outside catering department. This I loved, although I had to catch the 6am bus to be there on time. I would work a hard day setting everything up, serving and clearing everything up afterwards, usually getting back in time to catch the late bus home.

We went to some beautiful houses on big estates. Sometimes the events – usually weddings – would be held in huge marquees, beautifully decorated with flowers and ribbons, or in the house itself. Sometimes it would be a cold buffet, or canapés, or a sit-down meal.

A lot of work for the chefs, who sometimes had to bring in army-style kitchen equipment to cope. The clothes were beautiful, the people good fun, and the tips were good.

The job I usually got at the end of the day was to bring the prepared hamper for the honeymoon couple to take on their journey, as they usually hadn't eaten very much during the festivities. The surprise for me was that the beautiful dresses were usually just left on the floor where the bride stepped out of them; surely they could have hung them up.

# CHAPTER 24

—

Jen's parents and mine agreed we could go to youth club. Jen was to come down on the seven o'clock bus and go back on the 9pm one. I was to meet her and see her back to the bus, then run like hell down to the Withymead. On winter evenings, I had the devil behind me.

Youth club was a new experience, with all sorts to do. It was overseen by the vicar, who was great fun.

Skiffle was all the rage, so we decided to have our own group. Herbie from the town band found a brush handle and an empty tea chest. With some twangy thread, tied to the brush handle and tuned with drawing pins, he was able to make an agreeable double bass sound. Dougie always came with his guitar just in case, and we all sang 'My Old Man's a Dustman' and got a round of applause from the other members.

We were also introduced to square dancing, the vicar getting the Saturday night caller to come and teach us the moves. We had to have partners for this form of dance, which was interesting.

I found myself with a very nervous-looking Herbie, who stood before me and asked if we could dance. I just nodded a shy nod of agreement, the music started and we were off. A curtsy to my partner, then holding hands in a big circle, whizzing around the hall. Then the call came to do-si-do, which was going around your partner with your arms folded, back to back. This sent us into hysterics and had everyone collapsing.

After a few weeks we got the hang of it, and the caller invited us to come to the village square dance on the forthcoming Saturday. Herbie asked if he could take me. He had taken to coming with me, Jen and Pete to see Jen onto the bus after club meetings. Pete had a bicycle, so he whizzed off home to Wraxall, while Herbie walked me home. I thanked him, and he confirmed Saturday's date for the square dance.

Mum and Dad seemed to approve of Herbie, so they agreed for me to go. I wore my trusty tan skirt and jumper with scarf, and waited for Herbie.

When Herbie arrived I opened the door and my mouth fell open. Before me stood Herbie in tight trousers and a blue jacket with Lurex thread laced all over it, wearing a shoelace in place of a tie.

I blushed to the roots of my hair, and stuttered that I couldn't possibly go out with him dressed like that. He smiled and said it was the style of the moment; 'Teddy boy', he said they called it. I said I was sorry and closed the door.

Unbeknownst to me, Mum had agreed to help with refreshments, so when I came back in from the hall saying I wasn't going she was somewhat surprised. 'What's made you change your mind?' she asked. When I explained, she smiled and said, 'Come on, we'll go anyway.'

To my surprise, when we got there Herbie had changed into his usual cowboy style, so all was well.

*** 

I cannot recall the length of time we enjoyed the fun of the youth club, but it came to an end, as with all things, when Herbie went into the army.

As my job was residential, I was away from home now quite a lot, just visiting for a weekend once a month. Occasionally our weekends coincided, but I was aware I was no longer the star attraction for Herbie. My heart was broken. He would pass the time of day when we happened to be in the choir together, but I was so sad.

One weekend home Mum told me Herbie was getting married the next day. My heart went to my boots.

I couldn't help myself; I had to go to church, and sat at the back. Herbie came in with his brother as best man. He saw me out of the corner of his eye, then he was gone down the aisle to wait for his bride.

We came to the bit where the vicar asked for anyone to come forward if they knew of any just cause to prevent the wedding. I had to hang on to the church pew to stop myself running down the aisle and proclaiming my love for Herbie; I was too late. He left the church smiling at his bride, and I prayed she would give him a good life.

# CHAPTER 25

—

At college I had noticed that a rather rotund man with glasses seemed to be wherever I happened to be, whether revising on a bench in the abbey courtyard, in the canteen getting a drink or just by my work table in the kitchen. Chef Nichol had noticed it as well and gave me a wink. I was embarrassed, and eventually asked Chef Nichol who he was.

'He is of the Palmer biscuit family, and his name is David.'

David seemed very lonely, as he was never with the other male students, and so I decided to talk to him. He seemed very interested in me. I could befriend him but couldn't see him as a boyfriend, mainly because he lived in Somerset, and was possibly from a posh background.

With exams 150 and 151 taken and passed, now the big one, 152, could see me out into the big wide world. I was very keen to get the City & Guilds, then I would be fully qualified in hotel and catering management.

The day of the exam arrived. Everything was already on the work table, with an exam sheet describing the menu to be cooked. It didn't need much explaining, as there on my table was a live lobster. It was to be cooked in the thermidor style; I could have died. Spinach and ricotta cheese ravioli as the starter, so there was pasta to make, and mille-feuille for dessert. I had a lot to get through, so no time for squeamishness.

The exam over, we had a few weeks left to discuss placements. David, of course, didn't seem to have the need to find employment outside the family business, and invited me down for a weekend to meet his family and see the factory. I didn't see myself in a biscuit factory, so I gently said that I had no transport to get to Somerset, and I was more into hotel management than biscuits. I thanked him very much but declined his invitation. He walked away very sad, but at least I had been honest. As I write this, I wonder what would have been if I had said yes.

As it was, three of us – Rosie, Lorna and I – were placed at Winsley Chest Hospital. It was in Winsley, about six miles from Bath, and on top of a hill where the wind seemed to blow constantly. This was presumably why the hospital had been built there, as they catered mainly for patients with tuberculosis and cancer, who spent a lot of time wheeled out in their beds onto their verandas to get fresh air.

Each patient had their own room, as opposed to wards. There was A block for ladies, B block for men, E block for operating theatre, Matron and doctors, and the chalets, which male patients were moved to when they were getting ready to be released. Usually, patients were in residence for about nine months. Many of the patients were originally guards who swore they got TB from people huffing on them to see if they were real. D block was the kitchen, refectory, domestic accommodation (where we were), and the boiler house.

The residents of the chalets had nothing better to do than find ways to scare the living daylights out of us as we took it in turns to deliver the nurses their evening meal. They had named us the three graces; Lorna was 'Grace', Rosie 'Disgrace' and me 'Candle Grease'!

It was coming up to April Fools' Day, so we decided to fool the chalet residents by raising the fire alarm so that they would have to get up early. The alarm was on E block, so, with the breakfast trolleys delivered, we went to E block, raised the alarm and ran like hell back to D block.

It was at this point we realised that not only were the chalets alarmed, but the whole hospital. Beds were wheeled out onto verandas; walking patients were given a blanket and taken out into the courtyard. The fire brigade arrived, but no fire to be found.

It didn't take very long for us to be summoned to the matron's office. Obviously we had been observed going to or from E Block. We took off our aprons, adjusted our hats and proceeded to the office.

Matron and one of the doctors were standing behind Matron's desk; we were lined up in front of the desk. The doctor spoke first: did we realise the seriousness of our actions?

Lorna spoke for all of us. 'We didn't in the beginning; we just wanted to fool the residents in the chalets for all the jokes they had played on us. It wasn't until we saw the results of our actions that we thought, *Oh, my goodness, what have we done?*'

There was a long pause while the two conferred. We were then asked if we had anything to say.

We seemed to reply as one and said how sorry we were. Was anyone hurt as a result of our actions? Could we help put patients back where they should be?

Another pause. Finally, Matron stood before us. We all felt we were going to be sacked, and, horror of horrors, what would our parents say?

'We cannot stress the seriousness of your actions enough. You will be on probation for the next three months, so any misdemeanours will result in instant dismissal. Dr Lewis and I realise what you meant to achieve, and in this instance no one has come to harm. In fact, it has proved to be a very good rehearsal of our fire precautions. This in no way condones your actions, but in this case no harm has been done. You may go and continue your duties.'

We felt like wet rag dolls, all floppy, and just collapsed on the hot plate in the kitchen.

Miss Hopkins, our catering manager, came out of her office. 'Well do I still have some kitchen staff?'

We nodded.

'Well, then you had better get to work; we have got lunch to prepare.'

The incident was never spoken of again.

# CHAPTER 26

—

In the fullness of time I got over my heartbreak and met Alan; he was an apprentice on Mr Blake's farm. He was always working hard on the farm, or making trailers and such for when he had his own farm.

One day, when I was visiting, Alan asked if I would like to go to the pictures with him. He said he had a car, so we could go to Bath. I was not too sure about this, so, when he went out to do the milking, I asked Mrs Blake if it was a good idea. She seemed to be of the opinion that it could be fun. So I agreed to a date, got on my bicycle and pedalled like mad all the way home. I had given Alan Mum's telephone number and the date I would next be home.

True to his word, on my next visit home, he rang and asked to take me to the pictures in Bath. I had told Mum, who seemed okay with the idea, so we were able to arrange everything.

He duly turned up, but he didn't come to the door; he just waited in the car for me to go out. I felt a bit awkward and shy. It didn't help when he said they were showing *The Fly* at the Forum, and he thought it might be fun. I couldn't imagine how a film about a fly was going to be fun, but told myself to keep an open mind.

We got seated just as the film was about to start. This blessed fly was everywhere, including in an experimental unit just as the experiment was about to start on this poor man. I just could not watch any more, so I closed my eyes and tried to block out the music.

It seemed to go on forever, and, contrary to expectations, there was none of the hand holding or cuddling which, if I was brave enough to peek out, I could see was going on all around me. Alan was totally absorbed in the film.

Eventually the film ended, and Alan asked if I would like to join him for supper on the way home. I accepted, otherwise I didn't know how I was going to get home.

He stopped at a café on the way out of Bath. I had a mushroom omelette, while he had breakfast. He asked if I had had a good sleep through the film, as whenever he had looked at me my eyes were closed.

'That was because I didn't like the film.'

'Why didn't you say? We could have left.'

'Well, you looked totally absorbed in the film, so I didn't want to spoil it for you.'

'My, that's a first: a girlfriend who is considerate of me. Thank you.'

We walked back to the car hand in hand. A kiss goodnight when we got home, and the request to meet again.

Neither of us had money to spare, so a lot of our meetings involved window shopping in Milsom Street and supper at what had now become 'our café'. Or we would go to his aunt and uncle for Sunday tea, which I loved.

His aunt and uncle's farm in Tibberton, just out of Gloucester, had been in his mother's side of the family for three generations. His grandmother had her own part of the house; Sam and Gwyneth and their three daughters had the rest. It felt very loving and together. Alan's mother lived at Nupend with her second husband.

I was also taken to meet Alan's father, Brian, who scared me from the beginning. He had a hard mouth, and looked at me with suspicious eyes below bushy eyebrows. He invented things and didn't buy anything new if he could buy it at auction rooms and do it up. He was in the middle of converting a lovely town house in Bristol into apartments. I liked his lady friend very much; she didn't seem to mind his grumpy ways and joined in to help with the renovations.

One day Alan arrived with the news his father was to marry Alison.

'Who is Alison?' I asked. 'It doesn't sound like the name of the lady I've met with him.'

'No, she is my first cousin.'

I looked at him with concern. 'But is that allowed?'

He didn't know, but the wedding was in two weeks' time, and we were invited. Then we would be taking them to Southampton to go on their honeymoon.

'Oh, my goodness, what am I to wear?'

Alan just laughed. 'You will find something, I'm sure.'

My first thought was to ring Jen; she would sort me.

Jen and I arranged to meet up on my half-day, at her lunch break. Jen had already done a reccy and found two outfits in the same shop that she thought I would like. One was pale grey with a pencil skirt and fitted jacket; the other was a full skirt and fitted jacket in a ice blue brocade. I chose the latter, and a feathery hat. Job done.

The day arrived, and Alan duly collected me from Winsley. He greeted me with, 'Hello, my princess in curtain material!' I smiled, but was confused inside as to whether that was a compliment or not.

We drove in haste to the registry office, where family and friends had gathered. We were called into a room where a suited man stood behind a desk. He said a few words about the legality of the wedding; they made their vows and signed the register. There, it was all over; they were man and wife. I can't even remember what she wore, it was such a whirl. Then we were in the car driving to Southampton, no fuss, no bother.

On reaching Southampton I was secretly worried about how we were going to find the ship for the newlyweds! As we turned into the dock road, it turned out I need not have worried. Alan's father suddenly said, 'There she is,' as the ship loomed above the dock buildings. The nearer we got, the bigger she got.

The car parked, luggage unloaded, goodbyes said, Alan's dad turned to him and said, 'Find yourself a farm by the time we get back,' and they were gone into passport control.

'Let's wave them off,' said Alan, so we made our way through to the dockside.

The ship was enormous. I looked along its side and read, *Queen Mary*. I looked up to see the passenger rail that was gradually filling up with people; I had to hold my hat on, it was so high up.

A military-style band was marching up and down the dock. Then men were taking off the ropes that were holding the ship to the quayside, and the gap grew bigger and bigger. The captain blew the horn, which was deafening, as the *Queen Mary* very slowly and gracefully pulled out of the dock. The propellers started to churn up the water as she slowly moved forward on her way to America. We just caught sight of Alison and Brian waving as she passed.

We walked back to the car almost in silence as the experience soaked in. A quick look down the water, and there she was, much smaller now, and committed to sailing the Atlantic.

The route out of Southampton navigated, we settled down to our journey home, back to our café. Alan suddenly said, 'Did Dad really say to look for a farm?'

I confirmed what I had heard, then, deep in thought, he took me back to Winsley. What a day.

# CHAPTER 27

—

The haymaking season was upon us, so Alan and I only met up on Sundays now. His comfy Ford Consul was exchanged for a grey Ford van, and on rainy days we would visit prospective farms with Mr Blake to give advice.

One Sunday evening, having spent the afternoon at Birdsend Farm in Tibberton (I loved the name), we were doing our usual shop gazing when Alan stopped at the little jewellery shop at the bottom of Milsom Street. 'I know you girls are all romantic about choosing an engagement ring, so which one would you choose?'

I had had my eye on a ring in this little shop for some time: not as an engagement ring, as I was far too young at nineteen to be thinking of marriage, and Alan was only twenty-three, but I had been saving to buy it for myself. I pointed out the little ring, which had a gold cup that looked like a flower with a diamond in the middle; I thought it very unusual.

'Oh!' he said. 'I thought you would go for something big and flashy.'

'Shows how well you know me, then, doesn't it?' I replied, promising myself to make more of an effort to buy it.

\*\*\*

One Sunday Alan said we were going somewhere different today and headed off in the Gloucester direction. When we got to Stroud he turned off and went up a road signposted Bisley, then at the top of the steep hill he turned right for Middle Lypiatt, went along the lane and turned right again.

One field in, he said, 'The farm starts here and goes all the way along this lane to Nether Lypiatt, down both sides to the valley bottom, so we can grow corn and make hay on the top and have store cattle on the slopes. What do you think?'

I, having no idea, asked, 'No cows or milking?'

'Good question,' he replied. 'No; I thought if I bought in day-old calves and reared them for beef, that would free up days. We could have the occasional day out or go to market, and not be tied down here to milk the cows.'

'Where would you live?' I asked, as I had not noticed a farmhouse, just some cottages halfway along the lane.

Just then he drew to a halt outside a beautiful square Georgian house with imposing railings. 'This isn't the house, but it is stunning, isn't it? It belongs to a gentleman called Nettlefold and is just off what will hopefully be my land. It is known as the Haunted House.'

He quickly turned the van around and drove back along the lane, then turned right and stopped outside another beautiful house. 'This is Middle Lypiatt House, and it's owned by Mr Graham. He didn't want the farm but liked the house, so I hope to buy the land. There are three more cottages down this path; I thought I could live in one of those until I have made enough money to build a house. What do you think?'

'Well, I know nothing about farming except what I've learnt from Jen, but it sounds to me as if it's a good idea. You have got it all worked out. What did Mr Blake think of it?'

'Well, he seemed to be of the same opinion as you,' Alan said. 'He said to be aware that a lot of money would have to be paid out, buying calves, feed, corn seed et cetera, so I should write that into the equation when costing everything out.'

'Sounds like good advice to me. When does your father come home?'

'Any day now, I think.'

You could feel the excitement. I really hoped it would all happen for him.

I had to work the day Alan's father came home, so, reassured he would be able to find that big ship, off he went. I, of course, was not privy to the conversations that followed, but in the fullness of time a very excited Alan came to collect me and announced his father had bought the farm for him.

Alan's father's trip to America had been a success, as the honeymoon had also been a sales promotion for his latest invention.

This invention was a gauge that told you when whatever you were filling, from toothpaste tubes to huge flour silos, was filled to the required level.

I was so pleased for Alan. You could see his mind was a whorl of things to do: trailers to finish, a cottage to furnish and so on. There was an open-ended cattle shelter by the cottages in the field which he was planning on making into a corn store with corn dryer. I thought he was so clever.

Our stroll round the shops that evening seemed so insignificant to what he was trying to achieve; nothing really made sense, so we had an early supper and headed back to Winsley.

'When do you take over the farm?' I asked when Alan had stopped the van.

'I think it will be about the end of November,' he said.

*Oh, golly,* I thought.

'Penny for them?' asked Alan.

'Well, I was just thinking what a time of year to start farming, with the winter weather and all.'

'Well, it is the right time of year for my style of farming. Ploughing the fields and hoping the frost will help break the soil down to make a fine tilth to plant the corn seeds. Good time for doing repair work and building the corn dryer, too, so not to worry.' He took my hands. 'What I do need is a wife to keep me warm and well fed, and company on the long dark nights. What do you say; would you marry me?'

I was shocked. Never once had he mentioned love or wanted cuddles; all I had seen from him was this drive to have his own farm. I could cook, yes, but I knew nothing of married life, and I was just twenty.

He had been fumbling in his pocket while he waited for an answer. Eventually he brought out a small box, which he opened. There before my very eyes was my ring. I couldn't believe what I was seeing.

'Well,' he said, 'yes or no?'

I looked into his eyes and said, 'Yes.'

'Thank goodness for that,' he said. 'I thought for a moment it was going to be no, then where would I have been?'

He put the ring on my finger; it fitted perfectly. I couldn't stop looking at it.

'When do you think we could get married?' he asked.

'Well, I would like a church wedding, if that is okay, as I didn't go a bundle on your father's wedding.'

'Okay, but it's now October. Do you think December would be possible?'

I had no idea, but had a sudden thought we would have to ask the vicar. He would set the date, I guessed, especially as Christmas was looming. I shared this thought.

'Good idea,' Alan said. 'So make an appointment to see him when you are free.'

'What would your father say?' I asked. 'And, for that matter, what would my mother say?'

'Dad is fine. It was he who suggested it, as practical as ever.' He gave a wry smile. 'I'm sure your mother will be pleased to have you off her hands.'

I wasn't sure whether to laugh or cry at that comment. 'Have you asked my parents' permission?'

He looked somewhat aghast. 'Do I have to?'

'Yes, you do; I'm under twenty-one.'

'Well, I will call round tomorrow evening. Will they both be at home?'

'Yes, unless someone decides to have a baby,' I said with a smile, 'or up and dies!'

I walked down the windy drive not knowing whether to laugh or cry. I was engaged, but I wasn't walking on air; there was no spring in my step. Was it just a business arrangement, or was there love there?

Mum and Dad agreed – somewhat reluctantly, I gather – but wanted to be sure he would take good care of me. Mum insisted that she would give me away. I was horrified; how could I do that to the man I loved as my father? He had clothed and fed me and had been there for me when Mum had one of her moments. She was simultaneously furious and very sad at my reaction. I have tried to analyse that moment many times over the years, and still do not understand it.

# CHAPTER 28

—

The visit to the vicar went well. There needed to be three weeks to call the banns for any objections, and we were requested to attend a service during that time. I only had one weekend off a month, so the earliest date for the wedding would be 9 December at 2pm.

Alison had sent word via Alan that she would like to make my wedding dress. If I could meet her on my day off, we could go to buy the material. In the meantime, I should get a bridal magazine to have some idea of design, and how many bridesmaids would I like.

So many decisions, plus my bank account was going to have a shock. Mum would be making no contributions.

So, on my next day off, I would be taking a trip to Bath. I needed to find a magazine, visit Fortt's to talk about the reception, buy tins for my wedding cake and look at headdresses. For my going away outfit, I would need to talk to Jen.

I rang Alan to see if he would like his three cousins to be bridesmaids. I also wanted the son and daughter of my chef instructor. They were delighted; the page boy was happy to wear a kilt, and the little girl would be a small edition of the three older girls.

Fortt's were amazing and said, as I had done such good work for them, they would be pleased to do a canapés and desserts menu for sixty people with a sparkling wine, tea and coffee, plus the staff to serve it, for £150.

I met Jen, who had found the most lovely suit for me in a fine green tweed with box pleat skirt and fitted jacket. Perfect. A wedding dress shop proved successful with a neat false tiara and circlets of white flowers with ribbons, just right for the bridesmaids. Just a kitchen shop now for cake tins, and I would buy ingredients from Mr Bevan when I got home. It was tricky getting off the bus and walking down the drive.

The visit with Alison to discuss my dress was amazing, as I hadn't really known what she was able to do. We looked through the bride magazine until we came to a dress I liked, which she thought was ideal.

My main request was no zip at the back; could the zip be in the front, hidden by a plaque covering it? I suggested small material buttons from scooped neckline to hem, with a skirt that fell into a train. She was delighted. The bridesmaids would be the same with a large rose at the back, chiffon floaty bits the length of the dress, and long sleeves.

Off we went to the shops, and we found a lovely brocade for me. I hoped Alan wouldn't think I was in curtain material.

I had envisaged red velvet for the girls, but there wasn't enough in any one shop, and there could have been a difference in colour if we bought it from multiple places. We went for a royal blue taffeta instead, and I found three white mohair shawls. Job done. Alison was thrilled to bits and got to work straight away.

The first fitting for my dress went well. Now we had to get the bridesmaids to try on theirs; this involved a trip to Tibberton on the morning of my next Saturday off. The girls were very excited; Grandma loved all the excitement too, and busied herself making lunch for us. Dresses fitted, the colour looked amazing as they all had blond hair, the two smaller children looking resplendent in their little outfits.

Alison dropped me off at Mrs Blake's and shared all the excitement with her, then the men came in from milking, so all talk of the wedding stopped. I thought Alan might have been a bit more interested to know if the girls were happy, but I guess he just left it to me. So I had to remind him of his job, which was cars from my home to the church, and to take the two of us to and from the reception. And was there to be a honeymoon?

'Oh!' he said. 'I thought all I had to do was turn up!'

'Well, that as well,' I said with a giggle.

\*\*\*

The date was coming around very quickly. Alan's father had been to an auction and bought us a bed, settee and armchair, a cooker that needed a good clean, a manufacturing-sized sewing machine, and a kitchen cabinet.

Alan had been very busy moving his tractor and trailer to the farm, measuring up for the corn dryer, checking fences and so on.

Come the day, there had been a sprinkling of snow overnight, which was the last thing I wanted to see. Aunt Rene arrived early to be there for Mum and Dad. She made sure there were endless cups of tea.

While I had a bath and washed my hair to be ready for the hairdresser, Aunt Rene decided I needed to know the facts of life, and plonked herself on the toilet. I was glad she had, as I hadn't known half of what she was saying; the job was remembering all the advice. My brother Chris scrubbed up well to be an usher, and Mum and Dad made a very smart couple.

Sam and Gwyneth and the girls, already in their dresses, came in to use the toilet before going to the church, and collected their shawls and prayer book flowers. It seemed that Alan had asked Sam to be our main source of transport to the church. Mum and Aunt Rene went first, then the bridesmaids, then me and Dad.

When I got in, I sat on my veil, which made my headdress slip to one side. The road was also quite slippy, so Sam was taking care getting there. I had promised Alan I wouldn't be late, so I was beginning to get a bit panicky.

When we got to the church, the planned side door entry was now the west door into the vestry, but at least the girls were warm and I could adjust my headdress. Then the doors opened and the verger was waiting for us to line up and walk into the church.

By now I was desperate to get up to Alan, who was standing waiting for me. Dad was holding me back in the gentlest way.

I gave my flowers to the chief bridesmaid and held on tight to Alan's hand, tears streaming down my face. I looked at him, but he was looking straight ahead. I tried hard to pull myself together and get the words of the vows out without sniffing. Then we had to kneel for the prayers.

Alison had made my dress beautifully, and had made an underskirt to give it shape. When I went to kneel, the edge of the underskirt caught on the altar step and pushed my dress up like a tent in front of me, so I just hung on to the altar rail for all I was worth to keep from toppling over. It was a relief to stand up while the vicar said his piece. Sadly, I have no recollection of what he said.

Now it was just the register to sign in the organ vestry. We signed first and moved around the organ to let everyone in, then everyone backed out to let us lead the way out of church.

What a performance. I dreamed for weeks afterwards of doing it as planned at the rehearsal.

Photos next, with a moderate wind blowing; my veil just took off. The girls' teeth were chattering, so we asked the photographer if we could move to the reception and do photos there. Fortt's had done well, the hall was warm and looking good, and the cake, which I had made in the shape of a horseshoe, hadn't collapsed.

Speeches over, it was time to leave, the sun already setting. We drove off into the night and the rest of our lives together.

'Where are we going?' I asked.

'How about Weymouth?' Alan said.

'Oh! I love Weymouth.' I was thinking of Sunday school outings to a beach where the sea never seemed to go out, unlike Weston.

'We are staying one night at a hotel, then a week at Gweek in Cornwall with my aunt and uncle, who are looking forward to meeting you.'

'Sounds lovely. Thank you.'

It was nearly half past nine in the evening by the time the poor little van pulled up outside the hotel. We collected our luggage, Alan making sure there was no evidence of confetti, and went into the hotel. We were welcomed and given keys, and a porter showed us to our room. I asked if we could have a pot of tea and some sandwiches, as there had been no hamper left for us, and by now I was starving, not having eaten since breakfast. Alan thanked me for thinking of it, as he was hungry too.

While we waited for the refreshments, Alan produced a towel for me to stand on. 'To catch any confetti that may be in your clothes,' he said. I didn't quite understand his concern with the confetti but went along with it.

Refreshments over, I got the seductive black nightie that Jen had given me out of my case and proceeded to undress on the towel, Alan doing likewise on his towel. The towels were then shaken out of the window.

I was in bed when Alan turned around, put out the light and got into bed. And we both lay there like laid-out corpses: no kiss goodnight, no cuddles. Should I initiate it? But I was afraid of being rebuffed, so I lay there and must have drifted off to sleep.

Next morning he was up and using the bathroom while I came to. Breakfast eaten, cases packed, we were off to Cornwall and Gweek.

The journey itself was interesting, with lovely scenery, and it was a sunny wintery day. I had been to Cornwall before, having had family holidays in St Ives, but I obviously hadn't paid attention to what was happening outside the car window.

We arrived in Gweek just as the sun was thinking of going to bed, and were given a warm greeting by Alan's aunt and uncle, with a delicious smell coming from the kitchen. I seemed to be the main entertainer as I recounted all the incidents during the service. Eventually it was time for bed, but the same ritual occurred, with the exception of the confetti issue. No hugs, no kisses, and so it continued for the rest of the week.

Time to return home, and Alan dropped me off and said he would be over early next morning to go to his father's and pick up his van with all the furniture in it. It had snowed again overnight, but the roads seemed to be passable.

Vans exchanged and loaded, we set off for the farm. Mum had given me a whole lot of bed linen, towels, pillows and other essentials. We also had two chairs and a lovely drop-sided table we had been given as a wedding present, along with a collection of different-sized pans and saucepans.

We had done quite well, given the weather conditions, but now we had the steep hill out of Stroud. We had almost reached the top when the wheels began to slip and slide; no grip could be found, so Alan put the van in reverse. He went down the hill a short way and tried to find new snow to grip on. Again, nearly there and the wheels take on a life of their own. Nothing for it; we would have to go all the way round and come in from the other direction.

The winter sun was setting, and Alan was driving in poor conditions. I stayed very quietly beside him.

Eventually I recognised the lane we had just turned into, so we were nearly there. He turned into the path down to the cottage, and drove down the steep slope.

We started to unload the van, and eventually got everything in and the bed put together. Alan had thought to bring some wood and coal to light a fire. I had thought to gather some bread and a few cans of soup from Mum's winter store, so we were able to have something warm.

I made the bed, as Alan very carefully reversed the van to the top of the slope in case it snowed more overnight. Exhausted, we went to bed and slept very well.

Next morning we were off again, luckily with no more snow. Alan drove very carefully on the slippery roads back to Bristol. We did a big grocery shop in case it snowed and set off again in the little van to get home, leaving the van at the top of the slope again just in case.

It proved to be the right decision, as the worst snow for years decided to fall in Gloucestershire. The wind was a huge factor; it blew the snow off the fields into the lane, snowing us all in for weeks. The snow plough would come through the lane, blowing the snow over the hedge, only for the wind to blow it all back again. Luckily we had no livestock to worry about.

# CHAPTER 29

With the snow gone and a little more warmth in the sun, Alan decided it was time for me to learn how to drive a tractor. He brought the smaller of his tractors out into the flat field, where he showed me how to start it, how to change gear and how to use the pedals to control the speed and the brake. After a jumpy start I got the hang of it to the extent that Alan said I was ready to cultivate the small field he had ploughed, and drove us both to the field. I was in seventh heaven, but freezing cold. Before long, I would always remember to wear gloves and a hat, no matter what I looked like.

So now my days were filled with home chores. Feeding the new calves, cooking lunch, preparing veg for the evening meal, fire banked in with the peelings as my mother had taught me. Then off to the field to cultivate wherever Alan told me to go.

The suggestion that I should learn to drive also cropped up. 'I think you should have a course of lessons and hopefully pass first time.' This I accomplished, but I had no car to drive. At least I now knew how to.

Maurice Graham, from Middle Lypiatt House, had rented out his paddocks to a polo-playing friend of his. The ponies came with their own groom, a very flamboyant character with flaming red hair flying out behind her as she exercised them. Over time I notice these ponies were getting exercised around fields where Alan was working, and not on the bridleways, but in full view.

I decided not to say anything, not wanting to be a neurotic wife or read into things. Still no romance at home.

Then Mr Graham asked if it was possible for Alan to take the groom home in the evenings, as he was taking his South African wife home for an extended family holiday. He would pay for fuel and time. Alan thought this was an easy earner.

The months went on, and Alan's return home got later and later. One night he came home wearing the shirt I had given him for Christmas. As he passed me I grabbed the shirt and tore it down the back. He rounded on me as if to fight, but I ducked and ran upstairs. I sat on the bed crying my eyes out.

He came slowly up the stairs and into the room, taking his trousers off as he came. He threw me on the floor and entered me with such force it took my breath away and hurt like hell. When he was spent he went downstairs and slept on the couch.

I was too terrified to sleep and just lay sobbing. Was this what Aunt Rene was talking about; was this really married life?

The nightly trips didn't stop. One night I felt really ill and thought I had a tummy bug, as I could not stop vomiting. I came to being carried by Alan out to the van. After a drive through the night to our GP, he pronounced I had appendicitis and should be taken to Gloucester Hospital as soon as possible. He would ring to say we were on the way.

Appendix removed, I was taking longer than expected to recover, so rehab was required. I thought of my lovely aunt Mim and wondered if I could come to recuperate. Alan came in to see me, as did his aunt Gwyneth, who asked who the flame-haired woman in Alan's car was. I just felt my heart drop to my boots.

Aunt Mim and Uncle Perce would be pleased to have me if Alan could bring me down, and this he did. He told me that he had taken on Andy from one of the cottages to help with the harvest and calves. Otherwise the journey was in silence.

The relief at being safe with my aunt was so healing. Picnics in the park, the smell of new-mown hay, not to mention her delicious cooking. Waking in the morning to the house sparrows' song took me back to childhood summer holidays.

# CHAPTER 30

—

All too soon I felt I had to go back, so I rang Alan from the telephone kiosk next door to say I was well enough to come home.

'Don't bother,' was his reply.

With tears streaming down my face, I ran in to tell my aunt and uncle what he had said.

'Well, my dear,' said my uncle, 'you have no choice but to go back. If you don't, he can divorce you for desertion.'

I was so shocked; whatever was happening?

'When Stan comes in, I will ask him to take you back. I will come with you.'

The next day Stan agreed to take me back that afternoon. I was to ring Alan to tell him I was coming back anyway. I was really worried as I thought they would beat him up, but I needn't have worried; he had moved out, and left me the furniture. He had taken Lou, the beautiful labrador I had given him as a wedding present.

Andy's mum came over to see me, and was so sorry for what had happened. She told me Alan had bought Hill Farm and moved the groom in. 'If I were you, dear, I would get legal advice.' She told me where to go for advice and what times the buses went, and gave me her telephone number in case I ever needed someone to talk to.

I caught the bus into Stroud. I knew that the solicitors' offices were in Rowcroft, and that I shouldn't go to Lapage, Norris and Payne, as Alan's solicitor was with them. All the rest looked old and dusty except Winterbotham, Ball and Gadsden, so I decided to go in there.

The receptionist was very smiley and asked if she could help. I asked to see Mr Gadsden, as that was the easiest name to say. 'Would that be Mr Graham or Mr Peter?' was the reply, so I stumped for Peter, but, alas, he was out of the office.

'What is your need for a solicitor?' she asked.

I couldn't think of the legal term, so I just said, 'Marital.'

'Ah, our Mr Anson deals with marital. Would you like to see him?'

'Yes, please,' came almost like a plea.

'I'll try him for you.' She picked up the phone. 'I have a Mrs …' She waited for me to say the name.

'Barton.'

'… Barton in reception. Do you have a moment?'

'Please send her up,' was the reply.

'This place is like a rabbit's warren; I will show you the way,' the receptionist said.

She took me to a door and knocked, and, as requested, I went in. I was greeted with a handshake and offered a chair in front of Mr Anson's desk.

'How can I help?' he asked, so I related my sorry story.

After a while he asked, 'Are you hoping for a reconciliation?'

I looked directly at him. How did he know that was exactly what I wanted: my husband back, as if it had all been a bad dream?

'Right, well, I will write to him and see what he says.'

The wait for Mr Anson to ring was like forever. Finally the worst came; the answer was 'no reconciliation'.

I had seen Andy's mum, who could tell me Alan's groom was pregnant. When I related this information to Mr Ball of the solicitor's office, he said, 'Right, I will now write and ask him to sign an affidavit' – whatever that was – 'to say he has committed adultery, then we can go for a divorce. I will be in touch,' and he was gone.

I slumped in the chair, and sobbed and sobbed. Andy's mum came in and put her arms around me. 'He is never worth it,' she said. 'You are better off without him.'

'But all those promises, the happy family gatherings that we both wanted, it all meant nothing.'

She knelt in front of me, took my hands and looked me straight in the eye. 'I think you have been used to get what he wants: his farm. You were the suitable wife; now he has what he wants and he's just casting you aside.'

***

It was hard living in the cottage on my own with Andy now feeding my little calves, no tractor driving, no nothing.

*Stop wallowing,* said a voice in my head. *Get a job; you need the money.* A trip to Stroud was in order, so off I went to buy a Stroud newspaper and find a job.

I sat on a park bench and scanned the vacancies page. There before me was the very thing, and only in the next street. It was to assist in a specialist biscuit unit in Slad Road.

I closed the paper and set off to find the premises. There was an office, so I went in, told a woman I was applying for the job, waving the paper, and was asked to take a seat.

After a while she returned with a gentleman wearing a white coat. He took a seat and described what was required: piping almond biscuits. Had I any experience of piping? I explained my qualifications, and the experience I had of piping.

'Well,' he said, 'I think you are overqualified for the job, but come with me and we will see what you can do. I have just made a batch to be piped.'

We went upstairs to a white-painted room with stainless steel worktops, a stack of trays, a mixing machine, piping bags and nozzles. He handed me a white coat and I was off. Piping bag filled, I took a tray of biscuits and began piping the mixture. After a moment he said, 'Those are perfect; when can you start?'

'Well, I have another two hours before my bus, then I can do a full day tomorrow onwards.'

He shook my hand and said, 'You have got the job!'

On my walk back to the cottage I was passed by Alan with the groom beside him. I thought he might stop, but no; he drove on by.

When I was home, I rang Fran, as I knew Andy's mum now, and told her the news.

'Good for you, gal,' she said. 'I've been thinking: I've got an old bike in the shed. I'll get Andy to give it the once-over, then you'll have it to do that walk to the bus stop every day. Put it over the wall when you catch the bus, then, with a bit of luck, it will still be there when you get back. Better for you with the dark nights coming.'

So there I was, all set up and with an income, albeit small. I would make it work.

I had news from Mr Anson that the necessary paperwork had been filled in, so he could start divorce proceedings. 'This may take a little time, as the law requires applicants to have been married three years before you can proceed. I think if my calculations are correct you are just coming up to your first anniversary.'

'That is correct,' I replied. 'Have you any idea how much this will cost me?'

'Don't you worry about that,' was his reply, 'and well done on getting yourself organised so well.'

***

Christmas was coming, and arrangements were made for us all to go to Aunt Mim's. Magical. I was to get the bus down to Chipping Sodbury, and Dad would pick me up, having dropped Mum and Chris and Bruce off first.

He was there waiting when the bus pulled in. I, well loaded with gifts, was pleased to see him.

'You look like Father Christmas,' he said, with a big smile. He touched my hand and asked if I was okay. 'If Mum gets stroppy, just let it go over your head, okay?'

A warm fire was burning in the sitting room fireplace, and I had a lovely welcome when I went into their everyday room. The dining table had been pulled out into the middle of the room for us to sit round, and a delicious smell was coming from the kitchen. Big hugs from aunt, uncle, Stan and Mum, and a big smile from Chris, with a very waggy tail from Bruce. Happiness personified.

Stan was a dear; he was a cousin of Uncle Perce and was stud groom to the Duke of Beaufort, and had once volunteered to teach me and Christine to ride. Christine had refused, but I had loved it; I had soon stopped being a sack of potatoes on the poor horse's back, and had been allowed to ride out with the team some days to exercise the horses.

The sleeping arrangements sounded amazing. Dad and Uncle would be in Christine's room, Mum and Auntie at the head of Aunt Mim's bed and me and Christine at the foot, with a mattress in the bath for Chris. Stan would go back to his house down the road and come up for meals.

Supper over, we all set to work preparing for the big day. The kitchen was groaning with vegetables and goodies of all description. It was my job to do the Brussels sprouts, Mum did the potatoes,

Chris played at making the breadcrumbs. Uncle Perce and Dad got in loads of wood and coal for the two fires, and Christine laid the table when she came home. Aunt Mim stuffed the turkey and put it ready for roasting overnight in the slow oven of the kitchen range. I put my gifts under the Christmas tree in the window; it looked a lovely sight.

We all took a rest, as by now it was nearly time to go to midnight mass. The chaps had decided to miss out on that trip and poured themselves a beer. We all got muffled up as it was bitterly cold, then made our way to church.

It was very well attended. Christine didn't join the choir, so it was like having our own choir in the pew. The Duke and Duchess of Beaufort had been invited to Windsor Castle as guests of the Queen, so Auntie didn't have to work.

When we went up to the communion rail it was very crushed, and somehow Aunt Mim had got shoved into the corner behind the church banner. She peered out to see what was happening. When the vicar got to her, I lifted up the corner of the flag so he could see her. We had the most awful job to keep ourselves from laughing out loud. We were still laughing when we piled in through the door, as if we were drunk on communion wine!

Earlier, while Dad had been collecting me from the bus stop, Mum and Aunt Mim had put themselves in the front room and had made stockings for all of us with Uncle Perce's socks. These were now all placed along the fender.

We wished everyone a happy Christmas and made our way to bed. Mum and Auntie got into bed first, while Christine and I tried hard to slither down between them without touching. Of course it was impossible, and there was a great deal of giggling and 'oh!'s as toes or knees got in the wrong place, but eventually we dozed off.

We woke to the delightful smell of the turkey cooking. Auntie and Mum went downstairs to bring the fires to life, and came up with tea and stockings. Chris joined us and said he had slept well and hadn't heard us come to bed. Lots of fun opening the socks. A lovely day had by all.

Boxing Day, and the planned meet at Windsor Lodge was suddenly put on hold as we woke to a considerable fall of snow.

'Well, it looks as if no one is going anywhere,' so we made the fires up, gathered in the sitting room and listened to stories of

Christmases past, interspersed with I Spy. Cold buffet for lunch, and we all fell asleep in front of the fire.

After tea and cake, the sun having set, we launched into party games. Consequences gave the biggest laugh, with charades a close second, and so to bed.

# CHAPTER 31

With the A46 open, we reluctantly made our different ways home. My trusty steed was still over the wall, but now in a snowdrift. I decided to leave it there, as I had no shovel and wouldn't be able to ride it in the road conditions.

Home to a cold empty house, but I would soon get a fire going. I made a mental note to ask Andy to get some more logs. The TV was gone, but at least I had a radio.

I soon set into a routine of work and home, a meal, bath and bed. But, with the lighter nights coming, what was I to do?

The lawn needed cutting, but I had no mower. While planning how I could create a garden, I had a call from Mr Anson.

'I have some good news, I hope. You now have permission to leave the property without adverse effect.'

'Thank you; that is good news. How soon can I go?'

'Whenever you like,' was the reply, 'but I'd stress that you shouldn't go too far, as you will need to come to the office quite frequently now.'

I rang Mum with the good news, only to be greeted with, 'You are not coming here getting divorced; you haven't been married five minutes. What did you do, or not do?'

'Why does it have to be my fault?'

'You made your bed, now you lie in it!' and she was gone.

I was beside myself; why was Mum so cross with me? I put the phone down and slumped in the chair, then I thought of Auntie Mim. I looked at the time; I might just catch her.

I called Aunt Mim and explained what had happened.

'Oh, my dear girl, I am so sorry. I will speak to Stan and see if he can pick you up from Chipping Sodbury. Don't forget to give your notice. Give me a ring when you get home.'

The gentleman in the white coat, who I now knew as Mr Harris, was quite understanding and said that I was free to go, but that they would miss me very much. 'If ever you want another job, you would be very welcome.'

I rang Aunt Mim as soon as I got in and, yes, Stan would meet me at the bus stop. 'Just bring what you can carry, dear; don't worry about anything else. Look forward to seeing you tomorrow.'

Next I rang Fran and told her I was free to go. I thanked her for all her kindness and told her I would keep in touch, and that I would leave her bicycle in the calves' shed.

*** 

In Badminton, I was once more surrounded by the safety and calm of my dear Auntie Mim and Uncle Perce. Christine was not best pleased, for whatever reason.

I helped around the house and tried to get as much done as possible for when my aunt came home. Then we could have a quiet cup of tea and a chat before Christine would come in, demanding to know where her meal was as she was going out.

A week or so went past, and I felt I needed to get a job so that I could make a contribution for my keep. 'I think I will put a notice in the post office window to see if anyone wants help around the house.'

'You don't have to, dear; we enjoy having you around,' was Aunt Mim's reply.

'Well, at least I ought to try,' I said. 'If nothing comes of it, that's fine for the time being.'

I drew up an advert and went to put it in the post office. But, on the way in, I noticed another card already there: help needed with four little girls, aged between eight years and eighteen months. I took down the phone number and went back to Aunt Mim.

'What do you think?' I asked. 'Could I help with children? I've never done anything like that before.'

'Well,' she said, 'you will be working with the mother, so you would soon get into the routine. Why not give her a ring and see if you like the sound of her voice? If there's any question in your mind, say you've had second thoughts and leave it at that.'

The voice answering the telephone sounded very nice indeed, and I seemed to be answering with the right answers, so it was agreed that she would come and see me at 11am the next day. I spruced myself up and wore what I thought looked nannyish, and Aunt Mim was able to stay to meet her as well. The mother arrived on time, and we seemed to get on very well, to the extent that she invited me to come and meet her brood.

They all lined up like the Horlicks kids, and were very polite. They were obviously very fond of Vera, who was the housekeeper. Sally, the eldest, liked horse riding and had her own pony. Jane was quite shy but had a very gentle face; Gillian scowled and looked defiant, and Jennifer was just a delight.

We were just getting to know each other when the father came in and said, 'Hello,' then caught his breath. Looking me straight in the eye, he asked, 'Would your mother be Barbara and your father Leon?'

I was a little surprised. 'Yes.' It felt as if there had been some crime committed. 'But my father was killed in a road accident when I was a baby.'

'I know,' he said. 'Your father was my best friend, and your mother was in charge of me and my brother as kids. I am your godfather, Peter Lippiatt.' He held out his hand. 'I often wondered what happened to you.'

Well, I got the job. I rushed in to Aunt Mim and related the whole story.

'Well, I am blessed,' said Aunt Mim, collapsing into a chair. 'If he doesn't come, he sends. I knew he would take care of you.'

'Who are we talking of, Auntie?'

'Your guardian angel,' was her reply.

Mrs Lippiatt took the children to school, then collected me on the way back to Grickstone; the job was live-in. 'Do you drive, by any chance?' she asked.

'Well, I have passed my driving test, but I haven't had much practice since.'

'Well, we will have to get you driving again.'

So life settled down. An Austin 12 was bought for me to drive, so I practised going up and down their long drive with the girls standing on the seat, their heads through the sunroof, which was great fun.

Mrs Lippiatt came with me the first time on the school run with the girls squeezed in the back. Given her approval, I now took on the school run to Grittleton House School, a lovely old house in beautiful grounds. How different it was from school in Marshfield, I thought.

At tea time came the first of several phone calls from Mr Anson. 'Just a few questions,' he said.

With the questions over, he asked how the job was going.

'Fine,' I said. The worst thing had been catching Bashful, Sally's pony; apart from that, all was going well. 'We will be away in Dorset for a week at the beginning of the summer holidays.'

'Okay, but be prepared to come in the week after.'

The morning of the holiday was mayhem, packing and unpacking things with a train to catch. Eventually, the cases were closed and packed into the car. Mr Lippiatt was going to drive down, so that we would have a car there, and Mrs Lippiatt and I were to go on the train with the children. With the lack of sleep from excitement, and the rhythm of the train, they fell asleep, so we enjoyed a quiet time for most of the journey.

The Sandbanks Hotel was an absolute delight, catering for adults and children with the kiddie bar, sea and sand, and dining specifically for adults. It was an amazing combination: afternoon entertainment for children, adult entertainment after dinner. As a result everyone had a good time. All too soon it was time to go home with tanned, happy children.

A phone call that evening requested my presence at the solicitors' office the next Wednesday.

'Take the car, Cynthia,' Mrs Lippiatt said. 'It will make life easier for you, and you will be back to help with bedtime.' It sounded like a good deal.

The dreaded court case was looming, so, with the date fixed, I was talked through what would happen. I think this was meant to make the process less intimidating, but the very mention of a barrister for my case made me feel it would not be straightforward.

The case was to be heard in Gloucester Crown Court at 10am. Mr Anson drove me over, and I met the barrister, who introduced himself and explained how things would proceed.

My one question: was Alan going to be in court? They didn't know, but probably.

The thought sent me into panic mode. 'Can I ask for him to be removed?' I asked.

'Afraid not,' came the reply.

I was shown into the dock; the courtroom was full. Someone called, 'All stand,' and the judge came in and sat in his place.

The clerk to the court came and handed me a Bible, on which I had to swear the words written on the card: to tell the truth, the whole truth and nothing but the truth, so help me God. The judge asked me to look at him when answering questions.

The case began. Talk about dirty washing in public, I have never felt so embarrassed in my life; everything came out. The barrister would ask me questions, to which I replied, only for the judge to bellow in my ear to look at him. It was excruciating.

Eventually it came to finance. An award of £10 a week was made, to be paid monthly, and a life insurance policy taken out in Alan's name was also included, with me as beneficiary. Before I could stop myself, I was saying, 'If he doesn't want me, I don't want his money.' Mr Anson put his finger to his mouth to signal me to be quiet, and the barrister continued.

The judge declared a decree nisi was granted, with absolute in three months, and it was all over. I was sad beyond belief.

The journey back to Stroud was in almost silence. Eventually, I spoke up. I thought I should apologise to Mr Anson for my outburst, but it was as I felt. Plus the insurance policy was in case Alan was killed on the farm, so, if he died in mysterious circumstances, who was going to be the first suspect? I asked if Mr Anson would please say thank you, but decline the insurance policy.

This he agreed. 'Now we just have to wait three months in case either of you change your mind. Plus I have made legal history getting you a divorce after only two years of marriage.' Sounded like a good day was had by all.

# CHAPTER 32

—

Come the day the three months were up, I got the phone call to say the absolute papers were ready for signing, so I offered my usual Wednesday 2pm slot. When Mr Anson said he would bring them down for me to sign at about 6.30, if that was convenient, I got all flustered; that would be getting the children ready for bed time, plus he would be coming down out of hours, as it were.

Mr Lippiatt, who had overheard the conversation, gave the thumbs up. 'Ask him in for a drink, then we will leave you to sign the papers.'

'Thank you,' I said. That had made me feel like family.

Six thirty came, and, sure enough, sitting in his grey Jaguar outside was Mr Anson, reading his paper.

I opened the door and invited him in, but he refused and said, 'There must be a pub nearby.'

There was, but, out of respect for my mother, I had never been in one.

I went in and told Mr and Mrs Lippiatt he wanted to go to a pub. I don't think they were best pleased, but they went along with it. I grabbed my coat and got in the car.

'Now, where is the nearest pub?'

'Well, there is a hotel just at the end of the road which I believe has a public bar, or there is the Compass a bit further on.'

'Well, let's go for the Compass.'

We drove in silence while locating the Compass. He held the door open for me to go in, then led the way to the bar. 'Now, what will you have?'

I had no idea; a sherry didn't seem the right thing to ask for. He suggested a gin and tonic with a slice of lemon. At that moment, I felt I'd take anything.

With a table found, the drinks arrived and the paperwork was brought out. The glasses chinked and cheers were exchanged once it was completed.

'Your case has been very interesting for me,' Mr Anson said, 'and you were always so gracious. It was refreshing not to have warring partners fighting over money and possessions.'

'Well, it was just so demoralising to realise I had been used to secure his farm, then just cast aside with the rubbish.'

'Well, I have enjoyed working with you, and I wonder if we could meet sometimes.'

Well, my flabber was well and truly gasted; how dare he suggest such a thing?

'What sort of woman do you think I am, to cheat on another man's wife?' I asked, furious. 'I saw the photograph of two little girls on your desk. It is the most awful experience I have had and I wish it on no one.'

'I am so sorry; I should explain my wife and I divorced five years ago. I had custody of my girls, but we both felt they were better with their mother while so young, so I have them for high days and holidays. The eldest goes to boarding school; she is fifteen, and Caroline is ten and starts in the new school year. Their mother has remarried, so all is well.'

I calmed down and sipped my gin and tonic.

'I had been wondering if on a weekend you could come and meet my girls and maybe show them how to ride. I have hired two ponies from a client, but I don't have enough time to teach them myself. Is it something you would consider?'

'Well it would have to be on my days off, and I'll have to see whether Mr Lippiatt would allow me to use the car, as using the bus would involve someone having to take me to and from the bus stop.'

'Oh, I'm sure we can solve that problem if it becomes one.'

'Well, in that case I would be pleased to help after all your hard work. Oh, and when do I get your bill? I don't know if I'll be able to afford it, so maybe I'll have to work to pay it off,' I said with a laugh.

'The bill went to your ex-husband as part of the financial package, so no worries there.'

I have to say it was a huge relief to hear that, as I had been worrying about the bill for some time.

A weekend was chosen when the girls were next due to be with their father. The car wasn't a problem, but the suggestion was to park the car in the car park of the solicitor's office, which was locked at weekends, and Mr Anson would drive me from there.

This he did. Up the very pretty Slad valley we went, into the village itself, then a turnoff which read *Steanbridge Lane*. It narrowed to a single track with a few passing places. We passed beautiful scenery with a small lake and steep slopes, then uphill we went, but past the only house left in sight. I felt quite uneasy; what was I doing, with a relatively unknown man driving me out into the countryside?

At the top of the hill he turned the car around and proceeded to drive backwards down a very narrow lane. I was really now very nervous. The steep sides of the lane brushed on either side of the car, then suddenly there was a long low house.

A black and white dog dashed out of the first doorway, then two young girls tumbled out of the second door. Mr Anson stopped the car and jumped out to welcome his daughters. 'This is Cynthia, who I hope is going to help you learn to ride.' There was an audible groan from the eldest. 'Come on, let's get in and have a coffee.'

The girls introduced themselves, and shared their biggest fears about horse riding, which were mainly falling off.

'Well, when you are ready to have a go, I will help you,' I said. 'Do you know the names of the horses?'

'Yes,' said Caroline, the younger girl. 'The small horse is called Chocolate, and the big white horse is called Quizzy.'

'So, if I gave you each a carrot, would you be able to go into the field and give them the carrot?'

'No way,' came the joint reply.

'Okay, well, Dad, we have a problem: the girls are afraid of the horses.'

'Well, could you just try?' Mr Anson asked. 'Please?'

'But why is it so important for them to ride?' I asked.

'Well, isn't it what every young girl wants to do?'

'Quite clearly not, but we will have a go tomorrow.'

Tomorrow dawned a grey day. Mr Anson needed to go into the office, so I was left to see how I could encourage these young ladies to love horses. They came down to breakfast suitably dressed, which was encouraging.

Soon we could not put the moment off any longer. Armed with carrots, we went out into the field.

As luck would have it, the horses were as interested in us as we were in them. They came over to us and were pleased with the carrots being offered.

'Now,' I said, 'let's see if they are willing to let us touch them.'

Caroline put her hand out to stroke Chocolate, the brown Shetland pony, who was pleased to have human contact. When Ailsa, the elder daughter, put her hand out to touch Quizzy, his ears went flat and he backed away, then showed his hind legs and strode off. So he was a non-starter.

Caroline asked if I could demonstrate how to fall off safely, so I got on Chocolate, who stood still for me. I crossed my arms and went to slide off, going into a roll as I hit the ground. Stupidly, I instinctively put my hand out to break the fall, and the very thing happened that I was trying to teach them to avoid. All the fingers on my left hand folded onto the back of my hand – total dislocation!

'Go ring Daddy quickly; I need to get to hospital.'

Caroline quickly got a clean tea cloth and covered my hand. I was trying so hard not to faint; the pain was terrific. Ailsa went in and got Mrs Timbrell, the lady next door, who made a cup of tea.

Mr Anson took me to Stroud Hospital's emergency department, which was thrown into a quandary. It was Saturday, so there was a skeleton staff and no one to administer anaesthetic, meaning the only way to help me was local anaesthetic.

They cut off my wedding ring, where the injury was swelling fast. Gradually they pulled my fingers back, stitched the open wounds and bandaged my hand as if it were a boxing glove. An appointment was made to see the consultant on Monday morning, and I was sent off with a box of paracetamol to help with the pain.

My recommendation to Mr Anson that evening was that the horses should go back and he should accept that the girls did not want to ride. The look of relief on their faces was enormous.

Next I had to ring Mrs Lippiatt to tell her what had happened. She was horrified, and told me to ring when I had seen the consultant.

The news was not great. They had done a good job putting my fingers back together, and the circulation was good, but a long course of physical therapy would be required to get full use of my fingers again. I would be starting next week, with three sessions a week, possibly for the next three months. Where was I to stay to get the treatment, and how was Mrs Lippiatt going to manage while I was away?

It was as if Mr Anson had read my thoughts. 'You will, of course, stay here for the course of your treatment. The appointments are in the afternoon for the physio, so I'd suggest you walk into the village to catch the bus there, then I can drive you back afterwards. Does that sound a good plan to you?'

I felt so embarrassed, but I couldn't think of a better plan.

I rang Mrs Lippiatt to give her the news. She was very upset and said she was sorry, but she would have to find someone else.

Mr Lippiatt came on the phone and was concerned by the arrangements. 'Are you sure you will be safe?'

'Well, I don't seem to have any choice. Mrs Timbrell and her son Dougie live next door, and Mr Anson is a man of standing in the community, so I have to trust him. I'll ask him if he would be so kind as to run me down so that I can collect my things; the only thing I can't do is get the car back to you for the moment.'

'Don't worry about that; if we need it, I will arrange for one of the lads to come and collect it. Please keep in touch; we are very concerned for you.' And he was gone. I suddenly felt very alone.

# CHAPTER 33

—

T he treatment, which involved keeping my hand in warm wax before being gently massaged, was going well, and the movement slowly coming back. The shops in Stroud were looking very festive with Christmas coming fast, and an air of excitement hung in the air.

I rang home to see how they were, and they wanted to know what I was doing for Christmas. I didn't know what I was doing, but I felt I should not impose myself on Mr Anson and his family. I was hoping it was our turn to go to Badminton, but it didn't sound as if that was happening.

'Well, you had better come here, then, hadn't you?' Mum said.

I felt like nothing on earth, but said, 'Thank you.' I asked if Dad would be able to fetch me, as I still could not drive.

'I am sure he will, but you will have to give him some directions.'

I thanked her and added, 'I look forward to Christmas Eve. Goodbye.'

I told Mr Anson, who was sorry to hear I would not be with them for Christmas. 'Who is going to cook the goose?'

I said I would leave instructions and gave him my mother's phone number.

He added, 'Do you think you could call me Arthur?'

Dad did a good job finding me at the end of Steanbridge Lane, Arthur having driven me down to the main road with all my packages, as I hadn't wanted Dad to have to navigate the lane down to the house. He seemed pleased that I was going to be home for Christmas.

I wasn't a lot of help to Mum with my hand still bandaged. But I could lay the table and put presents under the tree, and I enjoyed going to midnight mass, although it was weird thinking of how it was the last time I was in the church. I saw Herbie, which was nice; he now had two little girls.

On Boxing Day we went up to watch the mummers do their play all down the street, culminating in the marketplace. The village was full of visitors to see the spectacle.

The actors all wore costumes that were remade every year, as they were all of torn newspaper. We all knew they were men of the village, but we didn't know who was who, and it was always kept a secret. This year, though, as the actor playing George lay dying on the ground, a dog came along and lifted his leg, to the uproar of the audience. Afterwards the actor came and stood by us, and we knew it was Herbie.

That lunchtime a plaintive call came from Arthur: 'Is there any chance you can come and sort us out?'

Dad came to the rescue. He once again took me to the lane, and Arthur was there to help me up the long hill home.

Arthur related their tale of woe: the goose had been burnt, they couldn't set the pudding on fire, and they were tired of egg mayonnaise sandwiches, so please could I help them sort something for supper?

After supper, Arthur came out to the kitchen as I was putting the last bits away. He took the plates and put them in the cupboard, turned me to look at him, and asked if I had realised how much he had come to care for me over the weeks I had been with him.

'Well,' I said, 'I have enjoyed the kiss hello and goodbye, and I enjoy your company and that of the girls, so something that was so awful has been very pleasant.'

'Enough to marry me? As that is what I would like, if you will have me.'

I was really quite shocked, as he had always been the gentleman, and nothing awkward had ever happened between us. 'Oh, my goodness, that is a surprise. What about the girls?'

'I have already asked them, and they would love it.'

'I don't really have a leg to stand on, then, do I? Yes, I would like to marry you.'

He gave me a kiss on the cheek and put his arm around me as we walked into the sitting room. 'She said yes,' he announced. The girls jumped up and down, with kisses all round.

As I sat down, Arthur came over and took a square box from his pocket. 'Well, as I can't put a ring on your finger yet, I offer this as an engagement present.'

I opened it to see a beautiful pendant of gold, set with seed pearls and a large aquamarine in the middle. It was absolutely beautiful; I couldn't stop looking at it.

'Now, I don't think there is any need for a long engagement, and I would like to get married in Bristol registry office, if you can make the arrangements.'

All of a sudden my head was whirling around, as everything seemed to be moving so fast. 'Could I have a gin and tonic?' I asked, trying to let all this sink in.

'I am sorry,' he said, 'to load you with so much information, but I have got a lot on for the next few months. And, if we wait, which I couldn't see any good reason to, you may slip through my fingers. Then where would I be?'

He suddenly looked so vulnerable I just got up and gave him a kiss. 'Let's dot all the i's and cross all the t's in the morning,' I said, 'and let's just enjoy this lovely moment.'

Next morning I was down first, and I had the kettle on and toast made when Arthur came down, closely followed by the girls. We all sat around the dining room table as if for a meeting. Ailsa spoke first, to ask how much longer was my hand going to be bandaged.

'Well, I am hoping the bandages will come off after the Christmas break; that is how it is scheduled. Then my hand should be ready for gentle use if the swelling has gone down, so I would think about the end of January would see it well on the road to recovery.'

'That sounds about right,' Arthur said. 'I am thinking about the twenty-third of January, as that will be a break in weddings for me to be free on a Saturday, and we have to give three weeks' notice to make sure we are both free to marry and anyone else feels they have a right to a say.'

'I didn't realise you did weddings as well,' I said with a smile.

'Oh, yes. I am a superintendent registrar for weddings, divorce lawyer, as you know, and county district coroner, which is why it is tricky getting a Saturday off. So I would rather not get married in Stroud, if you don't mind doing the trip to Bristol on the bus to speak to the registry office. And, while you are there, if you find a wedding ring you would like, please buy it. I will repay you; can't have you buying your own wedding ring.'

It was all sorted. Arthur could also tell me that Mr Lippiatt's men had been to collect the car. So they must have found someone else, I thought to myself.

The trip to Bristol went well; there was a slot for us at 10.30 on the twenty-third, so now to buy a wedding ring. There was a jewellery shop nearby, so I had a look; there was quite a selection in the window, so I went in. All the other people in the shop were couples, so I did feel a bit awkward, but it had to be done.

The assistant was an older man, which helped me not to feel quite so bad, and he took me to a quiet corner of the shop. 'Now, madam, how can I help?'

'I need a wedding ring, please.'

'Do you know what size the original was?'

The wounds on my hand were still quite obvious. He had clearly assumed I'd had to have my ring cut off and this was a replacement, so I went along with it.

I chose a twenty-four carat gold ring with a fine design going round the middle. He managed to measure my ring finger and said I might have to have it made smaller when my fingers had returned to normal size. I thanked him and left the shop with a ring.

I had an hour to wait for my return bus, so I went looking for something to wear. A browse in Lewis's, and I had found the very thing: a coffee-coloured coat dress that fitted perfectly. The hat from Brian and Alison's wedding would be fine, and I could wear the same shoes. Job done. Much simpler having a registry office wedding, I thought, but not nearly as much fun.

Mum wasn't surprised. 'Are we expected to be witnesses?' she asked.

'Would you like to be?' I asked.

'Yes, we would,' came back the reply. 'See what kind of mess you have got yourself into this time.'

I tried to let it go over my head, and asked, 'Would it be possible to have, say, Mr and Mrs Austin and Mr and Mrs Blake come for a drink and a piece of cake?'

She thought that would be okay, and asked if I would be getting the drinks and cake.

'Yes, I will, Mum, no worries.'

I related my Bristol trip to Arthur over a stop at the Woolpack Inn.

'Well, you have done well,' he said.

'I didn't recall any mention of the girls being involved,' I said. 'Will they be home that weekend?'

'No, that is not an exeat weekend.'

'So that means we will need two more witnesses.'

'That's okay,' he said. 'We will get two of the spare people who are usually wandering around these places.'

I had that same feeling I did with Alan: no romance or loving attention. Was it all a myth, or just in films or books? I consoled myself with the fact he was much older than me.

The twenty-third dawned a sunny but frosty morning. Mum had booked Arthur into a nice B&B, which he had retired to after dropping me off at home the night before. He came to collect me and my parents at 9.30.

'One thing I forgot to mention: you didn't by any chance book a photographer, did you?' Arthur asked.

'No,' I replied. 'Sorry.'

'That's okay; we don't need that.'

Apart from my giving directions, there was little conversation between the four of us. We managed to park quite near, for Mum, and walked into what had been a chapel, so it had a kind of religious feeling. We signed in and sat and waited to be called.

Eventually it was our turn; we were called into the office. The registrar, on the other side of the table, asked for the witnesses to come forward, then we were asked to come forward ourselves. We swore on the Bible and signed the register. Then congratulations, and it was all over. 'Next,' came the call.

Back in the car and back to Marshfield in almost total silence.

Mr and Mrs Blake and Mr and Mrs Austin were waiting, and soon we were enjoying a glass of champagne. Mum had made some of her special cucumber sandwiches, we cut the cake, and within an hour it was all over.

When we got to Slad, the Woolpack was still open, so we called in for a drink. No one noticed the ring on my finger. We drove home and I made a cup of tea.

While drinking the tea, Arthur told me he had mentioned to a couple he knew that we were getting married today, and they had invited us up for supper that evening. 'They are long-term friends of mine and are very pleased for us.'

That was a nice surprise, I thought, and I promptly fell asleep from all the tension of the last two days.

Helen and Dick were absolutely charming, and an enjoyable evening was had by all. The time to go home came: a lot of leg pulling, then we were off.

On the drive home, Arthur said that he would be paying all big bills and I would have £10 a week for housekeeping, and £20 a month for a dress allowance, paid into my bank with a cheque account. I thanked him. I was puzzled, as it seemed to be more a job proposition than anything else, but at least I knew what I was dealing with.

Come bedtime, I asked if Arthur would like me to continue using the room I had been staying in.

'Well!' he said. 'I suppose you will want me to make love to you.'

I thought that was an odd reply, but he opened the other side of the bed for me to get in.

Again, the act was nothing like I had thought it would be. I just thought I had read too many love stories and went to sleep.

***

Everything settled down to the routine of domestic life, and I was gratefully released from treatment for my hand, which thankfully was getting stronger. I had taken to running to the Woolpack for some exercise, coinciding with Arthur arriving for his evening pint before coming home. It was quite a convivial group that met at 5.55 each afternoon to unwind from the trials of the day.

Then, one evening, it was all very quiet. When I opened the door, there was Mr Gardner standing with a pink pot in his hand, which he then turned upside down over me; it was full of punched paper. The game was up; someone had spotted the ring, and a great evening was had by all.

That night I drove home with Arthur, instead of running to the bottom of the hill before he caught up with me. After a while gaining my confidence, I suggested that, if I went with him to the office one day, I could catch a bus to Cheltenham for something to do.

'Better still,' he said, 'drop me off at the office and take the car, then come and pick me up at 5.45.'

I looked at him, astonished; he was going to entrust me with his beautiful Jag. 'Won't you need it?' I asked, all of a jitter.

'No, not tomorrow; give you a chance to get to know her.'

In the morning he gave me the keys, and I got in and familiarised myself with all the knobs, then off we went.

'I will have to get this drive done now, won't I?' he asked, with a bit of a grin.

'Will you be able to make a turning point at the top of the house so we could turn around? I think the dustbin lorry would be ever so pleased, too.'

'Yes, I think that is the plan.'

I was feeling quite pleased with myself, as so far all was going well. I got to the office and dropped him off, and suddenly I was footloose and fancy-free.

Driving through Painswick, I recalled Mrs Timbrell's GP came from there, so I parked and went to the chemist to ask where the doctor's surgery was. 'Just a few doors down,' was the reply, 'under the arch.' So, as it was still surgery hours, I thought I should register.

Dr Tinker was the doctor's name, which brought a smile to my face. His receptionist said that Dr Tinker liked to meet his new patients, and if I would like to wait he could see me next.

Dr Tinker was a friendly grandfather of a man who put you at ease very kindly. He gave me a general examination and asked if there were any problems, I showed him my hand, which was now looking good, and mentioned I had missed three periods, which was unusual for me.

He looked at me and asked me to lie on the couch. When I had readjusted my clothes, he said, 'I am delighted to tell you you are three months pregnant.'

I thought I was going to faint. How could that be, from one peculiar attempt at lovemaking?

I went to the car, still shocked, and just sat there. I was parked just by the churchyard, and at that moment I would have happily exchanged places with any of them. Whatever was Arthur going to say to that?

I went back to Slad, parked the car at the top and walked down to the house. I plonked myself on the settee and just howled. I must have cried myself to sleep, as I woke to see the clock telling me it was four o'clock. I started to prepare something for our evening meal almost in a trance, then it was time to collect Arthur from the office.

I was a bit early, so I parked up and waited. Soon there he was, coming towards the car.

'Hello,' he said. 'How did the trip to Cheltenham go?'

'Well, I didn't get there,' and I related my story.

'Are you really?' he asked.

I nodded.

'Well, how good is that? Let's hope it's a boy!'

'You are not cross?' I asked.

'Why would I be cross? Are you okay?'

'Well, in a state of shock, but apart from that all is well.'

'Not even any morning sickness! Clever old you,' he said, with a big smile. 'Now, let's go for a pint; I am absolutely parched.'

'Well, mine had better be just tonic and a slice,' and I smiled. We decided to keep the news to ourselves until it was obvious.

# CHAPTER 34

Life at Arthur's home of Down Court calmed down after a while. I developed a routine of having a cup of tea with Mrs Timbrell to make sure she was okay, as, out of the blue, Dougie got married.

Mrs Timbrell's daughter Annie came up every Monday to do the washing and every Friday with her shopping. The baker called every Tuesday and Friday, and the butcher every Tuesday and Saturday. The milkman was Monday, Wednesday and Friday, and the postman came on foot every day there was any post, walking the same footpath postmen had walked for hundreds of years, so we were well served. A huge cheer went up when the drive was finished, complete with turnaround space.

The time the girls were with us was spent shopping in Stroud or Cheltenham, and sewing on name tapes for Caroline, who was starting boarding school. Ailsa got herself a little job in the office some days, and we gained a puppy, a labrador called Cilla. She was an absolute delight and went some way to get Ailsa over her fear of dogs, but not quite. A great deal of egg and chips, chocolate cake and green jelly was consumed, but, what the heck, it was all over so quickly, then back to Mum for the new term.

When it was time to take the girls back to their mother, Arthur asked me to come so he would have company on the way home, having stayed overnight in Braintree. The girls' mother and stepfather lived in a lovely village called Horkesley just outside Colchester, a long drive from Slad, with no motorways.

I didn't get out of the car as the girls piled into their home. But, sadly, Mum and Dad had a disagreement on the doorstep, which was not very pleasant to witness, and we drive back to Braintree in silence.

The next holiday for the girls was the long summer holiday, where they just resumed what they were doing in the Easter holidays – all quite jolly.

As the end of the holiday loomed, I had a phone call to go to the surgery. I was introduced to the new doctor taking over from Dr Tinker, who was retiring. The new doctor was going on holiday and had three pregnant ladies all due while he was away, so the plan was for us to be induced so that he could be on hand if needed.

Sally had Andrew almost immediately, while Carol and I waited for something to happen. A week passed, and neither of us had a baby yet. The threat was that, if we hadn't had them the next day, we would have to go to Gloucester Hospital. We walked the hospital corridors and did all kinds of chores to keep active in the hope of persuading baby to arrive. The girls were due to go back home on the Saturday; they were so sad that they would not see the baby.

That night, before she went off duty, Matron came and asked if I would like her to help me. 'Yes, please,' was my reply, so she came with a roller towel and said she was going to turn baby, as it was presenting the wrong way round. Having turned it, she used the towel as a bandage to keep it in place and gave me an injection of pethidine, and I went to sleep.

About one o'clock in the morning I woke wanting to push like mad. Doors flew open as they wheeled me to the maternity ward. There I was presented with the most beautiful little girl; my love for her was so strong I could have moved mountains.

The sister said she would ring my husband so that he and the girls could come in early to see us. I just lay back in wonderment at what had just taken place. I had a daughter who no one could take away from me; she was mine for always.

The wait for Arthur and the girls to arrive passed the time they would have left home to do the journey, and a sadness came over me as I realised they were not coming that morning. The afternoon visiting slot came and went, and no Arthur. I hoped all was well.

At the next day's visiting time, Mum and Dad arrived with Auntie Rene; the nurse had very kindly rung home. They were pleased to see us well, and proceeded to go through a whole load of family names my daughter could be given. Then in the doorway was Arthur: a peck on the cheek and a finger kiss for baby, who was totally out for the count.

The nurse came in; too many visitors around the bed, so Mum, Dad and Auntie said their goodbyes and left me and Arthur together.

'What happened yesterday?' I asked. 'I waited and waited for you to come, but no joy.'

'Well, for whatever reason the girls seem to take longer than usual to get ready, so if I was to get back in time to be with you I had to miss coming in the morning. Then when I got back it was after visiting time, so I took Cilla for a quick walk, collected Mrs Timbrell and went to the Woolpack to wet the baby's head. But here I am, and all is well.'

*** 

Ten days later we went home. I thought Cilla had gone mad; she turned somersaults and rushed around.

'Poor love,' said Arthur. 'She's been stuck indoors, except for me taking her for a walk on a lead, as she has been in season.'

Arthur put the carrycot on the settee, and Cilla sniffed and sniffed, then sat quite content by her. From that day on she didn't leave my daughter's side for all her days. Arthur said he would have to get back to the office now, and was gone.

Now what did I do, left in charge of a week-old baby that didn't come with an instruction book? I thought back to the talks the nurse had given us, then set about making cotton wool balls, putting them in a biscuit tin and putting them in the oven to sterilise them.

As soon as I could drive, I put Rose (which I was secretly calling her, as nothing would be decided without the girls' input) in the carrycot and whizzed down to Badminton on what I hoped was Aunt Mim's day off. She was so thrilled to see us, and couldn't wait to get Rose out of the cot and into her arms. It was lovely to have her welcome my baby so lovingly.

Suddenly there was a ring of her doorbell. I answered, but no one was there. It was raining, but there were no wet footprints in the porch; the bell was still moving from having been rung.

I closed the door, went back to Aunt Mim and related what I had found.

'Oh,' she said, 'that will be the Blue Lady, our village ghost, coming in to see the baby!'

# CHAPTER 35

—

Rose Clare, as she was finally christened, developed into a delightful little girl, who brought a lot of pleasure to all who knew her. Arthur was the youngest of six, two of whom were twins, so there were lots of welcoming relatives to visit.

With the years passing so quickly, it was time to think about school. The village school had been closed after the Aberfan disaster; with the steep bank behind it, it had been declared unsafe. So now village children had to go to Uplands School.

Arthur was in favour of private schooling, and we visited to see what the local schools had to offer. Some of them were very busy, but one struck a good chord with me at Woodchester, so Rose's name was added to the list to start in September.

It was at this time I discovered Rose was not a good car traveller, which was odd, as she had been okay going to her uncle in Cirencester, who used to have great adventures going around the world in a hot air balloon. Either that or it was nerves at starting school.

Arthur had found me a Morris Minor with a good engine. Unfortunately, there was a hole in the floor between the pedals; when it rained, water would spray up into the car. Eventually of the three partners it was Arthur's turn to have a new car, so he kept the Jag for me and had a Volvo sports car for himself.

This Volvo coincided with the arrival of the miniskirt. If we were going somewhere where there were drinks, I would refrain and drive us home. The Volvo had obviously been designed for men to drive, as the handbrake was inside the driver's door, so every time I had to drive it I would catch my skirt on the blessed thing.

One day Arthur announced that the BBC were going to make a film called *Cider with Rosie*. They were looking for locations, so he had put forward Mrs Timbrell's part of the house, which was now empty,

Mrs Timbrell having moved into a retirement bungalow. Someone would be calling round that evening. There was great excitement.

Four people from the film team duly arrived to look at the house and loved it; it was just what they wanted to build their set inside. It would take about a year to film, as the story was set across different seasons; in the days before imitation snow, they had to wait for it to actually snow.

Laurie Lee, the author of the original *Cider with Rosie*, and his wife Cathy had a daughter, Jessie, the same age as Rose, so we had become good friends and we had many an impromptu trip to Weston on sunny days. Plus the village lost the sun at about 2pm because of juniper woods, whereas our home of Down Court was at the head of the valley and had sunshine all day, so a G&T in the sunshine was often on the books.

A beam was brought into the house, walls were taken down, and a working range fireplace was built. Claude Watham was the director, with Rosemary Leach as the mother and many other well-known actors involved.

There was a mobile canteen permanently on site, so we lost daylight in the sitting room but we were kept supplied with meals from there. One scene had to have the milk boil over, but the fire in the set took a long time, so they would get the milk to boiling point in my kitchen, then rush the pan round to the set and film it. The finished film was shown on the BBC on Boxing Day.

*\*\*\**

It was time for Rose to leave her little kindergarten and make a move to Hopelands in Stonehouse. I discovered that all the while she had been at Woodchester she had not sat down, except when the headmistress let her dog into the classroom to sit beside her. There was going to be no dog at Hopelands, so I was concerned as to how she would settle down.

In her new school uniform she looked very smart, and joined in with all the new girls and boys. I left her in the hope that she would be okay. Come time to collect her, she came out smiling and seemed happy.

Eventually, the big change loomed: Rose would be going to secondary school. Stroud High School had a very good reputation, so I hoped she would do well and move on to that school. The government of the time wanted to make all schools equal by closing the grammar schools. The voters of Stroud worked very hard to make sure their two grammar schools remained. After a long battle the people won, but Arthur announced that Rose would be going to a boarding school like his other daughters.

I was horrified. I didn't want her to go to boarding school; she could have a good education at the high school, and make long-term friends. But he was determined, and if I stopped it I would be depriving her of the best education possible. I was absolutely heartbroken.

I made appointments at all the boarding schools in the area I could find, and set about seeing what they had to offer that Stroud High didn't. Most of them didn't interview Rose; they just wanted to make sure we could pay the fees. One of them even encouraged pupils to ride and take their own pony to school. At the mention of O and A levels, I was told, 'Oh, well, they do get their riding ability certificates.'

I had managed to visit all the boarding schools and found none to outshine Stroud High for education, so I produced my findings to Arthur.

'Well, I see you have done a good job of elimination, but you have missed the ladies' college.'

'Well, I am not going there unless you come with me,' I said, standing my tallest.

To my horror, he said, 'Fine,' took out his diary and gave me a selection of dates to book an appointment.

The three of us were to be at the porters' lodge door for eleven o'clock on a Saturday morning. A prefect was waiting for us and took us across the school quadrangle, where all the girls were coming out of the building, clutching their little bottles of milk. The prefect asked them to break line and they stopped for us to cross the corridor. Absolute silence was observed in this corridor, so all you could hear was the sound of their feet.

Up a flight of stairs, the prefect knocked on a door and opened it as commanded. Arthur and I were offered a seat on a settee to the side of Miss Hampshire's desk, while Rose was seated in front of her. Miss Hampshire explained how the school worked and all the different things Rose could take part in.

'Now, where do you live?' she asked Rose.

'In Slad,' came her reply.

Miss Hampshire turned around to look at a map behind her chair, which had a circle around Cheltenham. She found Slad and announced we were just over the boundary, so Rose would be a boarder. My heart sank.

'Excuse me,' I found myself saying, 'I know of girls in Painswick who are day girls.'

'Yes, you would,' she said. 'It is a very fine line, but one that has to be adhered to as we have so few day girl places.' She called the prefect back in. 'This is Anthea,' she told Rose, 'who will show you the school and a house where you will have lunch with the girls. Then we will see you and your parents back here at 2.30.'

We all stood, Rose went off and we made our way back to the porters' lodge. 'Could I have a stiff drink, please?' I asked Arthur, and we proceeded to the hotel opposite.

With drinks and a table booked, we sat in silence. Eventually I asked how he felt, and he was fine: 'A jolly good school, and an excellent headmistress.'

'Yes, but what is the point of having children for them to grow up in a school? We are just up the road, for God's sake!'

'She will have more opportunities going to that school; it will open doors for her in the future. How can you deny her that?'

I finally realised all this traipsing about had been a complete waste of time. He was determined that she would go to boarding school. I just could not find a good reason why not. 'Perhaps Rose will want to have a say in what happens.'

Back in Miss Hampshire's office, Miss Hampshire asked Rose if she had enjoyed the school and lunch, to which she replied, 'Yes, thank you very much.'

'And do you think you would like to come to our school?'

'Yes, please,' Rose said enthusiastically.

Miss Hampshire turned to us. 'There we are, Mr Anson. Shall I add Rose's name to the September list?'

'Yes, please,' he replied.

Job done. I could not believe something so enormous to me had been so simply decided.

# CHAPTER 36

The time was passing fast, and even our planned summer holiday in Portugal didn't stop the hurt of my daughter's impending departure. Saturday trips to the uniform shop did nothing to ease my dread, even though Rose was full of the joys of spring. The sewing on of name tapes whiled away the time, but it was all part of the inevitable.

I was concerned that Rose had led a comparatively sheltered life, so I joined an agency called Gabbitas Thring, who provided guardians to children coming to school from abroad with no family to go to during holidays.

Our first children were two female cousins from Nigeria, Ngosi and Obi, who were at Westonbirt School; they were great fun and loved cooking. So my grocery list now included sweet potatoes, plantain and something they called witches' fingers, which I think was okra.

One day I had a telephone call from school to ask me to accompany Ngosi and Obi to meet an uncle who wanted to give Ngosi a birthday present. We were to go to the Carlton Tower Hotel for twelve o'clock. This we did, but twelve o'clock came and went, then 1pm, then 2pm.

Finally the uncle arrived, looking absolutely resplendent in silver and sage green, with a young boy dressed in the same material carrying all his parcels. The two girls fell to the floor at his feet; I stood my tallest and introduced myself. No apologies for lateness. We were asked to follow them to the lift, from which we went to the top floor and were shown to his suite.

An assistant came and brought a briefcase which, when opened, was full of £50 notes. Ngosi's uncle handed her the briefcase. I couldn't believe my eyes. I said she would not be allowed to have that amount of money at school; she could have £150, but that was all, and he should open a bank account for her in her name. He shrugged his shoulders and gave her £150.

About two weeks later I had a phone call to say Obi and Ngosi had left school and returned home.

Next we had Clayton and Connie from Hong Kong, accompanied by their parents. The family were very nice and came with an interpreter, although Clayton's spoken English was quite good.

Clayton and Connie were going to Kingham School, Clayton to brush up on his spoken and written English. Then he would be going to Cheltenham Boys' College in sixth form. Clayton, at the age of sixteen, was quite tall and dressed beautifully in designer clothes, so he found wearing school uniform quite difficult.

Connie was going to the ladies' college in Malvern. She was a very meek and gentle girl who didn't want to go to boarding school, so we left a very sad Connie. Exeats for Clayton didn't always coincide with Connie's, so we would go to her for an afternoon so they could be together.

After a while I had a phone call from Connie's school requesting I attend. Connie would not attend classes she was not interested in, so I was asked to explain she had to go to her classes so that she would be prepared for O levels. She explained that she only wanted to go to physics lessons as that was what she wanted to pursue.

I then had a phone call from the physics teacher to say he would like to have Connie for her next exeat to meet his wife, who enjoyed horse riding and thought it something Connie might enjoy. He asked for the arrangement to be between ourselves. I was furious and said absolutely not, as I had never met him or his wife, and Connie would need the permission of her parents for such an escapade. Connie stayed in her room for the whole of the exeat.

After a week or so it was discovered that Connie and the physics teacher were having an affair, and the school requested that I remove her immediately. I didn't have the authority to do that, so the school would have to contact the parents. I did question why they didn't sack the teacher, to which the reply was that Connie was expendable; physics teachers were hard to find.

Connie's mother came to the school with her interpreter, and before you could look around Connie was moved to a relative in Canada.

Clayton stayed the course and applied for sixth form entry to Cheltenham Boys' College. On the day of his interview Clayton refused to wear school uniform, which all students were required to wear. The sixth form house master took him aside and explained that these were the rules of the school. In addition, Clayton had given Chinese as his second language in the application form, which somehow contravened another rule of the school application. So his application was turned down and his parents were notified. Clayton returned to Hong Kong, but not to his parents' home.

So, with great reluctance, I terminated my time with Gabbitas Thring.

\*\*\*

Finally the dreaded day came. Rose seemed to be up for it, although I did wonder if it was all to please Daddy. Trunk packed and in the car, teddy ready, there was nothing else for it but to get in the car and go.

When we arrived at Farnley Lodge there were other girls arriving as well, which made it a little easier. Girls and parents all met up for tea and to meet Mrs Ford, housemistress of Farnley, a friendly, motherly lady who had done all this many times. She reassured us that our precious daughters would be well cared for, and that the first exeat was in three weeks' time.

We said our goodbyes and to have fun, but by the time we drew away I was a mess. Now I knew how the cows felt when their calves were taken away; they bellowed for hours. I just could not speak. There was no way I could go to the Woolpack, so Arthur dropped me off at home. I poured myself a whisky and cried and cried.

What was the point of having children just to send them away to school? It was beyond me.

I bought loads of envelopes and stamps and wrote to Rose every day, relating all Cilla's antics and what was going on locally. In return I got letters saying not a lot, really, except dates of the next exeat. After the first three weeks, the exeats seemed to work out every weekend, usually a Sunday, so it wasn't so bad.

The one thing that was constant was dear Cilla, who was my faithful companion. She seemed to know my every mood and reacted accordingly. I vowed never to be without a Cilla.

Christmas was looming, and the usual whirl of parties helped pass the time. The end of term was 9 December. That morning there was a blizzard warning. I decided to go early to Cheltenham and do some last-minute Christmas shopping, and made a list of groceries to buy just in case.

I bought frozen turkey and Brussels sprouts, a Christmas tree, a sack of potatoes, a couple of bottles of sherry, whisky and gin, and six loaves of bread. If it snowed, we would be able to survive!

The first flakes of snow were falling as I drew up at Farnley to collect Rose. If it was snowing in Cheltenham, what would it be doing in Slad?

Goodbyes were said and presents distributed. Trunk loaded and teddy in situ, we set off, full of excitement and foreboding.

We luckily met a snowplough clearing the A46 to follow, but at the turning for the B4070 it was a quiet, white world. I just crept along in a low gear, trying hard not to slide as the Jag was prone to.

By the time we got to Steanbridge Lane I knew we would not get the car home. Better to park up facing out of the lane, and ring our farmer neighbour to see if he thought the tractor and trailer would get up the hill at some point. It felt as if he had been waiting for the excitement of such a call, and he came straight away.

When we got to the farm, he drove through the yard and out into the field that led to our house. 'Making tracks so the boss can get home,' he said with a big laugh. He drove off up the new road back to the farm.

Having got everything in, I rang Arthur to tell him to come home as soon as he could and to consider leaving his car at the end of the lane; I would walk to meet him if he rang when he was leaving. We had to do the same in reverse for going back to school, and we didn't get the cars home again until March!

# CHAPTER 37

I met our new neighbour Peggy, who had been renovating a former cow shed with her husband, and I was invited to tea to see what they had achieved. It was fantastic, and the garden was already presenting its new colours. Her husband, who she called Spud, was a quiet, unassuming gentleman with a lovely soft voice.

Peggy told me the village needed a representative on the parish council in Painswick. 'That would be something you could do very well, I will put your name forward. They are also looking for a guider at St Rose's.' I was blown away by all the information this lady had to hand.

Having heard nothing more from Peggy, I decide to see if there was a job I could do. I put an advert in the local newsletter offering to cater weddings, funerals, private dinner parties and so on.

Cake making for a local tea shop was my first enquiry. This was very interesting, but the quantity required was too time-consuming, and it was just me.

Next was to do dinner parties in Slimbridge. Was this for the whole village or an individual? When I rang the number supplied, the secretary told me it would be private dinner parties on a roughly monthly schedule. This sounded interesting, and I suggested I do a sample evening just for the host and hostess before making a big commitment. This was agreed; the menu was left for me to decide, with a cooking time of one hour.

I had taken Rose and the girls to Slimbridge Wildfowl Centre several times, especially when the baby ducks were hatching, but hadn't really taken any particular notice of buildings. So I made enquiries and realised the venue was Sir Peter and Lady Scott's, at which point I felt a sudden fit of panic. But I needn't have worried, as they were both absolutely charming. The evening went well, and an arrangement was made: they would ring to give me notice of their dinner parties, and on the whole I would be the one to choose the menu.

One thing I had to remember was not to move quickly in the kitchen. There were no curtains at the windows, as Sir Peter liked to enjoy the ducks and swans coming in to roost for the night, which meant any sudden move to catch a pan boiling over had to be avoided as it would frighten all the birds.

The routine settled down very well, and one evening Sir Peter came in to ask what was for dinner. I said grilled trout.

'Oh, well done; Prince Charles will enjoy that.'

'What?' said I in sudden panic. 'Your secretary didn't say who the guest was to be.'

'Don't worry, we have every confidence in you. It will be my publisher, Prince Charles and his equerry. Prince Charles has written the foreword in my book just published, so this is a meeting of friends.'

All went well, until I took in the coffee to serve it, then left the room. Normally Sir Peter and his wife would involve me in conversation to help them out, as they were both getting on in years. I was just finishing tidying up when the door opened. 'Well, if you can't stay with us, we will come to you,' Sir Peter said.

He introduced me to Prince Charles, who wanted to know where I had got the delicious trout from. 'Cranham Trout Farm, sir,' I replied. Did I think it would be possible for him to go fishing there? *Well, who is going to refuse the future king of England?* was my immediate thought as 'Yes, sir,' came out of my mouth.

I gave the equerry the trout farm's telephone number, and the conversation continued with Prince Charles relating how difficult it was for them to find local people to staff Highgrove, the house he and Princess Diana were moving into locally. Eventually they took their leave, and I went home in a state of shock and euphoria.

# CHAPTER 38

W hile taking a break with a cup of tea, I settled down with *Lady* magazine, where I had been told I might be able to find work, as sadly Sir Peter had passed away. Business was good, but I missed the regularity of going to Slimbridge.

The guide company Peggy had spoken of came to fruition, and I was needed once a week in term time. Peggy had agreed to give me a hand, which worked well.

As good as her word, she had also put my name forward to be parish councillor for Slad ward, which had been agreed at a village meeting in the Woolpack. This was a shock. 'What am I supposed to do there?'

'Oh, go to the meetings once a month and stand up for Slad; you will get the hang of it.' All well and good, but it was all voluntary, and no payment.

I leafed through the pages of the *Lady* until I came to the 'situations vacant' page. There it was: required in Gloucestershire, cook and housekeeper. Could I do that, and where would it be in Gloucestershire?

I decided to apply: letter sent, then the waiting game. No reply after a month. Then there the advert was again, so I applied again.

I came in from walking the dog to find a smiling Arthur. 'Kensington Palace want you to ring them. I took the call just after you left for your walk.'

I went to wash my face and brush my hair. 'Do you think it was someone playing a joke?'

'No. I did ask that, but they said they were genuine, and would be very pleased if I could ask you to return the call.'

I rang the number Arthur had taken down, and a very pleasant lady replied. They had received my letter, and they were very interested; would I be able to go to Nether Lypiatt Manor on Friday to meet Princess Michael and her assistant? I related the phone call to Arthur.

'Well, well done. Are you going to go?' asked Arthur.

Sudden panic set in, along with the realisation that Friday was just two days away. 'What am I going to wear?'

'Well, you're not going to a garden party; it's an interview, so just look your usual smart self.'

Friday dawned a bright sunny day, so a summer dress would be the answer. They had sent me a map, but I knew the way. I wondered if Alan would still be at Middle Lypiatt.

I had been asked to park in the stable yard, then Jane the groom would show me to the garden door. Jane was a very smiley lady who made me feel very welcome.

Just as I was about to knock, two bubbly ladies came around the corner.

'Hello; you must be Mrs Anson. Come on in,' Princess Michael said, opening the big green door. 'This is my assistant, who you spoke to on the telephone.'

We walked into the kitchen: a big square room fitted with units and a huge green Aga, with lots of light coming through two big windows.

'Do take a seat.' Princess Michael indicated the chairs around a big rectangular table.

I seemed to have given all the right answers, as she asked if I could come and work the next weekend to see how we got on together. She was really looking for someone to live in, but we would see how things went.

The next weekend came very quickly. I had boiled my white apron so it was gleaming, and wore a stripy grey silk dress as it would be my job to answer the door, so it looked a little like I was wearing a uniform. Rose had no exeat that weekend, so I didn't have to worry about collecting her, but I had to be sure to ring to let her know how I got on.

The weekend went well. Prince Michael had arrived with the nanny and two children, plus a Siamese and two Burmese cats. It was a lovely family country home.

On the Monday morning Princess Michael asked me to come to her office. She said how easily the weekend had gone and that the food had been delicious. They would like me to stay on if that was possible, but they were hoping someone who was willing to move in would apply, so they would keep the advert running for a while; if I could interview any possible applicants and explain the ropes, that would be fantastic.

She also explained that they wouldn't be down every weekend depending on family commitments, so there would be some weekends off. This was good news to me, as Rose was my priority. On the other hand, Arthur could collect her on my working weekends and the two of them could have some one-on-one time.

Life settled down to a lovely routine. I met people I would never expect to meet in normal life, who would come as invited guests. There were normally no extra staff, just me and the princess: a real family feeling.

Then one day our guest was going to be on duty and would need a retinue of staff to keep her in contact with her responsibilities; her husband would be joining us as well. This meant that there would be eighteen extra to be fed and watered.

'Get a chef from Buckingham Palace; you be front of house with me,' were the princess's instructions.

Come the day, I had prepped the lunch for the visitors to make for smooth running when the chef arrived. Tania, who was my assistant, was there to look after the dishwasher and so on. We were just about to serve lunch when the chef cut himself quite badly. A search of the first aid kit revealed that we were out of plasters. One of the retinue was responsible for emergencies, and was equipped for everything for gunshot wounds to heart attacks, but no plasters. Eventually a call to the nursery saved the day; the chef was patched up and service continued as normal. The princess left me a lovely note the next morning thanking me for a very happy visit. I still have it to this day.

Family would often come for an impromptu lunch, and on one occasion it was to be a sea bass barbecue by the swimming pool; Prince Michael enjoyed a barbecue.

When the sea bass arrived it was rather large, and the princess suggested starting to cook it beforehand so that Princess Diana, who was almost at full term with Harry, wouldn't get ill from eating undercooked fish. When they were ready to barbecue the fish, she would summon me to bring the half-cooked fish down and leave it at the side of the barbecue. This I did. As I turned to leave, the princess asked if I could stay to help serve.

Princess Diana was sitting comfortably at the table. She asked what the round container waiting on a side table was used for. 'That is for the biscuits for cheese,' I explained. 'A memento of Prince Michael's days in the nursery.' She smiled, and we continued in conversation until the fish was ready.

With the food taken care of, the children came down to play football on the croquet lawn. Soon Nanny Barnes and I were requested to be goalkeepers between two heaps of jumpers for goalposts, while William and Freddie and little Ella ran themselves silly, so much so that Prince Michael and Prince Charles came and joined in the fun. Lovely day, and again a lovely note of thanks.

When it snows in Gloucestershire we usually get a good downpour, that New Year's Eve being no exception. Usually the prince and princess spent Christmas with the Queen at Windsor, but that year the Queen was having Christmas at Sandringham. Not all the family could attend, as it was much smaller, so they took it in turns like any other family.

As the prince and princess were at home for the turn of the year, they decided to have a New Year's Eve party, and invited all their local friends and neighbours. Most of them were expected in spite of the snow, as they all seemed to have four-wheel drive vehicles. Arthur had just changed the Jaguar for a Subaru, so I was okay.

The two footmen arrived, but no chef, so I set to work to prepare the meal. It was to be a festive turkey stuffed with a goose, stuffed with a duck, stuffed with a chicken, stuffed with a partridge, with mushroom duxelles between the layers and stuffing sausage meat. Everything was prepped for the chef, so all I had to do was put it together and cook it, along with the accompanying dishes. I left them having a great time.

We had noticed the gardener and chauffeur David was very friendly with Nanny Barnes, so it was no surprise when they announced their engagement. Freddie and Ella were to be page boy and bridesmaid, and we were all invited. The only problem was that the wedding was going to be on the outskirts of London, at Potters Bar.

Prince Michael, who was a qualified pilot, organised a helicopter and we all flew to Potters Bar, where a chauffeured car and police escort was waiting. I had the staff car, meaning I was outside the escort but still had to keep up, breaking speed limits to do so round all those roundabouts. A lovely day enjoyed by all, but now we had to have a new nanny.

Having a Subaru parked in the stable yard did not sit well with Prince Michael, and a great deal of leg pulling went on about this, as he promoted British-made cars.

One day the chauffeur had been called to London, so, when the call came through to say Prince Michael would be landing at Badminton Airstrip, I had no option but to go in my Subaru. I got there just as the prince was coming in to land. No one else was there, so that spared his blushes.

While we were exchanging pleasantries, the car window suddenly opened on the passenger side. 'What is the Japanese for "close the window, please"?' asked Prince Michael. I blushed and said, 'Your knee is pressing the button, sir.' We had a good laugh and nothing more was said.

\*\*\*

I did my usual Monday morning visit to the princess's office to ask if the weekend had gone well with the prospective replacement for me, to which she replied, 'Yes, it went reasonably well, Mrs Anson, but there was just something missing.'

I had been with them for eight years. I loved my job, and had had many glorious moments to remember. But my husband had retired and was not enjoying the best of health.

'Ma'am,' I said, 'I am going to have to leave. Was she not at all suitable?'

She turned to look at me directly. 'Mrs Anson, did you not realise our little game? All the while we said, "No, not really," and you stayed.'

As I write this there is a great deal being said about how the royal family treated Meghan. In my time, Prince and Princess Michael hosted two royal brides-to-be with their prospective husbands, to help them understand some of the traditions and that they had a loving, caring family to turn to. I never saw Princess Michael being pushy; she was kind and fun and caring.

# CHAPTER 39

With A levels taken and universities visited, the dreaded envelope arrived, and Rose took herself off to the drawing room to read it on her own. After a while I peeped in to see if all was well, and she said she had passed but didn't want to go to university.

'Well, that's okay, but do you have any idea what you would like to do?'

'Yes, I would like to work with children.'

'In what capacity?' I asked.

'As a Norland Nanny,' was the reply.

This she did, and she had an amazingly interesting career. I still missed her as acutely as the first day at boarding school, but now she was a young lady busy in her training.

It was March; the days were feeling warmer, and the garden began to come to life, while the trees started to wear their brand new leaves. I rang home to wish Dad a happy birthday. He was going to be on his own as Mum had gone to day release, so I invited him to come on up and have some lunch with me. He was delighted.

Jack and Don, a couple of workmen, were busy painting the window frames and doors. I lit the fire, so that it would be good and warm when Dad arrived, and made tea for them. When Dad arrived, we all sat and had a cup of tea with the usual banter.

I asked Dad what he would like for his birthday lunch, and his face lit up. 'Do you know, I would love some fish and chips; is that possible?'

I invited Jack and Don to stay for lunch, and asked if they would keep Dad company while I went to get us all some fish and chips. I put a bottle of whisky and three glasses on the side table with instructions to enjoy themselves.

Fish and chips eaten, I left Dad to have a snooze while I did the dishes. But, before I could look round, Dad was beside me with the dishcloth.

After a while Dad said he needed some fresh air; I thought maybe the smell of the paint had got to him. As he went through the back door, I saw his hand slip suddenly down the wet paint. I yelled at Jack and Don to come, as by now Dad was on the floor, out for the count.

They lifted him onto the garden steps, and after a while he took a big intake of breath; he was a bit fazed. I went to open the garden door while Jack and Don helped to support him. We sat him in the armchair so he could breathe the fresh air and slowly come round.

Jack said to ring the doctor, so I did. The doctor pronounced that he had only fainted and should rest for a while, and definitely no driving.

I had to go to Hungerford to get Rose for the weekend, so I left Dad cosy on the settee, in the tender loving care of Jack and Don.

When we got home Dad had had a sleep, and was talking about getting home to be there for Mum. I tried to persuade him to stay, but that got him upset, so Don said he would drive Dad's car, while Jack came with me and Rose.

Mum was already home, and was quite annoyed with me for bringing Dad home not feeling too well. I made them sandwiches and a flask of tea, and had to leave with the instructions that they should ring any time they needed me.

We rushed back to Stroud in time to meet the London train, on which a friend of Rose was coming for the weekend. I reunited Don with his car and dropped Jack off at his house with many thanks for all their help.

The next morning I rang home to see how things were, for Mum to tell me Dad hadn't felt at all well, so she had called the ambulance and they had taken him to Cossham Hospital. She didn't know what the matter was. I said I would come down and take some things in for Dad. She told me not to bother as she had rung Christopher, and he was on his way to the hospital. I was knocked for six; how could she do that? 'Well, I am coming anyway,' I said, 'and I'll collect his washing and shaving things and spare pyjamas.'

When I got to the hospital, Dad was sitting in bed looking pleased to see me, and told me he had had a heart attack. He was a better colour but had no tubes or anything attached. I told him Chris was on his way and asked how long it took to get here from London, as Mum had said I was not to be here when Chris arrived.

'How sad; he would probably be very pleased to see you.'

So, with a big hug and kiss, I left Dad looking happy.

When I arrived home I was met by Rose and her friends. Rose threw her arms round me, then Emma, and Debbie told me they had just rung from the hospital to say Grandad had died.

I was so sad. That lovely man I was so proud to call Dad was with us no more.

Christopher had gone to be with Mum. Given that she was crippled with arthritis and could hardly walk, she managed to organise Dad's funeral very quickly at the request of the Three-Day Event committee. The event was about to start off, and the road to Little Badminton church would be awash with horse boxes and so on, so a funeral cortège would really bung things up.

I was delegated to go to the hospital and collect Dad's things and the death certificate, then to go to the registry office and register his death. I had no idea where the registry office was, so I had to ask at the hospital. They gave me a hospital bag with Dad's belongings in it. I suddenly felt very on my own, having lost my dear dad.

After requesting the death certificate, I was taken to a big room where I realised some twenty other people had all come to do the same thing. I heard them discussing how many certificates they needed.

When my name was called, I was shown into an office with a man sitting at a desk. He didn't look up, just asked, 'How many do you want?'

I said, 'I don't know; what would I want them for?'

He stopped what he was doing, and looked at me as if I were something off another planet. Eventually he said, 'Six is usually enough,' and handed me six copies of the certificate.

Come the day, Mum's instructions were that I was to look after Auntie Mim; Christopher and Ann, his wife, would look after Mum. I was pleased to look after Aunty Mim, but felt sidelined once again by Mum.

# CHAPTER 40

As things settled down it became obvious Mum could not stay in the house in Badminton on her own, and a retirement bungalow was allotted to her back on the Marshfield council house estate. Not a happy bunny, but she acquired a delightful carer.

Aunt Mim went to stay with Mum for a while when the warmer weather came. I got a phone call to ask if I could bring some travel brochures on my next visit, so they could enjoy dreaming of where they would like to go. This I did, and I left them to thumb through the selection.

The next day I had a phone call from Mum to say they had made a tentative booking, but they needed a carer, so they wanted to know if I would go with them.

'Where on earth have you decided to go?' I asked, taken aback.

'We would like to go on the QE2 to the Caribbean for three weeks.'

'Oh, Mum, I only brought that brochure for a laugh.'

'Well, we've got it all sorted, as long as you will be our carer. We think Aunt Cath would probably look after Arthur for you.'

'Oh, my, you really have got it all worked out. I must say it all sounds very exciting, and thank you for thinking of me as your carer, but I will have to ask Arthur.'

I rang Cath first, but Mum had already spoken to her, so she was prepared for my phone call. She was willing to look after Arthur as long as he was happy with the arrangement, so there was nothing left for it but to ask Arthur. *I'll wait until he's had a G&T after supper,* I thought.

'Well,' Arthur said, 'they seem to have got it all worked out. If you want to do it, that's okay by me.'

The next morning I rang home to say it was all systems go. 'When is this to happen?'

'It'll be at the beginning of November.'

'Well, gives me time to get Christmas organised.'

So I left two happy sisters to plan wardrobes. But my thoughts were of crossing the Atlantic in wintry weather.

During the weeks that followed, Arthur was not feeling too well, and the doctor asked him to have some tests. He put them off and put them off until they were to be while I was away. Rose said she would keep an eye out and would telephone me the day they got the test results.

As we were nearing America, a force 10 gale blew up, and the captain announced that the ship would be taking another course 200 miles south of the storm to try and avoid the worst.

Rose had worked out the time difference and duly rang at the appointed time, but got the message that the QE2 had changed course because of the storm and she would need to try again. This she did several times, to be told the ship was out of radio contact. That was it; now she and Arthur sat glued to the television news to see where the missing QE2 could be, and hoping it was not the bottom of the sea!

For us on board it was quite an adventure as the ship battled the tempestuous seas. Passengers were requested to remain in their cabins for safety, and to follow the voyage on the in-cabin television.

Mum was able to deal with travel sickness with the occasional tramadol, but I was not sure what I could give Aunt Mim because of her diabetes, so I decided to take her down to the hospital deck for advice. It was hilarious going down the long corridors one minute, rushing about everywhere the next, being pulled to the ground by the G-forces. All Aunt Mim could do was laugh.

When we got there the place was full of poorly people; we waited quite a long time before we were seen. The doctor said, if we were all right at the moment, chances were we would be okay, so back we had to go.

On the way back, I made a decision that we should remain in our cabin as requested, as the lifts opened onto the main staircase and I might not be able to control Mum's wheelchair very well. When we got back to the cabin and I recommended staying there, though,

Mum was having none of it; she hadn't paid all this money to stay in the cabin.

Just then, a knock on the door; it was the captain's steward reiterating that all passengers should remain in their cabins until further notice. All meals would be served in the cabins.

The door closed, and Mum said, 'And how much did you pay him to say that?'

I couldn't believe my ears.

I went to lie down on my bed, which by now had been folded back into a settee, but there was no view from my window except seawater in turmoil. All there was between me and it was a window with a two-inch-thick frame.

That evening the captain made himself available in the ballroom to answer questions, mainly about the storm. He spoke about the degree of force the weather had put on the ship, and he reflected that he had met many storms crossing the Atlantic, but it was the first time he had experienced waves breaking over the bridge. We all slept well that night, in safe hands.

Eventually Rose got through to say Arthur had opted out of his tests again, so there was nothing to report, but she wanted to know how we were getting on. All was well at home.

The next day the weather had calmed down a bit, so we were able to get out once again, but it was still very grey and overcast. We make our approach to Chesapeake Bay going into New York, but we had missed the tide, so there was an officer measuring the slow movement of the fathoms under the ship.

I decided to look for the Statue of Liberty, but she was very elusive. Then came an announcement that we would be passing her in about five minutes on the starboard side. With that it felt like all the passengers suddenly moved. I panicked; would we capsize? But all was well, and I spotted the statue once I stopped looking up, as she was much smaller than I had expected.

We finally crept into New York City, and anchored at the end of 32nd Street. How good was that?

In the afternoon it seemed a bit brighter, so I ventured out onto the deck. What greeted me was this wonderful warm air that wrapped itself around me like a silk veil. The sea was a midnight blue. I rushed back in to collect Mum and Aunt Mim so they could experience it as well.

'This is what we have come for,' said Mum, reclining in her chair, while Aunt Mim held her face to the breeze.

The next morning found us docked at sea off Saint Lucia, with the twin peaks of the Pitons on the horizon. 'No going ashore for us,' I announced, 'so we will just have to sunbathe.' The beautiful warm air was such a pleasure to sit in.

Mum and Aunt Mim both dozed off, and I asked the deck steward if she would keep an eye on them while I did a circuit of the ship. She happily agreed, so off I set.

I suddenly became aware that this huge ship was being turned on her anchor by the tide to face the other way; how amazing was that? The wind force below the bridge deck was seventy miles an hour, according to the gauge. I could hardly keep my feet on the deck.

When I got back, the two of them were still snoozing, so I saved the story of my adventure for dinnertime.

We spent a lot of time people watching, and I found myself interested in the operations of the ship. Fuel came in what looked at first like little boats, but as they disgorged their load it slowly became clear that the tankers were quite big vessels, and fare of all description was manhandled on board for the passengers.

Visiting dignitaries were given tours of the ship. All the while we seemed to have a steward just for us, supplying hot and cold snacks and drinks. I think we must have been the only passengers left on the ship. Soon, though, it was all aboard and we were off again.

Our next stop was Barbados, our first real taste of a Caribbean island as she had a deep water dock, so theoretically we could get off the ship. When Mum saw the angle of the passenger gangway, though, she refused to go. The crew suggested using the goods entrance, as that was wider and not at so steep an angle, but Mum was all for keeping her dignity for another day. She told us to go and leave her with the nice deck attendant.

So Aunt Mim and I escaped onto a tour of the island, which was fascinating with the colourful houses, cane plantations, and a stop at some well-known caves in the middle of a rainforest. Aunt Mim thought this was amazing. Her eyesight was very poor due to her diabetes, so she could only see what was in front of her; she didn't see the deep drops on either side of us. But she could feel the coolness of the air, and when we emerged into the sunshine again she was greeted by a very colourful parrot, which sat on her shoulder for the rest of the tour.

At our next stop, we were quite high up. The courier explained that the rougher sea on the right-hand side was the Atlantic, while the left-hand side with its calmer waters was the Caribbean Sea, and where we were parked was a British Army base. I had expected to see a dividing line of some sort where two seas met, but the merest ripple was all that made the difference.

Mums and grandmas were sitting on the doorsteps of their colourful houses, watching the world go by, while children played outdoors. Everyone had lovely smiley faces.

Next came a stop in Bridgetown, the capital of Barbados, and a chance for us to go shopping. But by now Aunt Mim was beginning to feel tired, so a little light refreshment gave us a flavour of what it would be like to live on this beautiful island before we returned to the ship.

Saint Kitts was our next and final stop. Again we weighed anchor at sea, so no going ashore today; that was until our friendly steward offered to look after Mum and Aunt Mim, letting me go ashore with a shopping list to see if I could find some Christmas gifts that reflected our trip.

We were greeted by a band playing Christmas carols on oil drums; this was very joyous and lifted the spirits considerably. The shops that surrounded the little bandstand were full of Christmas gifts, but mainly for children. So I ventured out of my comfort zone onto the main shopping street. This was a little intimidating as they had big burly men on the street urging you to buy things from the shops, which were mainly jewellery shops.

I managed to escape into a shop that sold table linen. Beautifully embroidered tablecloths and napkins were unfolded before me. I chose a selection of what I hoped would be acceptable gifts, found the rear entrance out of the shop, crossed the road, and sought out the safety of the transport back to the ship.

Mum and Aunt Mim were still asleep after their lunch, so I sat comfortably until they awoke. They welcomed the goods I had purchased, and somehow I got the impression that they were not going to be Christmas gifts.

That evening was a formal evening, so we all dressed in our finery and were greeted by the captain. There was a festive feeling as we waved goodbye to the Caribbean, and the QE2 started on her return journey. We soon lost the wraparound warmth of the

Caribbean Sea, and by the time we arrived back in New York it was back to the greyness of November days.

The next day, the final day to go ashore, we were once more on an empty ship with occasional visitors, watching her fill up with fuel and provisions. The day had dawned as if the sun might show herself, but a definite hint of winter hung in the air. We decided to go on deck to say goodbye to New York, and were met by a rose-coloured sky and a sense of frost to come.

The ship prepared to sail, and as we slid very gracefully out of dock the ship's horn was sounded in salute to New York and thanks for letting us stay. The sound hung in the air for quite a while, then it was time to put on the glad rags and prepare for the evening sail away.

The journey home was calm and grey. At lunchtime the captain told us we were approaching the loneliest part of the Atlantic, and that the sound of the ship's engines would not be heard as we paid respect to the place where the *Titanic* lay. It was lunchtime, and the silence as the engines were switched off was quite pronounced. It was a relief to hear them come back on as we proceeded on our way.

They were just serving dessert when the engines stopped again. We all waited for the reassuring voice of the captain. Just as consternation was beginning to grow, the familiar voice of our captain came to reassure us all was well, except that they had caught a whale on the bow of the ship. It was unusual, as whales usually kept out of the way. They were going to have to send down divers to assess the situation, and we would all be kept informed.

With that there was a great rush to the bow deck to watch, so we were left in a solitary state to enjoy our dessert. The opinion was that the whale must have been either dead or dying not to have avoided the ship. Carcass removed, we were free to continue our journey.

On arrival at Southampton there was no Rose to meet us, which was a surprise, and I hoped all was well. It transpired that the young driver of our limousine thought Rose fair game, and had given her an uncomfortable journey. I, as you can imagine, was all for giving him a hard time, but she was scared as he knew our address.

All was otherwise well on my return, and gradually my legs and head registered that I was back on terra firma.

Christmas was arriving fast, so planning for that became the priority. I began not feeling too well, and before I knew what was happening I was in Stroud Hospital for a minor operation. The recovery took longer than expected; Christmas Eve came, and I was beside myself with concern at not being able to make Christmas arrive.

A visit from Rose and Arthur soon put my mind at rest, as Rose had organised everything. While they were explaining everything, the doctor came and told us that, if they took good care of me, I could go home. It was the best Christmas present ever.

On Christmas morning there were stockings as always. Thank you, Father Christmas.

The smell of turkey cooking was beginning to percolate through the house, the fire in the drawing room lit, and I was allowed downstairs. There were no presents under the tree but a blanket box. My presents were still hidden in the attic, ready for me to wrap, so there would be a different present giving this year.

Then Rose and Arthur brought the blanket box to me. When I opened it, it was beautifully lined with purple satin and contained parcels all wrapped in glittering paper; it was absolutely beautiful.

Lunch ready, I could not believe my eyes; it was just as if I had done it, but it was all Rose's work. A really magical Christmas, and one I will never forget.

# CHAPTER 41

—

A friend of ours had bought Burley Court Hotel for his very glamorous wife to run as something to do. After a while it all became too much for her, and it was back on the market. I asked Arthur if he would consider buying it, and to my surprise he didn't say no, but he didn't say yes either. Nothing more was said for a while, then one evening after dinner he said he had mentioned it to David, his bank manager. After some deliberation, David had come to the conclusion that the catering trade was a bit rocky, so he didn't advise it.

'Are you going to take his advice?' I asked anxiously. 'I have got it all worked out. I feel sure I can make a profit for you, otherwise I wouldn't ask, plus we'd have a lovely Georgian house to live in. I would even let David do the books to keep you reassured.'

Sadly his mind was made up, and my chance to run a hotel was just a dream.

\*\*\*

The house tidy, the garden in good order, with Rose away at Norlands, time on my hands, I asked Arthur if we could run Down Court as a bed and breakfast. He wouldn't have to do anything except maybe have tea and cake with guests when they arrived, and I would promise not to let anyone sit in his chair. It could be interesting.

'Where on earth are you going to get any passing trade out here, one mile up a country lane?' he asked, as if I had finally lost the plot.

'Well, I have found this book, *Staying Off the Beaten Track*. So I could apply to be considered for inclusion, and notify our local tourist offices that we're open for business.'

'Well, you seem to have it all sorted out. See how it goes.'

The lady who came to interview us for possible inclusion in her book was very precise and insisted on staying the night to experience it for herself. We would have to supply an evening meal if required, and that evening it was required. Being a good Girl Guide, I was prepared, and an enjoyable evening was had by all.

After a full English breakfast she asked us to join her for the result. We had a beautiful home, and she had been made very welcome after navigating the lane. The bed was very comfortable, and she suggested trying to fit an en suite in the twin room. She would be delighted to include us in her book. I thanked her very much, and wondered if I should make a charge, then thought better of it.

I was thrilled to bits. It was going to be hard work, but at least I could make some pocket money and be busy. I gave invitations to all the ladies in both tourist offices to come for a meal and see what we had to offer, so they knew what to tell visitors.

Authur seemed to enjoy meeting the different guests from all over the world, all marvelling at our view and wondering what life was like in the winter.

One visitor came with his secretary and guide dog. He disclosed that he was here to interview Laurie Lee for a radio programme and was anxious about meeting him. I suggested joining us for a drink on the terrace before dinner to calm the nerves. In the meantime, I rang Cathy to see if she and Laurie would like a G&T that evening, and they appeared as if by magic. When our guests came down to join us, it gave me great pleasure to introduce them. A good evening was had by all, and the interview went well the next day.

On another occasion, with all the guests enjoying breakfast, I busied myself tidying up in the kitchen. I gave the kitchen sink a really good scrub, and to my dismay the plughole came away from the sink.

I must have let out a shriek, as one of the guests came into the kitchen to ask if I was okay. When he saw what had happened, he realised that the sink and units were an imperial size and now everything was metric, so we would need to replace everything. I panicked like mad, as I knew Arthur would be furious at my causing a big expense.

After a quick trip to see how much it would cost, it was time to go to Stroud and face the bank manager. I would need a loan.

The bank manager had apparently been interested to meet me, as Arthur had related all my escapades. 'So, how long do you expect to borrow this money?' he asked, once he had his business head on.

'Well, that really depends on how many guests I have, but I would hope five months would see me clear it.'

'Very well. I expect your husband is your guarantor?'

'Yes,' I said tentatively.

'There we are, then. I will see you in five months' time.'

The time passed, and, five months to the day later, I got a call to come into the bank.

'Well, how is business?' the manager asked.

'Not as busy as I had hoped,' I replied. 'Something to do with the Olympics and the rain, I understand.'

'Well, I am afraid I am going to have to call Arthur to ask him to pay,' he said quite firmly. 'I am sure he won't mind.'

'Please don't. Can't I extend the time?' I pleaded.

'No. He will be fine.'

I couldn't bear waiting to hear the result, so I collected my things and left before the manager returned with the answer. I got to the car, checked the fuel. I had enough to get to Mum and back, so off I went.

Mum had moved to Badminton to be near Aunt Mim, and to be out of a council house. The door was locked, so down to Auntie I went, only to have the shock of my life: to my absolute horror, Aunt Mim was now blind.

My aunt was sitting in an armchair in the corner of what had been her lovely sitting room, but it now had no other furniture. Her budgerigar was in the window; there was birdseed all over the floor, and mice were happily eating the seed.

I took Aunt Mim in my arms and gave her a huge hug and kiss. I wanted to wrap her up and take her with me. 'Where is Christine?'

'Oh, she will be in when she gets home.'

'Can I make you a cup of tea, and have you had something to eat?' I asked.

'A cup of tea would be lovely, dear, if you have time.'

I went to her kitchen and wept. How could I have neglected my dear, lovely aunt? I had been so busy with my own needs.

I took the tea in and helped her to drink it, while she told me Mum had been taken to hospital to see if they could get her ulcers to heal by keeping her legs elevated. 'She went in this morning, so I expect you will get the message when you get home, dear.'

When Christine came, I went up to Mum's and let myself in with Aunt Mim's spare key. I rang Arthur to say where I was and that I wouldn't be coming home tonight.

'Why?' was the question.

'I just can't cope with a row tonight, and they have taken Mum to hospital, so I must go to her in the morning. There are no guests booked for the B&B.'

'Please come home. I promise there will not be a row. I have paid for the kitchen.'

I rang the hospital, and Mum had managed to bring some things with her, so I went home.

No hugs or kisses or even playfulness, just the usual silence.

# CHAPTER 42

—

Coming of age was still an important date in young people's lives at the age of twenty-one, as they were now figuratively entitled to the keys to the door, and to all the responsibility that went with it. Rose decided she would like to invite all the girls from her year in Farnley Lodge. They had all kept in touch, so it was easy to send them an invitation.

Ten of the twelve were able to come, so we planned a dinner party. With the menu decided, flowers arranged, table laid and beds made up, all that was left was what Arthur and I could get Rose to celebrate the occasion. Eventually we decided that she would probably need a set of luggage for her career, and that she would appreciate two tickets to fly to Venice for a long weekend, as a break from end-of-course exams.

Some of the girls were driving down; the others we met at Cheltenham station. The excitement at seeing each other was deafening, and so set the tone for the weekend.

Rose waited to open her present from us until we were on our own once again, and she was thrilled with the luggage. When she found the tickets inside one of the cases there were tears all round, she was so pleased.

'Now, who are you going to take with you?' was the question.

I expected her to say Emma, as they were good friends. But it was, 'You, of course, Mum; you've always wanted to go there as well.'

She was quite right; I had, but it wasn't a must for this occasion. She was quite adamant that it was to be our jolly, though, and Arthur agreed that he could survive for four days.

Unbeknown to us, the first Sunday in September was a grand fiesta in Venice, with gondola races on the Grand Canal. The world and its wife were there for the celebrations. Tiers of seating hung from the sides of buildings overhanging the canal.

We had a high-speed boat from the airport, which delivered us to our hotel. The boatman said that the hotel was the turning point for the races, then you could rush indoors to see who had won on the TV. It all sounded very exciting.

We dumped our cases and went to explore Venice. We soon realised the canals, over 125 of them, were like roads. Some had footpaths and bridges; some just had bridges. At the crossroads the sign would sometimes read *St Mark's Square* going in either direction, so we had choices!

Eventually we found St Mark's Square, more by luck than judgement, and were not disappointed. We entered by an archway with a square café to our right and with the cathedral of St Mark straight ahead, the afternoon sun glinting on the windows.

I was admiring the clock to my left, over an archway that looked inviting, when Rose caught sight of it as well. 'I think that's the shops, Mum; come on, let's go!'

It was shopping as I had never seen it. Beautiful clothes, jewellery, shoes, handbags, all designer and apparently going for free, as there were no prices anywhere.

Rose's eyes lit up when she saw the shoes, and she was in the shop before I could look round. After quite a lot of deliberating she decided on a pair of beautiful soft leather shoes that looked lovely on her. I can't recall who paid, but they came with us out of the shop, along with a very happy Rose.

'Now,' I warned, 'before you wear them you must get some fine rubber soles put on the leather, as they will be so slippery.'

'Yes, Mum,' came the reply, and you just had that condescending feeling of *poor old soul*.

We explored the cathedral. I was very aware of the water level marks on the walls, and tried to visualise the square and cathedral flooded. We saw the beautiful treasure on display, but no more services for today.

We came back out into the light and warmth of the sun. Found the gondolas and where you caught a boat to go to the islands. Saw the Bridge of Sighs and could feel the atmosphere of those poor souls crossing it, not knowing if they would ever cross back again. An amazing place; I was so glad we had come, and Rose had chosen me!

The next morning the sun was shining in a clear blue sky, and people were already gathering to see the spectacle of the races. 'Come on, Mum, let's be quick and get a place.'

I grabbed sunglasses, Rose got her camera, and a moment later we were in the lift down to the ground floor. Out in the sunlight the waiting crowds were already four deep, all down the bank of the canal. We found a space and waited, intrigued by all the antics of fellow tourists. Some were hiking their girlfriends up onto their shoulders for a better view, others hopped up and down, but there was nothing to see just yet.

Eventually cheers and applause came up the canal, following the most huge gondola I had ever seen. It took fifty men to row it and needed a six-point turn before it could go back down. When the next one appeared, it became clear that the first was winning by two lengths.

That spectacle over, the crowds sorted themselves out again, leaving two steps free. Rose rushed forward to claim them for us, and everything went into slow motion as she very gracefully entered the Grand Canal!

Everyone stood back with open mouths as they viewed the spectacle. Rose wasn't panicking, as she was a good swimmer, but with the straight sides of the canal there was nothing to gain purchase on. In my very best English I asked for help to get her out, as everyone was still gaping. Eventually some strong young men pulled her out, holding on to the handrail.

'Thank you, thank you,' was all I could say as I tried to spare Rose's blushes and get her into the hotel.

Rose stood dripping on the doormat as I got the room key. The manager appeared to see what all the noise was, and I asked for two glasses of brandy to be brought to our room. I opened the door and just ripped her dirty clothes off, ran the shower for her and collapsed in a chair.

The phone suddenly rang; it was the hotel manager. The onlookers had brought Rose's handbag and camera, and had rescued her shoes from the canal. I rushed down to thank them, but they had gone.

'Could I have a pot of tea?' I asked.

'Looks as if you need something stronger than that!' the manager said.

'Tea will be fine, thank you, and I am sorry about the puddle in the lift.'

I drank the tea while Rose sipped on the brandy, hoping it would act as a disinfectant, and we watched the races on TV from the safety of the bed.

I had nightmares about it for weeks. Rose was just annoyed about ruining her lovely shoes. We had an Italian supper in a restaurant next door to the hotel, which was delicious, and retired early after all the day's excitement, but sleep seemed to escape me that night.

# CHAPTER 43

—

At Christmastime we always eagerly anticipated the arrival of Auntie June's Christmas parcel, and this year was no exception. Auntie June was Ailsa and Caroline's mother's sister. Sadly, June and her sister were not too happy in each other's company, and so Arthur, Rose and I had adopted her. She was great fun, although she could only visit once a year because she lived in Toronto, Canada. We would look forward to her annual visit with pleasure, and always hoped to have it fall while the girls were with us.

When June came this year, she had good news: she had met Les, who she described as a bear of a man, and was obviously very much in love. They were going to be married. We were so thrilled for her, and hoped she would bring him on her next visit. This she promised to do.

A great deal of shopping was required. As good as Toronto shops were, some things could only be bought in England, according to Auntie June.

Auntie June had had TB as a child, rendering her lungs in poor shape, so she required a nap after a shopping spree. An hour later, once she had been revived with a cup of tea, we set about putting the world to rights. Suddenly there was a huge gust of wind that shook the house; we were quite shaken by the strength of the gust, but not enough to stop our crusade.

That evening, when I went to our bedroom to change for supper, I noticed lots of dust. I looked up and saw the big old oak beam across the ceiling had snapped at the foot of my bed. A quick phone call to Jack, who could explain the 'wind' had been an earthquake in Slad!

I picked Jack up with acrow props and such to make the situation safe. Jack proclaimed that the beam would need a shoe to give it its

163

strength back, so a shoe it would be. In the meantime I didn't like any high winds, especially at night.

***

Auntie June returned to Canada and had a lovely wedding with friends in attendance.

To help June's health, she and Les eventually decided to try living in a drier, warmer climate, and decided on Spain. They sold their house and put everything in storage, ordered a caravan from a company in Cheltenham, arranged for their Karmann Ghia car to be shipped over to England, and booked an extended stay with us before setting sail.

While we were waiting for June and Les to arrive, a very large parcel came for them. Les also asked us to contact a company that would come and wire up the house to supply oxygen to June. We would need a supply of oxygen cylinders to top up her mobile handset as well, so she would be able to go out on trips. This bothered me somewhat, as it meant June's health was deteriorating.

With the oxygen supply installed, I received a new instruction: I would be given permission to board the aircraft when it landed, so I could connect June to a portable oxygen supply for the journey from the aircraft to my car. The oxygen cylinder was concealed in a bag that looked just like a handbag, so apart from a thin plastic tube there was nothing obvious. I thought this was so good for June, who took such pride in her appearance.

All went smoothly, and a safe arrival in UK. The first item on their agenda was to visit what would be their new home until they found somewhere in Spain to live.

The large parcel revealed a large quantity of Hamilton tartan, June being Scottish. The plan was to use it to upholster the caravan they would be living in, so to the caravan we went. Les measured the floor space for a carpet, noted the measurements down and gave them to June. 'Now, you two, off you go shopping!'

I had hired a wheelchair for June to save her energy. We set sail for Cavendish House, carpet department.

After a good search of the selection June decided on a carpet. We found an attendant, and June proudly announced she wanted to carpet her entire home in her choice. The look on his face was memorable.

Space was made for her at the counter and a chair brought for me. 'Do you have the measurements, madam?' the attendant enquired.

She gave him the note Les had given her. Talk about crestfallen. 'Is this just one room?' he asked.

'No,' she replied, 'and we would like it fitted. You see, it is a caravan, so for the time being it is our only home.'

Eventually the attendant smiled. 'You had me going there, madam.'

She just smiled graciously.

Collecting Les, we returned home for lunch and bed rest for June. With the dogs walked, it was tea time. I took June a cup of tea, and soon the usual girly talk had us laughing.

'Did you enjoy your Christmas box?' June enquired.

'Yes, it was a lovely surprise, all those Christmas lights. I hope I sent thanks.'

'Yes, you did, and you were so polite, as we realised I had sent them with Canadian fusing. Were you able to use them?'

'No.' I laughed. 'The electrician I asked to install them thought it was an April Fool's trick in December!'

The car arrived in Portsmouth, so we took a trip to collect that. A tow bar was fitted and strengthened to pull the caravan. Then, cupboards filled, boxes and cases packed, passage booked, it was time for June and Les to set off. It was a fine day, so, roof down, off they went on their new adventure, June's blonde hair blowing in the breeze, with a boot full of oxygen cylinders.

It was quite a while before we heard from them again. We were almost at the point of worry by the time Les phoned to say they had found a Spanish cottage in a lovely position near the sea at Majorca. All was well, with a huge thank-you for all we had enabled them to do.

# CHAPTER 44

—

Life continued at Down Court, with a steady stream of B&B guests to keep me occupied.

One weekend, when Rose came home, she brought a big smile and brochures for a holiday in Hong Kong and Thailand. She said she had tentatively booked it for the two of us for two weeks in October, as she could be free then and thought the B&B would be tailing off. So, with Arthur reluctantly in agreement, and Cath once more booked to look after him, it was all arranged and paid for, which was a lovely feeling of achievement.

Connie and Clayton's mother, Mrs Mo, invited us to visit while we were in Hong Kong. Plus Mrs McMeeken, who I had been looking after at weekends, arranged for me to visit her son so that I could check on his furniture and she could decide what treasures to leave him in her will.

The date of departure soon came around. The flight was long, with our first port of call being Bangkok. We were met at the airport by a cream Mercedes and a chauffeur in cream and gold livery, who navigated the streets and people with expertise.

We eventually arrived at the hotel, right beside the Chao Phraya river, which was filled with floating hyacinths. Amazing boats sped up and down the river; they looked like hollowed-out trees with a bus engine on a pole.

Our hotel was very luxurious, with beautiful lounges and waitresses wearing beautiful Thai silk saris, who knelt at the low coffee table to serve you. Our room was stunning; it overlooked the river and the image of a temple in the setting sun.

Our dinner that evening was the most delicious I had tasted for a long time. Back in our room we were welcomed by a most tempting-looking arrangement of fruits of all kinds. A quick shower, and so to bed.

We decided to breakfast in our room and study our day's excursion: a trip to the former capital of Thailand, Ayutthaya. Rose rang for room service, which was almost immediate. Breakfast enjoyed, we got ready to head out.

The traffic was amazing and scary. Two or three people on a pop-pop motorbike, balancing everything from groceries to children, was the norm. If there was an accident, the traffic just drove around it.

Ayutthaya was as I imagined Thailand to be, with graceful buildings, primarily temples, and courtyards of statues to the Thai Buddha, all dressed with the golden sash across the chest for autumn. Then on to Wat Phra Si Sanphet and the magnificent buildings to Buddha. Quite a lot of sightseeing.

Back to Bangkok, and the peace of our hotel, and the amazing room service.

That evening we asked the concierge if it was possible to have a tour of the city at night. We were asked if a man was travelling with us, and we said no, so a car and liveried driver were put at our disposal.

Our driver told us the city was arranged in a wheel, and if you wanted to buy a fridge you would go to the street that sold fridges. As we were looking for Bangkok at night, he took us to the red light district, and the street to go to if our handbags were stolen. So, all in all, quite exciting.

Next day, it was the Grand Palace, which was fascinating. What was also interesting was the wide street, like our Mall, with the current royal palace at the end.

We had been asked to cover our arms and legs in respect when visiting the Grand Palace, which we were already doing, and to take our shoes off when entering the temple. The guide described the various services that took place here, and how, when a member of the royal family died, they would be laid in state.

There was a lot of walking, and we discovered that October was the rainy season when we got absolutely soaked with warm rain. On returning to our hotel, we stripped off our wet clothes, showered and were ready for the afternoon trip. I decided to deal with the wet clothes all in one go when we got back, so I left them in the bath. When we came back, the clothes had vanished from the bath and were hanging in the wardrobe, all washed and ironed; I was well impressed.

Next day our trip was on the river and up the Thonburi khlong, a canal coming into the river like the Grand Canal. As we entered the canal the water coming down it was black. I looked at Rose and hoped she would stay very still in our hollowed-out tree; I was sure that a fall into the canal would be curtains.

The khlong market was all on boats and sold everything you could want for everyday living. The houses were on stilts, and everything seemed to involve the canal, from washing vegetables and clothes to washing the baby. No visible signs of furniture, except for maybe a chair on the veranda.

The boat slowed and pulled in for us to get out to see the serpent house. None of us left the boat. I was aware of people strolling with snakes coiled around them as if taking the dog out for a walk. At the end of the canal was a wider area where they had filmed the race scene from a James Bond film.

Finally back out on the river, we travelled along its wide flow until we came to the stables, but not for horses: for the king's boats. There were stately canoes and long rowboats, beautifully painted and carved, and I was sure they would make a statement when in use.

Our last day's excursion was to the reclining Buddha and the temple where the king of the film *The King and I* was buried. Apparently the book and film are banned in Thailand, and his grave is inconspicuous and sad, but the king's son had carried out his requests and brought Thailand into the twentieth century. We returned to the hotel and reluctantly packed our bags for Hong Kong.

Our arrival in Hong Kong was frantic, but mercifully there was a car waiting for us. I wondered if Rose had arranged all this, as it made life much easier than fighting for a taxi. Our transport this time was a green Rolls-Royce that transferred us at speed to the Peninsula Hotel. Fellow travellers gazed into the windows to see who was inside, so we decided to do the royal wave, with a laugh.

On our arrival at the Peninsula, Mrs Mo was already waiting for us in reception. She invited us to join her family for dinner at a hotel; I had begun to write down the name when she said her car would come to collect us at 6.30. It felt more like an order than an invitation, so we were careful to be ready on time.

The car duly arrived, a gold American-style car, and again there were inquisitive faces outside the windows, but we thought we had better behave. The car brought us through a double-gated entrance to a block of flats. The lift seemed to go up forever, but finally there was Mrs Mo, smiling in greeting.

Their home was palatial and furnished in French regency style. Mr Mo was waiting, as were Clayton and Connie, by the most magnificent view from their drawing room window. Here we realised we could see the journey we had just taken, as the window was looking straight at the chequerboard that all pilots had to aim for before turning hard right for descent between the blocks of flats into Kai Tak Airport. Below this was a sign for the tornado shelter.

'Do you get tornadoes here very often?' I asked.

'Oh, yes,' replied Clayton, 'in the tornado season. They really make the building sway.'

Mr Mo announced the car was here to take us to dinner at the hotel.

When Clayton had stayed with us, we had gone out for a day in London, and of course a visit to Chinatown was compulsory, so we felt confident that we would enjoy the food. We were not disappointed.

At the end of the evening Mrs Mo asked if she could take us shopping, so a time was arranged for the next afternoon.

Rose wanted to see if she could get a suit made by the time we left, which was just three days away, so in the morning we set off to find a tailor. In one window was a lovely suit, just what she was looking for, so in we went: measurements taken, cloth chosen and deposit paid. A very happy Rose!

We needed to get some cash, so we went back to the hotel and collected our passports to go to the bank. Transactions finalised, we were shocked to have our passports thrown back at us with a demand to know why they couldn't have one of those. We both felt very threatened.

Back in safety, we strolled through the underground shopping area, where Rose's eyes lit on what were described as 'happy diamonds'. They were loose in an attractive pendant, and as the pendant moved these diamonds sparkled. A quick calculation proved neither of us could afford them, so we just had to gaze and reluctantly leave them.

Back in the hotel, it was almost time for Mrs Mo to take us shopping, so a quick room service and we were ready. Perfectly on time, we were off again in the limousine.

Rose was asked what she would like, so she related the story of the diamonds.

'I have a friend who has a jewellery shop,' Mrs Mo said, so the driver was given instructions, and off we went.

Rose was shown into the jewellery shop, and I followed in her wake. Mrs Mo was in charge of operations, so I sat and watched as happy diamonds were produced and a chain selected. The pendant looked lovely around Rose's neck, and it was just the right length. While Rose admired it in the mirror, Mrs Mo turned to me. 'There we are, Cynthia, at a bargain price.'

I felt my mouth fall open, but nothing came out. Even at the bargain price, I could not afford it, and in an attempt to cover my embarrassment I said I did not have that sort of money on me.

'That's okay; my car will take you to the bank.'

Passport collected, money withdrawn, passport thrown back once more, but now no contingency fund in case of difficulties. Back at the shop a beaming Rose greeted me.

When we were back at the hotel, I disclosed that I would not be able to make any contribution to the suit, which was fine as she was able to pay. So off we went to collect it.

That evening we changed to have dinner with Mrs McMeeken's son John, who we were to meet at the top of the Peak to see the sunset. This we did, but we had not realised how long it would take to get there. Looking out-of-place in smart dress on the ferry, we missed the sunset, and a fed-up John met us. What was more, his wife was already at the yacht club when we got there and was not amused at having been kept waiting. Plus the whole purpose had been for me to do some reconnaissance and report back to Mrs McMeeken, which was an awkward motive in itself, so a difficult evening was had by all.

What was worse was that, when I visited Mrs McMeeken after our return home, she asked me to read her post to her, as she was blind. There was a letter from John asking her to stop sending all these ridiculous people to him, wasting his time. She was embarrassed that I had to read such a comment, and sad that she could not make a decision for her will.

# CHAPTER 45

—

O ur adventures over, it was time to prepare for Christmas once again, alongside the parish council work.

One evening, while I was preparing to go to a school governors' meeting, Arthur asked if I had to go, as he was not feeling too well. I was so surprised I rang and gave my apologies. He asked me if I would help him to the kitchen, as he felt very nauseous and had difficulty in walking. I managed to sit him on a kitchen stool and went to ring the doctor.

The doctor's decision was that Arthur had vertigo. He helped me get him upstairs to bed, and told Arthur that he would be back in the morning. In the meantime, if he needed the bathroom, he would have to let me help him with a container.

Arthur slept well. When the doctor came, he said that the tests they had wanted to do for some time were now important and Arthur needed to be on a drip. He was sending for an ambulance, and would be back once he had collected the paperwork for the ambulance workers.

Arthur said nothing while the doctor was speaking. When the doctor left, he asked me not to let him go to hospital. I felt between the devil and the deep blue sea, as he had needed these tests for ages but had never kept the appointment. I suggested he tell the doctor on his return.

The doctor and ambulance arrived at the same time, but Arthur didn't say a word. He was taken to the ambulance, and I had to follow in my car so that I would have transport to get home. I got in the ambulance to say I would be following, and Arthur gave me the filthiest look I have ever received. I had rung Rose the night before to tell her what had happened and that I would keep in touch.

I let the dogs out for a quick walk, then locked up and called in on Jack, who had seen the ambulance come. I asked if he could let the dogs out if I didn't get home tonight.

When I got to the hospital, Arthur was not where the ambulance men had said he would be, and I was told to go to casualty to see if he was there. As I walked there a taxi came by and stopped, and out got Rose. I was pleasantly surprised. The doctor she worked for had told her to get the next train home, so we walked into casualty together. We were asked who we were looking for and were shown into a side room.

'This does not look good, Mum,' Rose announced.

I replied that she had been watching far too much *Casualty*.

A doctor in a white coat came in to tell us Arthur had a bleed in his brain and had been sedated in preparation for a scan, and that he might not know us. Rose was told to hold his hand, and Arthur was asked to squeeze her hand to say he knew we were there. Then he was off for the scan, and we were asked to remain in the waiting room.

Suddenly Rose turned to me and said, 'If anything happens to Dad, you will never survive.' I was quite shocked, and said that I would have no option but to survive.

The scan over, we were told which ward he had been moved to, so off we went to find him. We were shown into a side ward, where Arthur was struggling for breath. This upset Rose, and she asked to go home. I notified the nurses' desk to tell them I was taking her back, whereupon the doctor told me how ill he was. I said I would have to look after my daughter and would return as fast as I could.

When I got back, the gasping had stopped and shallow breathing had returned. All I could do was hold his hand and watch the pulse in his neck.

I can't recall how long I sat there, as I had forgotten my watch in all the rush, but I suddenly could not hear his breathing or see a pulse. I went to the desk to ask if my husband had passed away.

No one had come in the room all the while I had been there; suddenly it was all go, and a doctor leapt on the bed, ripped Arthur's pyjama jacket open and began resuscitation. It looked brutal, and I asked what he was doing. He asked if I was refusing resus. I asked if Arthur had died. When he stopped, Arthur looked very obviously dead.

I was invited into a room and asked to sign a form confirming refusal of resuscitation. I felt as if I had murdered him; I went into shock. A cup of sweet tea soon had me recovering, and I was told to come back the next day to collect the death certificate.

It was now past midnight, and as I walked through the hospital to the main doors I could see that there was a whole group of people outside. I thought if I opened the door they would all rush in, so I turned around and walked back into the hospital, where I met a couple coming out, obviously having lost someone too. I asked if I could walk with them to the car park; we walked through the throng and went on our way.

When I got home Rose was still up. I wondered if she had thought to ring the girls; she had not, so I left it to the morning to tell them.

I decided to sleep in the spare bed in Rose's room so we could give each other company. Then there was a patter of dog paws on the stairs; Holly never came upstairs, but she came between the two beds. I patted her; she lay down and stayed with us all night. But sleep would not come; it all kept going over and over in my mind, and I felt bad that I had not rung the girls.

The next morning, I rang the girls. They were both very angry with me for not telling them before. I was very sorry; I hadn't meant to exclude them, but it had all just unfolded.

I rang Peter, Arthur's working partner. He said he would look for the will and take me to the hospital to collect the death certificate.

When he came, he told me he had not been able to find a will, so we were dealing with intestacy law, which meant I had no home or money except what was my own and the £125,000 allowed the widow. The girls would inherit equally, with one third being invested, the interest being paid to the widow. The hope was that the house valuation for probate would be lower than street value, enabling me to purchase the house from Arthur's estate. But then I would have no money, so I would be totally reliant upon the B&B, and perhaps making the house available for dinner parties, weddings and such.

The day of the funeral arrived. The girls had thought it a good idea to have the hearse leave from the house, so this we did. The journey to and from the crematorium was in almost silence, as the girls were finding it difficult to forgive me for not telling them that their father was not well, and so far there was still no will, with the contents of his desk having been emptied that morning in a last desperate attempt to find one.

On our return to Down Court, our home of thirty years, it was full of well-meaning members of the congregation, all saying kind things of Arthur. Then I saw one of the clerks very upset in the corner. I went to comfort him, and he looked at me with pleading eyes. 'Didn't you know, Cynthia, didn't you know we were partners?'

I was confused, as I had not heard he had been made a partner in the firm. 'I am sorry, John; Arthur must have forgotten to tell me. Congratulations.'

'No, not in the firm, together, we were together.'

My mind went absolutely blank. What was he talking about? Arthur had been here all the time since he had retired; what was he talking about?

I remembered a time when Caroline had come home, put her head around the kitchen door and asked if I could join her and Arthur in the sitting room, as she had something to tell us.

'You are pregnant,' I had volunteered.

'I sincerely hope not,' was her reply.

Her news was a shock to us both; she said she was gay and had a partner she would like us to meet. Was it that kind of partner? Arthur hadn't ever said he was gay. but it did give a reason for the lack of affection between us.

Now, at the funeral, Caroline came to put her arm around me and asked if was okay. I asked her if she knew her father was gay, and she said yes; their mother had told them. I felt such a fool, and so many whys filled my mind.

I was brought back to reality by people saying goodbye and telling me to keep in touch. I just felt numb.

Was that the reason there was no will? And why crucify me, when I had kept house for him for thirty years? It was still illegal to be gay in 1964, when we had married. He must have felt unhappy to be the way he was, and not be free to be himself.

The meeting to finalise everything was in the office and felt very formal. All three girls came with me, which was reassuring. Rose had elected to have her inheritance in shares, which was no surprise, as she and her father had made quite a study of it. I was able to buy Down Court with my allowance, and then a big surprise: Ailsa and Caroline wanted to lend me a considerable sum to help repair the house and set it up for B&B guests. It would be a debt on the house, repayable when I sold. But Rose refused to join them. I was taken aback by her attitude; I felt really embarrassed. She gave no explanation, just 'No.' I didn't recognise this side of my daughter.

It was after the meeting that the whole reality of the last month sank in. The girls left for their various destinations, back to their lives. For the first time I was really on my own with my faithful dog Holly by my side. Now to make the house pay for itself.

# CHAPTER 46

—

I was given the telephone number by the proprietor of our local music centre when trying to decide how best to sell my piano: an Érard 1821, beautiful burr walnut case with satin wood lining. Was it a musical instrument, or a beautiful piece of furniture?

'Look, here's the telephone number of a delightful gentleman who will, I am sure, come along to play your piano, and will give you an unbiased opinion of its musical ability. His name is Douglas Smith. He will probably make no charge for coming out.'

This last point was a very important one, as far as I was concerned, having been widowed in February of the same year. With winter looming fast I had decided I would have to raise some money to get through the cold season, hence my needing to sell the piano.

I rang the number only to get an answering machine, so I left my details as requested and waited. Two weeks passed, and I came to the conclusion that I wasn't going to get a reply.

I was sitting quietly, drafting an advert to be published in *Cotswold Life* magazine, when the telephone rang.

'Hello! Sorry to be so long returning your call; I have been up to Skye playing in a concert, and it was so beautiful I stayed longer than expected. How can I help?'

His voice was like velvet, so warm and comforting; his words just seemed to wrap themselves around me. I explained my dilemma, and after a pause he said, 'I have a free day on 8 August; how does that suit you?'

'Perfect,' I replied, and I gave him instructions how to find the house.

'Great. See you about twelve noon, okay?'

'Thank you,' I said, and he was gone.

The eighth dawned with a thick layer of fog all down the Slad valley into Stroud, leaving us in this rarefied atmosphere as if we were floating in some magical sea. The heat of the sun usually soon burns it off and reality returns, but not this day. It started to lift, then settled in a veil of cloud that still allowed the sun to shine through, making driving difficult; visibility was almost nil.

I was waiting for a party of six B&B guests that night, who would be expecting dinner. I had just laid the dining room in readiness when the phone rang. I looked at the clock; it was 12.20.

'Hello,' came that lovely voice again. 'I am having difficulty finding you in the fog; I have tried twice.'

'Where are you now?' I asked.

'In the Woolpack, having a pint.'

'Did you find the lane?'

'Yes, but I couldn't find an exit at the top of the hill, only a notice saying *Private Road*.'

'That's the road to take,' I said.

'Okay, I'll give it one more go. Hopefully I will see you in about five minutes. If not, I will have to give up, I'm afraid.'

There was a kind of desperation in me all of a sudden, as I realised there was a strong chance I was not going to be able to put a face to this wonderful voice. What could I do? The drive went down an incline to our house. On your first visit you didn't know where to look to see the house, and in the mist it would be almost impossible. All I could do was hope.

I went to the front door and listened. Eventually I heard the sound of a car climbing the hill; the sound tailed off as it reached the top. The wait seemed to be forever as I willed it to continue down the drive to my house.

To my great excitement the engine started again, and I could hear the car's cautious approach in the fog. Suddenly there it was, its headlights emerging through the mist. I gave a wave and the car came to rest.

'Hello; I have made it at last, if you are Mrs Anson.' His handshake was firm, and a wonderful smile greeted me.

As we went into the house, Douglas related that a fellow musician he had known for years had moved into the area, Alexander Kok; did I know him?

'Oh, yes,' I was able to say. 'You have just driven past his house at the bottom of the hill.'

We walked through the house with such ease; it seemed as if I had known him for always. He was very relaxed and declined my offer of tea or coffee, having had the pint in the pub.

'Do you go to Skye very often?' I asked.

'Not as often as I would like,' he said. 'But now I have retired I hope to spend more time there, as I have bought a timber house in Ardvasar, a village to the south of the island.' Whereupon he produced a photograph of this little wooden A-frame house with the most amazing view. 'It has been my salvation since my wife died in an awful car accident on New Year's Eve. My daughter Anna and her boyfriend of the time were also in the car, but mercifully escaped with minor injuries. That was all of ten years ago, but it still seems like yesterday. Now I can escape the agony of all the memories around me, and walk in the Cuillins and watch the eagles soar. And, joy of joys, I have met a local doctor who plays the violin really well, so now we have musical evenings when he is free. Have you been to Skye?'

The conversation just flowed and flowed. His enthusiasm for life and his music and the beauty around him was almost tangible.

'Did you earn your living as a musician?' I asked.

'Sadly, no. My father was of the opinion that music was not a "proper" job, and that I should be a dentist like him.'

The sound of the doorbell was a sudden intrusion into the place I had been transported for the last three hours. When I glanced at the clock on the mantel shelf, it told me it was half past three and my B&B guests were arriving.

'Heavens, is that the time?' Douglas exclaimed. 'I must be on my way. We have a full rehearsal this evening for a concert in two weeks' time, so I must catch up with my practice to be on form for tonight.'

'Will you have a moment to look at my piano?' I asked tentatively, as we walked through the drawing room to answer the door for my guests.

'Oh! My dear lady, I had completely forgotten about the piano,' he said. 'Can I give you a ring tomorrow? Now that I know where you are, perhaps I could come again.'

He shook my hand, said good afternoon to the waiting ladies, and was already turning his car by the time the guests had introduced themselves. A final wave and he was gone.

The ladies reassembled in the drawing room after breakfast, and we were having the usual fuss over who was paying for what, all falling over each other's luggage, when the phone rang.

'Hello,' came that velvet voice again. 'I am so sorry about yesterday. You must have thought me very rude. Would it be possible to pop over this afternoon before you get busy, about half past two if that is a good time for you? I promise to give your piano a once-over this time.'

'Thank you, that will be fine,' I replied.

I replaced the phone slowly, as I tried to analyse why I felt weak at the knees just hearing his voice again, my heart all aflutter.

'Thank you so much for a lovely stay, really comfy beds, thank you. We will recommend you to our friends,' were the words that brought me back to reality in the drawing room. 'Can we just use the downstairs loo, just to be sure?'

'Yes, of course, and thank you,' I found myself replying automatically. 'Have you signed the visitors' book? And don't forget the map; won't get too far without that.'

With the final waves goodbye, they were gone.

The silence in the house seemed to add to my confused state. I slumped into the armchair by the old inglenook fireplace and became lost in my thoughts about this lovely man.

*For goodness' sake!* I heard a voice in my head. *You are an old woman, and very fat; who on earth is going to look at you? Get on with your work; you have no time for daydreaming.*

Preparing the rooms seemed to take forever today, and the only thing that motivated me to get the job done was the realisation that, if I didn't get my act together, I wouldn't be finished by the time he arrived. The fog of yesterday had gone, so he was likely to be on time.

The washing machine was still whirling away when the doorbell rang.

'Hello! Sorry if I'm a bit early, but I had a bit of free time, and as it's such a lovely day I thought I might take my dog for a walk, if you don't mind my parking. Looking on the map, you have some lovely footpaths through here.'

'Of course,' I replied.

'I'll be back promptly by 2.30,' he said, with a wonderful mischievous twinkle in his eye.

He opened his passenger door, and out jumped the biggest, hairiest rough collie I have ever seen. She shook her coat, which added volume to the hair.

'What's her name?' I asked as she pranced around on four very delicate paws.

'Barley,' he said.

How aptly named, I thought, as her coat was just like the colour of a barley field, from shades of cream to the golden browns of the ripened ears of barley. 'Would you like some soup and a sandwich when you get back?'

'That would be lovely, if it's not too much trouble, but I mustn't forget the piano today,' he replied.

'No, I won't let you forget today,' I said with a wave as they set out on their walk.

My two dogs, Holly and the puppy Poppy, were set into action defending the boundaries, with a whole cacophony of barking as they chased through the garden and paddock.

Tea trays had never been laid so quickly, nor washing hung out with such gay abandon. Vacuuming seemed to become a new dance as I went through the chores of running a B&B.

In no time at all, it seemed, Douglas and Barley had returned, and we enjoyed lunch on the terrace. The conversation was so easy.

Douglas related how his music was so much part of him. He had known at the age of six that he wanted to play the piano, and had pestered his father for lessons, like Tom, his elder brother. Eventually his father gave in, and so started a whole new world for Douglas.

His piano teacher was a lady of considerable age, as he remembered her, but she loved her music too. She had encouraged Douglas each week, and he in turn had wanted to please. Practice for him was something to look forward to, and getting him to take some time with the piano was not a battle like the one between Tom and his father. It got to the point at which Tom's reason for not practising was that Douglas was always playing, and so their father allotted times for each to do their practice.

Suddenly it seemed as if World War III had started in my back garden, as fur and bared teeth were all that could be seen of the two older dogs, and the puppy was now shivering between my knees.

'Oh, Barley, you have let me down again,' Douglas said as he separated them. 'You will have to go into the car if you behave like that.' He led Barley by the collar to his car. 'I really don't know why she does that. Are your dogs okay?'

Holly was standing so close to me that I had to twist around to see if she was all right. 'I am so sorry,' I heard myself saying. 'I have never seen Holly fight before. As a rule, labradors are a pretty laid-back breed.'

'I'm sorry. This is not the first time Barley has done something like this. She had been lying quite contentedly at my feet; I didn't worry when she got up for a wander. I really must be more aware of her tendency to dominate. If no harm is done, should we go and have a look at your piano?' he asked, with an impish grin.

My two labs kept very close, and made sure they were between me and Douglas as we walked back into the drawing room.

I was quite curious as to why Douglas had made no comment on the Érard, as he had passed her several times now. To me the piano was such a dominant part of the drawing-room furniture; nearly everyone made comment as they entered the room. She was a very slender eight feet long, with an exaggerated waist.

'How did you come by this brute?' Douglas asked, and I found myself gently patting her to console her after such harsh words.

'She graced the drawing room of my sister-in-law for a good many years, and when she was downsizing to a smaller house, the piano just wasn't going to fit in. She tried to sell it, with no joy; the only offer was from Duck Son & Pinker, who offered £25, the cost to take it away. We had just finished the renovations here, and, having admired it often, I offered the £25, which Lottie accepted. She was pleased it was going to stay in the family, as it had been so much part of her two sons growing up; they both loved jazz.'

'So a lot of hard use, would you say?' Douglas asked as he moved to the front of the piano, lifting the lid with care. He pulled out the piano stool and positioned himself to play. His hands moved over the ivory keys with such lightness, and suddenly my beautiful piano came to life. He was playing the opening movement to a Mozart concerto I now know as K488. I was absolutely spellbound.

'Do you play?' he asked.

'Oh, my goodness, no,' I said with more than a hint of panic, lest he should ask me to play. 'I had been having lessons with Russell Brandon, but he disappeared to Wales, I think, and I have not had any further tuition.'

'Oh, yes, I know Russell! He used to organise the Guiting Music Festival each year, and would invite me and the orchestra to be involved.'

'Really?' I enthused. 'We – his students – were encouraged to attend to watch the pianist perform.'

'Well, that's one way to fill the hall, I suppose,' Douglas said, with a laugh.

'I remember coming to one concert when the soloist was going to be a Russian pianist Russell was particularly pleased to have engaged,' I said. 'The concert took place in the village hall. By the time you had a fifty-plus orchestra in on a summer's day, plus an audience, all the windows needed to be open. The soloist made his entrance and took his seat at the piano. The orchestra was brought to life as the conductor raised his baton and started to play the introduction. We all settled down for the concert. Suddenly there was a disturbance at the front of the hall, and a call went out for a doctor. A very imposing lady strode to the front of the hall, and after a brief moment announced that all was well, but the soloist had fainted.'

'I know, I know, I remember it very well,' Douglas said, as he stopped playing and jumped up from the piano. 'I was in the front row and caught him as he fell.'

'If I remember correctly,' I continued, 'the mood became more lighthearted when a concert pianist in the audience … volunteered … to play – "Unrehearsed, you understand," he said – and he proceeded to play … the very piece … you have just been playing.' My voice tailed off as I realised who the man with the velvet voice was. 'You are that Douglas Smith, aren't you? Concert pianist, and founder of the Cheltenham Symphony Orchestra?'

'The very same,' he said, bowing from the waist. 'Now, about your piano: if it were mine, I think I would be looking to sell it as an historic piece of furniture. It really needs restringing and new felts, which could be very expensive, to bring it back to concert pitch.'

I thanked him profusely and volunteered to pay for his time and travel, whereupon he volunteered that he had never taken money for his music, and if he had been able to help, he was delighted. He had to be off now to return to his practice for his concert at St Barnabas in Gloucester.

He was on his way to the front door when he turned to me and asked if perhaps I would like to go to the concert. If so, he would be delighted to send me a ticket, and perhaps we could meet afterwards for a drink and a critique of his playing.

I rushed off to my diary to make sure I would be able to go. No B&B guests, but a ruby wedding meal to cater for in Uley. It would be a lunch, and if we were quick with the washing up I could possibly make it.

If I wouldn't mind sitting at the back of the church, he said, he would come and find me after the performance, as he would be on too much of a high to sit through the symphony. He thanked me once again for lunch, and apologised for Barley's bad behaviour.

'What will you be playing?' I asked as he got into the car.

'The *Emperor*,' he said with a wave as he started up the drive.

# CHAPTER 47

—

I t had been a whole week since Douglas Smith's visit. The ticket had arrived, with a note to say that he hoped it was still possible for me to go, and to give him a ring if I wasn't going to make it. It added that perhaps I could give him a ring anyway.

I lifted the receiver and dialled the numbers. My heart was racing. *For goodness' sake,* came this intruding voice in my head, *you are behaving like a lovesick teenager. He is just being friendly, nothing more than that.*

'You are quite right,' I heard myself saying out loud. 'Pull yourself together.'

The phone was now ringing. Perhaps he didn't answer the phone when he was practising. *The answering machine will cut in in a minute; what are you going to say then?*

I was just going to put the phone down, when a very out-of-breath velvet voice answered. 'Hello.'

'Hi, it's Cynthia Anson from Slad. Have I made you rush from somewhere?'

'Oh, my dear lady, how nice to hear from you. No, I had just got back from walking Barley; I could hear the phone ringing, and my key just wouldn't unlock the door, for the simple reason that it was the wrong key!' I could visualise his smile as he added, 'Silly me. How has life been for you this week? Have you sold your piano yet?'

'No, I haven't, although I did ring Cambridge University's music department to ask if they would be interested. They were very nice and especially interested in the age of it, but added that they did already have one in the storeroom, so they would have to pass. I have the feeling they thought I was donating it to them, on reflection.'

'Well, that's all very well, but that won't help you, will it? In the meantime, enjoy it,' he said. 'Are you still able to come to the concert?

I've been practising like mad, as you may be the only person in the audience, and I want to get it right. Worst of all, I have agreed to play a piano that has been made by my piano tuner. Why I agreed I don't know, as it doesn't sound anything like my Steinway, but he is very good to me, and there can't be anything worse than spending all that time perfecting your creation and not having it played in concert. I just hope the soundboard doesn't explode.'

The very thought made me laugh, as I visualised a Victor Borge act with the piano collapsing.

'It's all very well for you to laugh,' he said, with a chuckle in his voice, 'but it is always a possibility.'

I assured him I was going to do my best to be there. 'I hope my clients will not realise they are being rushed. My team have been primed for a quick turnaround, so I hope all will go well. I will wear my red coat,' I added, 'so you will be able to spot me, and I will look out for you.'

'Looking forward to meeting you again,' he said. 'Bye for now.'

The day went well for me and the team; all we had to do now was clear the dining room, and we would be away. The plan had been for the guests to retire to the upstairs drawing room for speeches and present opening. The team were poised to clear and I had loaded my car, and we were in good time. Then to my dismay I realised they were having their speeches now, and in the dining room, so all we could do was wait.

The relative over from Australia especially for the occasion had gone to a lot of trouble doing a family tree, and went on forever. At the end I tiptoed in to our client and asked if we could clear as we had another function. She was most apologetic, and asked everyone to move to the drawing room. The team went into action, and we soon had everything looking like home again, with the supper buffet laid, but we were now an hour behind schedule.

My now well-loaded car struggled to get up Uley Bury, with a certain amount of complaining as the china readjusted itself when we went around the corners. I had three quarters of an hour to get changed and be there before the concert was due to start. There was no time to wash my hair, but a quick dash into the shower was a necessity.

My clothes were difficult to get on with so much moisture still on my body, and my urgency didn't really help. I grabbed my red coat and sprayed my hair with my best perfume, and was about to rush out the door when I remembered Rose was now living with me. I scribbled her a note to say not to wait up for me, and that I had my keys, with Douglas's phone number. I hadn't had time to unload my car, so the china continued to complain all the way to Gloucester.

I got to St Barnabas church just after 7.30, and the concert had just started. I slid into an empty seat at the back of the church, and tried to keep my racing heart from making me breathe too loudly.

Douglas had played that wonderful opening movement, and the orchestra were now enjoying their turn. I had made myself familiar with the work by listening to a recording of the *Emperor* played by Peter Katin over and over, and was very aware of the fact that Douglas was going to be playing the piano for the next forty-five minutes. As I started to relax, I sat back in my seat and allowed the music to wash over me.

After a while I became aware of a clicking sound: quite gentle, but a definite click. It seemed to be coming from my left. I slowly turned my head to see that the lady sitting next to me was knitting. *Well, that's a first,* I thought to myself, as I put my concentration back onto the music.

It was the end of the first movement, and in the pause people coughed, adjusted their seats, clothes and feet, and settled down for the second movement.

I looked at Douglas, who was looking calm and composed as he concentrated on the conductor, Mark Foster, waiting for the cue to begin. He looked immaculate in his tails and white bow tie, his white hair giving the impression of Beethoven, the composer of the piece he was playing.

He very slowly and accurately began the slow, measured notes that opened the second movement. There was no other sound to be heard; even the *click, click* in my left ear had stopped for a moment. Suddenly tears welled up in my eyes, as this beautiful sound played with such feeling spread up through the church, fixing us all in a trance. I don't know how long it took for him to play this movement, but it was the most beautiful moment of my life, and one I will never forget.

There was no shuffling of feet at the end, no coughing and readjusting: just a feeling of being suspended before the orchestra brought us back to reality with the grand opening of the final movement. Being aware of wetness dropping from my chin, I reached into my pocket for a handkerchief.

I was suddenly aware of a hand on my coat. I looked to my left to see the knitting lady looking at me with concern. 'Are you all right, dear?' she asked.

'Yes thank you,' I whispered. 'It's just the music.'

'Oh, I know,' she said. 'He's the same.'

My eyes followed the knitting needle now pointing to the gentleman sitting next to her, whom I presumed to be her husband. He too was applying a handkerchief to his face.

Before I could gather my thoughts again, it was all over, and the audience broke into an overwhelming round of applause. The conductor turned to the audience, and then Douglas, and acknowledged his masterly playing of such a great work.

Douglas bowed to the audience, then turned to the orchestra and bowed again. The conductor brought the orchestra to their feet as the applause rose again in appreciation. Douglas and Mark left the platform, and the orchestra sat down, but the applause continued. Douglas returned to the platform to rapturous applause, followed by Mark, who bowed and brought the orchestra to their feet again. Douglas left the platform once again, but the audience wanted more, and when he returned they stood and clapped with all their might, the orchestra stamping their feet in appreciation. Douglas gave a deep bow to the audience, turned and did the same to the orchestra, and with a final bow to the audience he was gone.

The look on people's faces were of absolute joy and contentment as they rose from the unforgiving church pews for the interval. Douglas came bounding through the rear entrance, grabbed my hand and said, 'Come on, let's go!'

Our cars were parked on the spare piece of land opposite the church. 'Can you follow me back to Cheltenham?' Douglas asked. 'We could stop for a quick pint in the Slug and Lettuce, and it seems silly to come all the way back to Gloucester to collect your car.'

'Of course,' I said. 'Lead the way, as I do not know the Slug and Lettuce.'

He laughed as he jumped into his car, flicking his tails up behind him. He drove cautiously back to Cheltenham, following the ring road, and soon we were coming to rest in the pub's car park. Before I could get my act together he was by my car and opening the door; he stood to attention as he held the door open for me.

The Slug and Lettuce was heaving with young people enjoying themselves. I suddenly felt very overdressed, and Douglas seemed even more so in his white bow tie and tails, but no one took any notice.

'A pint, please,' Douglas was instructing the barman, 'and for you?'

'A gin and tonic would be lovely, no ice,' I added.

We collected our drinks and found a table in the far corner. He took a long, hard drink, replaced his glass on the table and exclaimed that that was much needed, and he was now feeling much better.

'How did your day go?' he asked with interest.

I related the day's events, to which he listened with concern; he was very interested in how I achieved so much in a day. We tried to have a conversation, but the noise of young voices laughing and chatting meant we were shouting at each other to be heard.

Did I have time to join him for some bread and cheese at his house? 'It's just around the corner,' he said.

I looked at my watch; how could it be quarter past ten already? Reluctant to leave, I agreed to join him, but added, 'Then I must be on my way.'

We turned our cars, and I followed him out of the car park. We came to a stop outside a white-painted house with a tall double gate; as the lights of the cars had swept into the road, I had caught a glimpse of a well-established wisteria draping itself across the house. He opened the gates and, as we walked across the small brick courtyard, he turned and joked that he hoped to get the right key this time.

He switched on the lights, which revealed an immaculate white kitchen, its white marble floor set with small black tiles. 'Welcome to my humble abode,' he said with a deep grin, and for a moment it was Uriah Heep standing in the doorway. 'Come on through and make yourself comfortable.' He gestured with such ease.

He bent down, and before my eyes a fire sprang into action.

'Gosh,' I exclaimed. 'An instant fire, how splendid. I could do with one of those; it would save a lot of work and dust. What a good idea.'

By now he had turned on another switch, and the room was now lit with a selection of table lights. There was a settee and two easy chairs flanking the fireplace, the rest of the room being dominated by the most enormous black piano I had ever seen. The music stand still had the music that he had played that evening resting upon it, with neat beige piles of music manuscripts across the top.

'Oh, my goodness, if you are going to have a piano, have a piano,' I said, standing now by its side.

'Isn't she splendid?' he asked. 'She is my pride and joy. When my wife died ten years ago I knew I would never marry again, so I took out her half of my pension and bought my Steinway full concert grand.'

I could understand now how he had been able to walk past my piano seemingly without noticing it, and how my piano was a piece of furniture, while his was a musical instrument.

The rest of the piano was covered in photos, I presumed of his family at various stages of their lives. There was one lovely photograph of him with a very attractive lady and a handsome younger man, whom she was looking at with pride.

He must have followed my eyes to the photograph, as he was now turning it to himself, and with a wistful glance he introduced me to his wife and his eldest son Mark, on Mark's wedding day. Close by was another photograph of Mark with his bride, looking absolutely radiant. 'Oh, he has given me a hard time, one way or another, but he is a good man. This is my lovely daughter, Mim – she lives in Australia – and this is my other lovely daughter, Anna, who also now lives in Australia.'

Both girls were strikingly good-looking, with the most beautiful long wavy auburn hair. As I commented on their beautiful hair, I looked at his now receding hairline. He patted his head and said, 'I think it must have been the milkman,' with a big smile.

He picked up a small photograph frame and, passing it to me, said, 'This is my youngest son, Julian. I really must get a bigger photograph of him. Ju has some real issues about being the youngest, as he wasn't christened, wasn't breastfed, and it always seemed to him that he was a tail-end Charlie. Nothing could be further from the truth; he was very much wanted, but I suppose, with Mark being ten when he was born, there was so much more demand on our time. When he was born I left my wife in hospital and came home to supervise breakfast and the school run, but as we were all rushing around in the usual headless chicken act before leaving the house, a taxi drew up at the door. Out jumped my wife with Julian under her arm, exclaiming, "I couldn't rest in there wondering how you all were." So I guess he picked up right from the start that he was going to have to fit in to survive, poor Ju.'

He replaced the photograph, and seemed to reflect for a moment. 'Ah, well, those were the days. They all pass so quickly, don't they? Come on, let's have our bread and cheese.' He pulled out a chair for me at the table in the dining part of the kitchen. 'Do have a seat. Would you like red or white wine?'

'Oh, I think I will pass, thank you, as I will have to drive home in a minute.'

'Just one will be fine, as we're going to eat. Red or white?' He was now standing by me with a bottle in each hand.

'Red would be lovely,' I said.

Before I could ask if I could help, two wooden platters were on the table, one with cheese, one with bread – real fresh bread, I observed – quickly followed by a butter dish and a dish of chutney. A small pile of plates were already on the table with some knives and napkins.

'I can't eat on a concert day,' he was saying, 'but later, of course, I am always starving, so I put something easy in the fridge ready for when I get home. I am usually joined by Christine and Ray, two members of the orchestra, but I have told them I have a guest tonight, so they probably won't turn up. Do help yourself.'

He sat down, and suddenly I felt his hand on mine.

'I am so sorry,' he was saying. 'You have been dealing with food all day; please don't feel you have to eat. But it's nice for me to have company, so I hope you will stay for a while.'

'Well, I suppose it is a little similar for me: surrounded by food all day, I don't eat. When I get home I wonder why I feel a little queasy, then realise I haven't eaten, so thank you for inviting me to join you.'

We tucked in to the beautiful fresh bread.

'Where did you find this lovely bread?' I asked.

'Oh, in my butcher's,' he said, as if it were the most usual place to buy bread. 'And the cheese. He is the most fantastic butcher; they look after me very well. They're just by the post office in Montpellier, so they're very convenient.'

I was just about to ask about the evening's performance when the kitchen door flew open and in poured two people, very rushed and excited.

'Hi,' Douglas greeted them. 'Here are the two reprobates I thought might call. This is Christine, and this is Ray.'

I stood, and we shook hands and all sat down to the table. Douglas poured the wine, and the bread and cheese circulated.

Christine was very slim, with blonde hair; she was probably in her early fifties, and very smart in her black performance wear. Ray was also slim and blond, and looked as if he came from a film set where he would have been the matinée idol.

'Christine is leader of the orchestra,' Douglas was saying.

'And I play second fiddle,' added Ray. 'I know my place!'

Much laughter all round. The conversation flowed and so did the wine, and the general conclusion was that it had been a good performance. 'Even if you did play the G when we agreed it should be an A,' concluded Christine.

'Sorry,' said Douglas. 'It's time I retired.'

Much laughter followed; another bottle of wine was opened, and my glass was filled before I could cover it. I made a mental note not to drink it.

'So which agency did you come from?' Christine asked, looking at me.

I looked at her and then Douglas, somewhat puzzled. 'I am not a musician,' I offered. 'Douglas invited me to this evening's concert.'

Douglas came to my aid, touched my hand, and replied to Christine, 'Don't give all my secrets away.'

Christine was not happy with this. 'Was it Saga or the Lady?'

The penny dropped, and I laughed. 'Neither, I am afraid. Douglas came to see my piano, then invited me to the concert this evening.'

'Good on you, Douglas,' Ray interjected. 'See, you are still able to pull the birds.'

Much laughter followed, but my thoughts couldn't help contradicting the statement. I hadn't been pulled; I had practically rushed, and I felt more like an old boiler than a bird.

Douglas's hand was on mine again, with a slight look of concern. 'Take no notice of these two; I can't take them anywhere.' He smiled and gestured to the door, looking at Christine and Ray. 'Time you went home. Thanks for a good evening, and I think that bowing was a great improvement, Christine; you must have put a lot of work into that. Thank you.'

Waves goodbye followed as they bustled out into the dark night.

I had stood up to say goodbye, and found myself a little dizzy. I thought I was perhaps tired after a hectic day, but a glance at my glass told me I hadn't done as I had told myself, as it was now quite empty.

Douglas came in and closed the door. 'They are very good friends,' he offered, 'and have been there for me in those dark days; they mean no harm.'

I smiled and thanked him profusely for a wonderful evening, and added that I really had to go. The big kitchen clock struck just once; I thought it might be half past something, but a quick glance told me it was one in the morning.

'I am going to have a cup of tea before I retire,' Douglas was saying. 'Will you join me?' He hesitated for a moment when he switched on the kettle, 'Are you okay?' he enquired. 'You look a little pale.'

'Nothing a cup of tea won't put right,' I replied, 'then I must be on my way.'

We chatted quite lightheartedly as we drank our tea, mainly about the different characters in the orchestra. It was very clear just how important the orchestra was to him, and how much part of his life.

I got up to go, and he took my hand.

'Are you all right?' he asked. He seemed to be taking my pulse. 'I had to qualify as a doctor when I was training to be a dentist,' he said, 'and my recommendation is that you should not drive tonight.'

I must have given him an old-fashioned look, as he assured me his intentions were honourable, and that the spare bed was always made up in case Ju decided to drop in. 'I can even offer a pair of pyjamas, if that helps.'

'Thank you; I will accept your kind offer. My main problem is that I'll need a clock, as I must be home before my daughter wakes and realises I have been out all night.'

He smiled. 'No problem.'

We went up the stairs that led from the kitchen onto an L-shaped landing.

'My room is just here.' He indicated the room at the top of the stairs, then walked down the long side of the L to the bathroom and, opening the airing cupboard, gave me a towel and a pair of pyjamas. Proceeding down the short part of the L, the guest room was next. We went in, and he put the light on, drew the curtains, picked up the clock, looked at his watch and adjusted the time. 'What time shall I set the alarm for?'

'About 5.30, I think, then I will be home by 6.30, and all should be well.' I thanked him for a most enjoyable evening, and assured him that I would just slip out and try not to disturb him.

'No fear of that; I shall sleep like a top tonight.' After a little hesitation he asked, 'Can I ring you again? I have so enjoyed your company tonight; perhaps we could take the dogs for a walk if I promise to make Barley behave herself.'

'That would be lovely, and thank you so much for this evening,' I replied.

With that he pulled the door to and added, 'Sleep well.' His footsteps went off down the landing.

As I started to undress I was aware of the outside light going on, and footsteps across the courtyard, and assumed Douglas was taking Barley out for her night duties before going to bed. I got into bed and put out the light; as I did so the outside light went off, and after a short while I heard Douglas come up the stairs and close his door.

I awakened to a telephone ringing in the distance. I looked at the clock to see it was 5.30am; with that the alarm went off. I was then aware of footsteps down the landing, a tap on my door and Douglas standing there with the telephone in his hand.

'It's your daughter wanting to know where you are,' he said, handing me the telephone.

'Hello, darling,' I said.

'Where are you?' Rose demanded. 'You haven't been home all night.'

'I'm fine and will be with you within the hour,' I said, and ended the call to stop any further conversation.

Douglas smiled, and said she had asked, 'Where's my mother?' in a very cross voice. 'I told her you were in my spare room and that I would take the phone to you. There was an exasperated sigh in reply.' He laughed, and touched my hand. 'Not to worry.'

I had to smile. 'It sounds like a role reversal. So much for me slipping away quietly.'

'I'll leave you to get up,' he said, closing my bedroom door behind him.

I went downstairs, where Douglas had made himself a cup of tea. He gestured to a mug. 'Will you have one?'

I laughed and said that I thought I should be on my way. He smiled and nodded in agreement.

'I will ring again, if I may,' he said as he held the door open for me. I thanked him and said I would look forward to it.

# CHAPTER 48

It was a bright morning to drive home, with the sun rising well, and the promise of another lovely day. Was I being silly or was there an attraction?

I felt as if I were walking on clouds. I couldn't believe my ears when he asked if he could ring again. Perhaps he was just being polite. I would just have to wait and see.

I just loved every moment of being with him; he was so easy and relaxed. What was amazing was that he was interested in me, when after all he presumably had a whole orchestra to choose from.

My mind wandered back to last evening and all that wonderful music, and how easy he was to talk to about it. He was so talented, yet so unassuming. His hands had interested me, as always; I had been very surprised to see he had quite small, square hands, with relatively short fingers for a pianist.

I had taken myself off to a concert in the cathedral so many times, and had been desperate to share the experience with someone, only to come home to a husband not interested. What a luxury if Douglas and I did become friends, I mused to myself.

I had driven home in a daydream. As I returned to Down Court, where I had lived for the past thirty-one years. Rose was still being Rose. I couldn't believe she could make me feel so guilty at having enjoyed myself. Not to mention having the audacity to have left her in the house, at the tender age of twenty-seven years, all night.

'How did your evening go, darling?' I asked. 'Did your friends turn up?'

'No,' she said with a huge sigh, and my heart sank for her.

'Oh, darling, I am sorry to hear that. What did you do in the pub by yourself?'

'I had a drink,' Rose related, 'and as I asked the barman if there were any messages for me, I noticed a very tall man waiting by the bar. I sat down to finish my glass of wine, and the tall man came over to ask if I was waiting for friends as well. I told him I was, and hoped they wouldn't be too long. He took a seat at the table, and before too long we were enjoying another drink. Neither his friends nor mine came, so we carried on talking. When I said I had to go he asked if I would like to meet him there again, and I agreed.'

'That's fantastic, darling,' I said, giving her a hug. 'So not an entirely wasted evening, then.'

Rose had decided to come home in the July after her father died. I am not really sure why to this day, as she seemed very happy with life in the fast lane in London, where she had been the personal assistant to a doctor based in Harley Street. I was very concerned that she would come home and be buried alive with me, so I was quite determined that she should have a job and make a life for herself with her age group. I needn't have worried on the job front, as financing her lifestyle was a priority for her after she came home from her friend's wedding in Barbados, and without further ado she was looking in the evening papers for jobs.

After several interviews, Rose would finally accept the position of personal assistant to Lord Dulverton's son and heir at Batsford Park, Moreton-in-Marsh. This was going to be a good sixty-mile round trip per day, and in winter could be a very difficult journey, so I took her to Tetbury to buy her a four-wheel drive vehicle. We also bought her the latest form of communication in the form of a mobile phone to have in the car in case of difficulties. In the meantime her relationship seemed to flourish with the tall man I now know as Philip.

*\*\**

The rest of the day went slowly, and was very restful after quite a hectic week. The concert the evening before just kept coming into my thoughts. I just couldn't believe I had been in Douglas's presence before, and had admired from a distance his skills as a pianist. So near, yet so far. Then, last night, I had been there at his invitation. Why did I have this strange feeling that meeting Douglas was meant to happen?

My friend Isabelle Danks had been married to Alexander Kok, whom Douglas had asked about on our first meeting. As a friend, she would sometimes invite me to come along to a concert, and likewise with my piano teacher. I would trot along, and thoroughly enjoy the concert, but never in my wildest dreams had I ever thought I would be there at the soloist's request.

The gentle tap-tap of Holly's paw on my lap reminded me it was time for their walk, and back to reality.

I spent a whole week rushing to the phone every time it rang. Very welcome bookings, but not the call I had been hoping for.

Eventually, I reached the stage where I was telling myself it was a one-off. He was a very kind man who just happened to have a spare ticket for that night. I had become quite accustomed to the little voice in my head telling me I had read more into it than there was, and to move on. Tempted as I was, I didn't ring him, as somehow it felt like an intrusion. It was a lovely thing to have happened, and a lovely memory, but now I had to move on.

Rose had met Phil again, and seemed very happy and settled. She came in with quite a glow on her face after their meeting, which was good to see.

I locked up and put the dogs to bed, and was about to go to bed myself when the phone rang. *Who on earth is that at this time of night? Rose is in, so no trouble there. Hope it isn't Mum – I don't relish driving to Marshfield at this time of night—*

'Hello,' I said, quite abruptly.

'Hello,' came the velvet voice. 'I am so sorry; I've just looked at my watch and realised the time, but I have just got back from Skye and I thought it would be nice to touch base. How are you?'

'I'm fine,' I replied. 'How are you? Have you driven down from Skye today?'

'Yes, and a good journey it was. Sundays are good, as there's not so much heavy traffic, but it does mean I have to go all the way round the top, as the Armadale ferry doesn't run on a Sunday, which adds almost 120 miles to the journey. Never mind; it was all worth it. Would you have any free time tomorrow? I just wondered if you would like to join me for a spot of lunch; nothing fancy, just some pâté and toast.'

The B&B guests had left this morning, so everything was all right there, I thought to myself. 'That would be lovely, but I must be back by half past three for my B&B guests.'

'Of course. Look forward to seeing you tomorrow.' And he was gone.

I found myself just staring at the phone. I hadn't just dreamt that, had I? I replaced the receiver and went over the conversation again. My heart was racing; how was I going to sleep now?

\*\*\*

'Ah! Hello, you were able to find me again,' Douglas greeted me. 'I wondered if I should have checked you knew the way. Isn't it a lovely day? Barley and I have had a lovely walk up Daisy Bank, haven't we, Barley?'

Barley was by his side, giving her curious singsong welcome. I patted her head, and she wagged her tail, while Douglas ran his fingers through her coat.

'I had a lovely journey over,' I said. 'It was so clear from Birdlip you could see for miles. Thank you for inviting me over; it's really good to get away for a few hours.'

The French doors in the sitting room were open onto the little courtyard, and a gentle breeze subtly moved the voile curtains.

'I keep meaning to get a little table and chairs to go out there,' Douglas said. 'But, as soon as the sun shines, I usually pop up to Skye and cut the lawn, and go walking with Barley and my camera.'

All around his sitting room walls were lovely photographs of mountains. 'Did you take these?' I asked.

'Yes, I did,' he replied with a hint of pride. 'Now, dear lady, before we go any further, what can I get you to drink?'

I asked for a soft drink, as I would have to be working on all cylinders tonight. He went off into the kitchen with a chuckle. 'First time I've heard that reason not to have a drink,' he said from a distance.

I walked around the room looking at the beautiful pictures, and mused to myself at being a 'dear lady'. There were also some pictures of churches. 'Are these local?' I asked as he returned with my drink.

'Oh, that was great fun. A friend of mine wanted a calendar to give to his customers, and asked if I could come up with some ideas, so I took myself off around the Cotswold villages and photographed all the churches. It was something I had wanted to do for a while, so

I thought I would give it a go. A bit different from nude ladies!' He laughed, with a lovely glint in his eye.

Before I knew it the clock was striking three.

'Oh, my goodness, where has the time gone?' I asked as I got to my feet. 'I have enjoyed myself very much, and thank you for a lovely lunch.'

'I have enjoyed it too.' He took my hand. 'I haven't felt so relaxed in female company for a long time. Is it possible to see you again?' He was looking into my eyes with such intensity. 'Forgive me for asking, but I am terrible on names, and I can't go on calling you "dear lady", as much as you are.'

I smiled and said, 'I'm known as Anne, but my first name is Cynthia, so you choose.'

'Well, I'll stay with the Anne as well, if I may, but please do not be offended if I call you Mary, as we were married for over thirty years; it may just slip out.' He took a pencil, and in large letters he wrote *ANNE came for lunch today* on his calendar. 'I'll give you a ring if I may, and please feel free to ring me; it would be lovely.'

We walked to my car, and he held the door open for me to get in. With a big smile, he said, 'Thank you for coming,' and, as if to make sure I had heard it, added again, 'I have enjoyed your company. See you soon, I hope.' And with a wave we said goodbye.

What a lovely, lovely man, I thought to myself, and what was truly amazing was that he was interested in me: fat old me.

I was brought back with a loud beep, as a motorist was frustrated I hadn't noticed the lights changing to green. *Better pay attention,* I said to myself. But his lovely smile kept creeping into my concentration.

# CHAPTER 49

I had been invited for lunch with Douglas and was dashing to the car, as I was late, only to twist my ankle on a stone. *Oh, that hurt!* I said to myself in surprise. *Better sit still for a moment.* I tried to make myself comfortable in the car.

I tried to put the car in gear to start, but the pain came back worse. I decided not to drive, and to sit with my leg up for a bit to see if that would ease it. I rang Douglas to apologise for not coming. He was of the opinion I had done more than sprain my ankle, and decided to come over.

On arrival and examination, Douglas decided a trip to A&E was required. The result was that I had broken a bone in my ankle. With a leg in plaster, crutches handed over and instructions not to put my foot to the ground for twenty-four hours, he drove me home while I wondered how I was going to cook dinner for six hopping about.

My hero in shining armour came to the rescue and said he would be waiter while I cooked, resting my leg on a stool. He was great, and everything was done in good humour.

Off to rescue Barley, then back to serve breakfast. Luckily I had help coming in to prepare the rooms, so Douglas did a mass dog walk, went home to practise and came back to help with dinner; it was all go for him.

The next day I tentatively put my foot to the ground and, using the crutches to get around, I soon got into a rhythm. But I needed assistance with things like shopping, so I still had a lot of help from Douglas.

\*\*\*

The last two months had passed so quickly, in a whirl of B&B guests, washing and ironing, dog walking, grocery shopping, lunch taking, and now a new activity, and one for which I felt ill qualified: music critic to Douglas Smith, LRAM. Douglas was to play the *Emperor* again in November in the Pump Room, Cheltenham. He had probably forgotten more than I could remember about playing the piano.

We had spent several happy lunch hours having a quick sandwich, then I would sit and turn the pages as Douglas practised – not that I could always keep up with his playing in the very fast movements. But he tolerated my bad timing, and with a quick swish the page would turn, as I had obviously lost my place again.

I was very surprised by the amount of time he spent practising, especially when he had played the same piece in concert in August. He would sometimes practise for eight hours a day, only punctuated by walking Barley, and now by entertaining me for lunch.

He did have another hobby of making beer, but, as he made that in a large container, it was a once-a-month occupation. Having a quiet pint for an evening's relaxation was a very important part of his day, although this was interspersed with friends coming in to practice cello or trumpet playing. But one evening was sacrosanct: the evening he went to Leckhampton Court to entertain the residents, many of whom were terminally ill.

As the concert approached, publicity was also added to his schedule, as he liaised between orchestra on practice nights and Cheltenham Town Hall, which sold tickets for the concerts, while wearing his other hat as orchestra administrator.

How quickly and easily it seemed I had become part of his life; how comfortable I felt in his company, and he seemingly in mine. No airs and graces, no drama, just sheer love of life and his music.

One day was proceeding as usual, when out of the blue he said he would like me to meet his son and daughter-in-law. They were coming round for supper on Wednesday, an evening he thought I could be free of B&B responsibilities, and he would like it very much.

I was very hesitant, as it seemed this would take our friendship into a different place, but I wasn't sure what.

He could see I was somewhat concerned, so he took my hand. 'Would it be easier if your daughter joined us as well?' he asked, with a big smile. 'You wouldn't be so overwhelmed by us Smiffs then.'

*Oh, heavens to Betsy,* I thought to myself, *how is Rose going to interpret that?* I had told her each time I had seen Douglas, but she had paid little attention. Her life seemed very settled at the moment, and Philip seemed to be very much part of it.

'I'll have to see if she is free,' I said at last.

'Oh, thank goodness for that!' He gave me a quick kiss on the cheek. 'I thought I was being turned down, and I really wouldn't like that.' He was looking at me intently now, holding both my hands. 'I have really enjoyed these last few weeks, or months even, and to be honest Mark and Joanna have seen a change in me and want to meet the person responsible. Do you mind?'

'Do they think I am from an agency too?'

'Well, yes, they did jump to conclusions, but I soon put them in the picture, and they were agreeably surprised that their old dad could still "pull the birds", as they put it.'

'That seems to be the in phrase,' I said.

'They are good fun, and Joanna is expecting their second child in November. "Had no idea how it happened," they said when they told me. Wind pollination again, I expect,' he said, with such a comic attitude I just couldn't stop laughing. 'Will you think about coming on Wednesday, please?'

'It would be lovely for you to meet Rose and for me to have her company,' I said. 'But I will have to ask her, as she may have arranged to see Philip, who I have yet to meet.'

'How about if we all have a big meeting?' he said excitedly.

'Well, I will put it to her, but I rather think it will be too much to ask. I'll let you know.'

Rose arrived home a little earlier than usual that evening, and we enjoyed a cup of tea together before the usual rush of the evening meal. She had me in stitches, as she described how the wife of her employer, who was into alternative therapies, treated a headache by putting a pill on her head and bandaging it on, instead of taking it, and no one seemed to think this odd. 'I expect I will get used to it,' she added.

Eventually I felt I could ask the question.

'Would you like to meet Douglas?' I asked, somewhat tentatively.

She just shrugged her shoulders. 'I don't mind. Would you like me to meet Douglas?'

'Well, his son and daughter-in-law have asked to meet me, and Douglas thought I might like to have your moral support. I think he might like to meet you, too. He did ask if Philip would like to join us as well, but I thought that a bit much, as I haven't met him yet.'

My last comment seemed to hit a nerve. 'Oh, Mother, don't let's get too complicated. Phil and I are just friends. I'm sure he won't want to be involved in a family gathering.'

I hated it when I got the 'oh, Mother' treatment. It usually meant a rocky time, but I was surprised by her next comment: that if I would like her to come, she would. 'Better see what you're getting into now,' she added as she got up from the chair.

'That would be lovely for me. Thank you. The invite is for next Wednesday; is that a good day for you?'

'Yep, that's fine,' she said, leaving the room. 'Put it in the diary. I'm going to change; I'm meeting Phil tonight.'

I rang Douglas later that night to tell him, and he was delighted. 'I have planned the menu in anticipation,' he said. 'How about curried parsnip soup, beef in red wine, and my special crème brûlée, if I can find my blowtorch?'

'That sounds a veritable feast,' I said. 'Can I be of help?'

'No my dear lady, you do enough cooking. This is my treat.'

'Can I ask where the blowtorch comes in?' I asked curiously.

'Ah! All will be revealed on the day,' he said, and I could imagine him tapping the side of his nose.

***

Wednesday seemed to come around very quickly. I took particular care with my hair, and took ages to decide what to wear. I was still pondering when Rose came home.

'You look lovely,' she offered, as she came into my dressing room. She had a quizzical look on her face. 'Is tonight very important to you, Mum?'

'Well, it's been a long time since I last had to "meet the family",' I said.

'Is this friendship serious? Dad only died in February, Mum; are you ready for another relationship?'

I took a little while to answer that question, as it was one I had been asking myself all day, if not the last few days since he had offered the invitation. I enjoyed Douglas's company very much, and all that beautiful music I just couldn't get enough of. Plus I had received more love and affection in these few short months than I had in thirty years with Rose's father. But I couldn't tell her that.

'Well, I do enjoy his company very much,' I said, 'but, hey, we are getting very serious here. His family may not like me, and it could all fade away, so let's just enjoy ourselves. I'll drive, then I shall have to watch my drinks!' I added with a smile.

'Okay, I'll go and freshen up. See you in twenty minutes,' Rose said as she whirled out of the door.

She looked absolutely lovely as she came down the stairs, with a lightness in her step. Her makeup was something I had admired for a while, and I wished I could have the same effect with mine.

We went off like two giggling schoolgirls, but as we got in the car my confidence was fading fast. I negotiated the lane to the main road as if on automatic pilot. The light was fading; it must soon be time to change the clocks, I was musing, when Rose said, 'It will be all right, Mum; if they don't like you, it's their loss. Don't worry. As you say, let's enjoy ourselves; we haven't been out together since I came home.'

She was quite right; we hadn't been out together. With the B&B and her work, life had mainly been in the fast lane. 'The B&B guests will be dropping off soon, so maybe we'll have some time to do things together. By the way, I had enquiries today about Christmas. Do we fill the house with strangers for Christmas?'

Christmas at Down Court had always been great fun; I just loved Christmas. There had been the grey side as well, though, as I always had to fight my corner to have my parents to stay for Christmas. Every year, as the planning started, Arthur would say, 'Anne, we are not having your parents again this year.' Inside I would die a death; how on earth did he expect me to tell my disabled mother and stepfather that they were not welcome? How I wished my brother would ask for them just once to save this awful feeling each year. At least I wouldn't have that problem this year.

'Okay, Mum, penny for them; you were deep in thought then.'

'I was just thinking about Christmases past, and how at least this year I won't have to argue about having Mum to stay for Christmas.'

'Oh, Mum, do we really have to have her?'

I couldn't believe my ears.

'Well, she has never been a grandmother to me, always so full of her needs, and not always very nice to you. Let's go away for Christmas.'

'Go away?' I asked, taken aback. 'Where on earth would we go, and how would we afford to go anywhere? And what about the dogs? I couldn't possibly put them in kennels for Christmas.'

'Well, at least it gave you something different to think about while driving over.' She smiled. We were nearly at Douglas's house.

'It all looks very familiar,' she said as we turned into Bayshill Road. The ladies' college was well illuminated, and must have brought memories back for her. 'Looks as if the house backs onto St Helen's.'

'Oh, of course! All the times I have come here now and seen the green-uniformed girls going in and out. I hadn't given thought to what was beyond the hedge.'

'Typical,' she said, 'n'est-ce pas?'

We looked at each other and smiled.

'Are we here too early?' I asked.

'Perfect timing, Mum,' she said.

'I do hope you like him,' I found myself saying. 'I have enjoyed his company very much, and the thought of it passing makes me feel very empty. I wouldn't want it to end.'

She squeezed my hand as she joined me to go through the gateway Douglas had left open for us. She was so confident. 'Come on, Mum, let's enjoy ourselves.'

We had arrived before Mark and Joanna, and I couldn't make up my mind if that was a good thing or bad. Then Douglas was at the door to greet us with his big smile and velvet voice.

'Well, who's a lucky man having two beautiful ladies joining him for supper tonight?' he said, holding the door open, and with a bow ushered us into the sitting room. He took my hand and gave me a kiss on the cheek.

'My daughter Rose,' I said proudly.

'My, how alike you are. Thank you so much for coming this evening. Do come and sit down; can I get you a drink?' His outward appearance was very relaxed, but could I sense a little anxiety in him too? 'Mark and Joanna won't be long; their son William has decided not to settle tonight for the babysitter, but it shouldn't cause too much of a delay.' And he was off to the kitchen to get the drinks.

He had just handed us our drinks when there was a commotion in the kitchen; it sounded like children tumbling in from school.

'Hi,' said Joanna. 'Sorry we're late; you know how it is with young children.'

'Hello,' said Mark with a big smile, and those perfect teeth, just like his father.

Rose and I got to our feet and shook hands, and waited for Joanna to take a seat that was convenient for her, as she was very pregnant. 'When is the baby due?' I asked.

'The beginning of November, if not before,' she said. 'It's all got a bit uncomfortable; it can't happen soon enough now.' She also had a lovely smile, with a very endearing gap in between her front teeth. Mark had gone with his father to help with the drinks, and much laughter and leg pulling was coming from the kitchen.

The meal was delicious; I was much impressed. The company was very convivial. All too soon, with the meal over and the coffee brought in, Joanna suddenly looked at her watch and said they must go for their babysitter. Douglas got up to help her. Mark patted his father on the back and promised to give him a ring, and said how nice it had been to meet us.

Douglas went over to Rose. Giving her a very direct look, he asked if she would mind if he took me to Skye with him soon. I was surprised, but Rose said she thought it a good idea.

Joanna said it was lovely and she thought I would enjoy it. 'Don't forget to take your walking boots!' she added.

'But how can we go to Skye when the baby is due?' I asked Douglas. 'Won't you want to be here for that?'

'Oh, I think they can manage without us,' he said, with a big smile, 'and we have a lifetime to wet the baby's head.'

'It's all right,' said Joanna. 'I expect you have noticed he has a concert coming up, and he always has to escape to Skye afterwards to unwind. He's quite right; he can't do anything, and my parents are coming to hold the fort, so no problems this end.'

Mark shook my hand and Rose's and bade us farewell. He turned to his father and said to keep a couple of concert tickets for them, then they were gone.

Douglas turned to me and said that he hoped I would be able to go with him to Skye. I looked at Rose, and said that I would have to make arrangements for my daughter to have company, and the dogs to be looked after, and that there was a definite return date for B&B

bookings: all the things that had been rushing through my mind since he had asked.

'Of course,' he said. 'I forget all those sorts of arrangements have to be made, having been on my own for so long. I just throw some things in a bag, put them in the car along with old Barley and lock the door, and away I go.'

'I would like to come very much, but I will have to be sure all is well at home first. Thank you for asking me.'

I was suddenly aware of dishes being collected. We both turned around to see Rose clearing the table.

'No, no, my dear girl, that is my job. I have to have something to do after you have gone to keep my feet on the ground.' He gave his big smile, and we thanked him for a lovely meal and said how nice it was to meet his family.

'Let's hope it is the first of many,' he said.

We both gave him a kiss on the cheek. He opened the car door and said, 'That was nice; I could get used to that,' with that wicked smile.

There was much general discussion on the way home, which sort of weaved in and out of the fact that I seemed to be getting into a serious relationship. There seemed to be some resentment to this. Or was I reading too much into the general conversation?

# CHAPTER 50

Elaine, who helped me with catering, had agreed to look after things while I was away, so I would be going to Skye with Douglas after the concert.

Douglas had explained the ritual that he had adopted to make his journey to Skye after a concert as easy as possible. The day of the concert he would take Barley for a good long walk early in the morning, having packed his bag the night before and put it in his car. He would pack Barley's bowl and food, practise for the rest of the morning, then meet up with the orchestra for a brief runthrough. Home for a bath and a rest, then he would dress and go to the concert venue. After the concert, straight home, change, and with Barley he would set off for Skye. The adrenaline that inevitably flowed with the excitement of playing such wonderful music would make sleep impossible, along with his need to be in the place he loved most, so what better way to unwind?

This time, however, taking me, it was going to be different. We would make an early start the day after the concert – four in the morning, to be sure – and drive up to Mallaig to catch the last ferry of the day to Skye. I was to stay the night in the spare room, and he would make a fish pie to take with us so that we would have a meal ready for our arrival, with no cooking after the long journey.

So, with all arrangements made, we set off for the concert. I was meeting friends and Mark there, so Douglas was comfortable in the knowledge that I would not be on my own. Joanna, still not having had the baby, decided that that kind of excitement was not a good idea, so she put her feet up at home.

The Pump Room, a beautiful Regency building built for the taking of spa water, was full to capacity. Mark Foster came out of the green room and, with his baton raised, the orchestra sprang to life with the overture. I thought of Douglas having to wait in the green room by himself: something he had done many times, I was sure, but this time I couldn't help feeling concerned for him.

The overture over, the applause rose and fell twice while Mark made his exit and reappeared, bringing the orchestra to their feet. Mark gave a deep bow to them and the audience, then returned to the green room.

When the green room door opened again, Douglas came out, followed again by Mark Foster. When they got to the piano and the podium they both turned and bowed to the audience, who were now in full applause. Douglas arranged himself on the piano stool, then, poised, he waited to be given the cue from Mark that the orchestra were ready. Then he was off on that long solo introduction to the work that was to follow.

The orchestra had a long piece to play before Douglas played again. I don't know why, but I felt a little anxious for him. After a while he was back in business again; the music ebbed and flowed with the score, and Douglas seemed very confident. He was coming up to a run that he had practised and practised, then I heard the missed notes and hoped he would collect himself. He did, and I hoped no one had noticed.

Then, mercy of mercies, it was the slow movement. This was such a beautiful movement, and Douglas played it with such care and feeling every time, even when practising, that I was deeply moved each time I heard it. There was total silence in the hall, as everyone seemed to be held in the spell of this beautiful music. I found myself thinking of Beethoven and wondering if he had been able to hear what he had written at this point. Then, all too soon, it was over.

After a moment came the final movement with all its fury. Douglas missed a few more notes that I hoped no one would catch, but he seemed to be confident. As if Beethoven himself didn't want it to end, the final part had the piano and orchestra having a kind of conversation as to whether to go on or call it a day, until the final page was turned and the piece came to an end.

Douglas's hands rested for a moment on the keys, then he stood and bowed to the audience, who were applauding loudly and appreciatively. Douglas held his hand out to Mark, but Mark was still looking at the orchestra, and seemed to take forever to turn and shake his hand. Was he showing his displeasure at Douglas's missed notes, or was he giving the audience time to show their appreciation? Eventually, though, he shook Douglas's hand and brought the orchestra to their feet.

Douglas returned to the green room, but, with the applause still continuing, he returned and gave a low bow. He turned and gave a low bow to the orchestra, turned once more to the audience and walked back to the green room, not to reappear.

The audience were now on their feet to take a stroll in the interval before the symphony. Douglas came and found me, accepting compliments on the way. He took hold of my hand very firmly, while joking with Mark about the missed notes he had 'fallen off'.

We went to the car, and I volunteered to drive, but that was not an option. 'Not my best,' he said, and for once I did not know what to say.

We did the short journey to his home almost in silence, except for Douglas saying how good a house it had been, and how it would help with the orchestra's expenses, as it was getting more and more expensive to hire music, arrange advertising, book venues and so on.

As we went in I asked if Ray and Christine would be calling. He said he wasn't sure, but he had said to them that we would not be going to Skye until tomorrow, so they might.

Douglas poured us both a drink, and we sat on the settee. He took my hand and looked me in the eyes and said how pleased he was that I had been there tonight. He had felt my support, which had given him the strength to carry on. I asked if it had been the first time he had missed notes, and he said yes, then, after a pause, he said, 'It must not happen again.'

We both sat in the near-darkness, sipping our drinks, looking thoughtfully at the flames of the gas fire that, along with the light on the piano, formed the only source of light in the room. All the while Douglas was still holding my hand tightly.

After a while Douglas said that the symphony was a long piece tonight, and he didn't think Ray and Christine would call. He put his glass down on the side table and turned to me. Holding both my hands, he asked, 'Would you please stay with me tonight?'

\*\*\*

The alarm woke us with a start at 3.30am. After a quick cup of tea and a bowl of cereal we were off, with Barley safely stowed in the back.

I was really surprised to see so much activity at four o'clock in the morning, and that was before we hit the motorway. I had always imagined everyone fast asleep at that hour if I had reason to be out of bed at that time.

A short run down the hill, and junction 11A was all lit up, with clear signs to the M5 north shining out. This suddenly felt like a big adventure. I looked at Douglas; the smile had returned to his face, and there was an almost little-boy excitement about his being.

'Is all well?' he asked as he caught me looking at him.

'Great,' I said.

'Well, here we go; next stop Southwaite services.'

The lights of the motorway lit the central reservation until well after Birmingham. Then it was just the dipped headlights of the oncoming traffic, and the red taillights of the rows of lorries all travelling at the same speed, making overtaking a lengthy business for them. I wondered how they kept awake; I was having trouble with my eyelids, as they continually tried to close. I asked Douglas if he was okay, and whether he would mind if I nodded off.

'No, I'm fine,' he said, with a smile. 'I'm usually doing this by myself, so it's a bonus to have you with me, even if you are asleep. Would you mind taking the top off the travel sweets and leaving the tin handy?' This I did, and I settled back in the seat to rest.

When I awoke there was a thin streak of light across the early morning sky. 'Good morning,' said Douglas.

'Where are we?' I asked.

'We're about to go over the Manchester Ship Canal,' he said, pointing to the straight-sided ribbon of silver that was off to our left.

I had heard so much about this canal in my school days: how it was the highway for all the cargo ships bringing cotton and wool to the mills, and iron ore to the great blast furnaces of the steel industry. Now, in the cold light of early morning, it looked small and insignificant, and empty.

The traffic was beginning to get busy now, with the early rush to work, but Douglas looked calm and relaxed. The signs on the motorway were now reading *Blackpool* and *Wigan Pier*, which set me wondering how Wigan had a pier when it looked as if it was a long way from the sea; perhaps it was on a canal?

I must have pondered on this for some time, as the next signs declared *South Lakes*, and *Services in 5 miles*. *Thank goodness for that*, I thought, wishing I hadn't had that cup of tea.

When we went past the service turn-off, I looked at Douglas in surprise.

'We get off at the next services; they are just twenty-five miles on, then we have done the bulk of the motorway.'

My 'Oh' in reply caused Douglas to ask if I was all right.

'Well, I could have made good use of their facilities,' I said with a smile.

'Can you hang on?' he asked, smiling back. 'I will go as quick as I can.' He leant forward on the steering wheel, with an earnest look on his face, to see if it would make the car go any faster.

We were now in open countryside, with the early morning sun just lighting up the peaks of the mountains in the far distance, and the fields glittered from the overnight frost. Small round patches of green showed through where the sheep had been sleeping, as one by one they got up and started grazing.

'On our way home I thought we might have a stopover in the Lakes to break the journey,' Douglas said, 'as it always seems further coming down again. Would you like that?'

'That sounds lovely,' I said. 'So many treats.' I had just realised how relaxed I was with Douglas driving. It had always been me at the wheel before, as Arthur hadn't enjoyed driving, but now I was able to look around and enjoy the scenery.

'Here we are: Southwaite services.'

I made a dash to the loo while Douglas gave Barley a walk to stretch her legs. They had just returned when I emerged from the conveniences. With Barley safely stowed once again, we left a window open for her and headed off for our breakfast.

When we had returned, fed and refreshed, we were about to get in the car when Douglas swore under his breath, as he discovered his hub caps had once again been removed from the front two wheels. 'I had just replaced those,' he said, 'after losing them on my last trip north. What can they be doing with them?'

Several things came to mind as Douglas and I made ourselves comfortable for the next stage of our journey. Hoping someone wasn't building a battleship with Douglas's hub caps, we negotiated the exit from the service area, having filled up with petrol, and were once again on the open road.

In no time at all, it seemed, we had crossed the border into Scotland and signs for Gretna Green appeared, bringing memories of the awful rail crash.

I don't remember when we left the motorway, as I had been so busy taking in all the changing scenery, and it all seemed so smooth and uncomplicated. But we were now on a dual carriageway with a great many roadworks, and signs for Glasgow were quite frequent.

'Do we have to go through Glasgow?' I asked Douglas, who so far hadn't needed to consult a map.

'Hopefully not. The trick is to find the very small and insignificant slip road that doesn't seem to need a second warning of its approach, but will take us away from Glasgow and head us for Sterling and the Road to the Isles,' he said with a roll of the tongue, his excitement obvious.

The slip road found, and Sterling now on the signs, there was again a change of scenery. We were now on two-way A roads, and making much slower progress.

Sterling Castle rose out of the scenery perched on its rocky pinnacle, defying anyone to challenge its right to be there, as we bypassed it and headed for Callander.

What a joy Callander is, with its long street full of interesting shops, displaying everything from walking sticks to tartans to beautiful crystal glasses. The local chapel had been converted to a Rob Roy museum, which included the tourist information centre; I made a note. The whole area was backdropped by various shades of green, as the pines and conifers growing on the higher ground surrounding Callander seemed to stand guard, bringing back memories of *Dr Finlay's Casebook*.

Were we going to stop? I looked at Douglas, who seemed to read my thoughts. 'Perhaps we will have time to stop on the way down,' he said, 'but for now we have a ferry to catch; let's have a sweetie.' I felt as if I had said, *Are we nearly there yet?*

The fast-flowing river that I had caught glimpses of through Callander was now flowing close to the road, and seemed to be in full spate.

'Our next stop is the Green Welly,' Douglas said with some glee, as a little encouragement that there would be another stop. 'That's at Crianlarich. I try to stop every four hours, for a break for me and Barley, and I hope you will enjoy it too.'

'Are we making good progress?' I asked.

'Excellent,' he said, 'and the weather is perfect; you're a good talisman.' He winked. 'Usually this time of year we run into fog, or torrential rain that can cause problems, and here we are, bathed in autumn sunlight.'

We passed beautiful countryside, and the road signs had started to read like a tourist guide, when suddenly Douglas was indicating to turn off right. There was a huge car park filled with cars and coaches and transport of every kind. 'Here we are at the Green Welly.'

Barley was now giving her singsong call; she obviously knew exactly where she was and was ready for her walk.

'First things first,' Douglas said with a wink, as he let Barley out of the car, her tail wagging. She had a good shake to straighten out her fur, then ran off to the nearest patch of grass. Douglas walked her around the perimeter fence, which was quite an area, and gave her a drink, then she obligingly jumped back in the car for us to go for our break.

The area was quite flat after all the hills and valleys we had driven through, with a strong smell of pine from the trees that surrounded the area. I took a good deep breath, and my wheezy old asthmatic lungs seemed grateful for such a luxury.

We joined the world and its wife, all going in and out of what looked like a very large agricultural building, which did not give a clue to what we would find inside. As we went through the doors there was an area for people to sit and enjoy a coffee or tea, and to the right were two shops that obviously would have to be explored. Straight ahead was the sign to the toilets, then off to the left was a restaurant from which were coming the most tantalising smells.

'Which do we do first?' Douglas asked, as he watched me take it all in.

'Well, I am for the loo,' I said, 'then the restaurant, then the shops.'

'Sounds like a good plan,' agreed Douglas, and off we went.

An hour passed very easily, and, with the purchase of a paper and some more travel sweets, we returned to Barley and the car. We filled the car with more petrol and headed for the Highlands, as the signs now read.

Within a few hundred yards of leaving the petrol station the road divided into two. To the left was Oban, to the right Fort William; we took the right.

As we started up the hill there were gates, open, but the sign on them read, *If these gates are closed, so is the road ahead.* I looked at Douglas.

'You have read the sign; it's very true. We are now entering the most beautiful and, in bad weather, the most difficult roads to travel.'

As we rounded the corner at the top of the hill it was like opening a book on an adventure. The hills rose steeply now on either side. The railway started to follow the road, went inland a little way, then decided it was a bit tricky and came back to the road, as there was no obvious reason why it went inland to start with.

The road was now a steady climb; every now and then there was a glimpse through a break in the mountains to reveal yet more mountains in the distance, with no visible means to get there. We passed the Bridge of Orchy Hotel and the fast-running waters of the river Orchy, and at the end of the road, as far as we could see it, was a big white bridge over the river. The railway was now nowhere to be seen, having been there at the hotel with a halt sign to stop the train if needed.

We climbed ever upwards, with views of faraway mountains opening up before us. On the corner at the top stood a monument to soldiers fallen in the great wars, where a lone piper, splendid in his kilt and full regalia, played his lonesome lament. A sign on the side of the road told us we were now in Argyll and Bute District.

The road now seemed to be going down slightly, and ahead was a large conical mountain that I realised I had seen before. 'Is that the mountain you have a photograph of on your wall?'

'Oh, well spotted,' said Douglas. 'That is the Buachaille Etive Mòr, known locally as the Shepherd of the Glen, as we are now about to go through Glen Coe. It was difficult to take that photo, as it was very cold with all the snow around; even the small stream at the bottom was frozen. I waited for the sun to rise, and as the shadow of the other mountain slid down the side of the Buachaille I was able to photograph her in all her majesty. In the meantime I had to keep popping in and out of the car to keep my camera warm, so it wouldn't freeze up as well.'

'Golly, weren't you cold, all that popping in and out?'

'Absolutely frozen; took my hands a week to defrost,' he said, shaking his hand at the thought of it.

Glen Coe was absolutely breathtaking, very desolate, with many ghosts of the awful massacre that had taken place there. Not the place to break down, I decided. Eventually we descended into the village of Coe and back onto normal roads, and I was aware of my heaving a big sigh of relief that we had made it.

We arrived in Fort William in good time, enough time Douglas thought we could go to the local supermarket and stock up on goods to save a journey to the shops the next day. Then he remembered that it was a Saturday, and no shops would be open on Sunday on Skye, so shopping was now a must.

Shopping done, and both of us grateful for the walk around the supermarket, Douglas gave Barley her own walk around the car park. I reflected on how normal it had seemed to Douglas to do the shopping, and how he had known just what would be required, not forgetting a bottle of whisky in readiness for anyone who might call.

'Splendid,' said Douglas, looking at his watch. 'Just over two hours to get to Mallaig; perfect.'

As we moved through Fort William, I noticed several businesses with the word *Nevis* in their name, and asked if we were anywhere near Ben Nevis. Then almost on cue there she loomed, big and dark. She really did not seem as forbidding as some of the mountains we had passed, yet there she was, the tallest mountain in Britain.

'The Ben is notoriously deceptive,' Douglas was saying, 'and many people get into difficulties on her for not giving her the respect she deserves. I have met people in ordinary shoes and summer clothes walking up, when I know that at any moment she can change, and launch into a howling gale with snow before you are aware. She is also pleased to see you, as usually she hides in the clouds, so you are honoured.'

'I thought she would have snow on her summit, given the time of year, and the other mountains having a covering,' I observed.

'Ah, but like any good lady she doesn't reveal all, just enough to be tantalising. Her summit is further back, and I don't think easily seen from the road.'

I found myself blushing, and hoped Douglas did not see.

We turned left past the Ben Nevis distillery, and ahead I could see a road sign with a picture of a boat.

'Ah!' Douglas exclaimed. 'Good; that means the ferry is sailing today, so no problems there. If there were any doubt the ferry would sail they would put up a sign saying *No Ferry*, which saves us all a long unnecessary journey.'

We turned left at the traffic lights, then we were on the road to Mallaig. With the loch on our left and the sun glittering on her rippling waters, we set off down the road to the Isles.

I looked at Douglas, who was showing no signs of tiredness after what was now almost ten hours' driving. He looked so happy and contented I just wanted to give him a big hug. Amazing that this same man could make such beautiful music.

There was a sign on the side of the road declaring a gathering of the clans this weekend. Now on either side of the road cars were parked. We slowed as people were walking, all in their different tartans, the men carrying varying sizes of staff; they were too long, I felt, to be walking sticks.

As the road wound around and down the hill we could see a huge gathering of people all around a monument. The man on the monument was looking down the most beautiful loch with steep sides covered in forestry. It all looked as if we had moved into another time.

Gradually the congestion cleared, and once more we were on our way again.

The road went into single track after about ten miles, and I was now aware of the railway having come to join us as if agreeing we had taken the best route after all. Douglas drove with great care around the blind summits and what seemed to be square corners.

Eventually the views opened out as we passed through Arisaig, with the fishing boats bobbing on the water of the loch. Then there on our right was a golf course. On the left the most beautiful white sand was now beside us, with the clearest blue water I have ever seen; it just took my breath away. There in the distance were the snowcapped Cuillins.

Douglas pulled off the road. 'I must take a photo,' he said. 'In all the years I have been doing this run, I have never seen the Cuillins look so magnificent.'

He got back into the car, and declared it was a cold wind as usual. Taking my hand in his cold one, he said, 'These are the white sands of Morar; isn't it just beautiful?'

He moved off somewhat reluctantly, but the timetable had to be obeyed; the ferry wouldn't wait.

We arrived in Mallaig to see the ferry coming in to dock, so without further ado Douglas was out of the car, into the terminal and buying the tickets. We joined the queue as the last cars were disembarking.

The ferry was a big ship in my eyes, built to endure the treacherous seas that could happen here, especially in the autumn and spring. Today, though, it all looked calm and inviting, with a little wind blowing enough to ripple the water. Skye was sitting, waiting gently on the sea, making the opposite shore look most inviting, with small white-painted buildings dotted about beneath the wooded hill, the Cuillins now hiding behind the trees as if they were not there. As we passed I noticed the ferry's name emblazoned on her side, *Lord of the Isles*, which seemed a contradiction in terms, but she was majestic.

The cars and lorries, and just one coach, were all safely stowed. Douglas spoke reassuringly to Barley as we were instructed to leave the car and travel on deck. We climbed the steep stairs to the seating area, but we both decided it would be nice to be outside. We found a suitable railing and huddled up together, with the cool autumn wind blowing in our hair.

The ship manoeuvred carefully out of dock and made a big curve to avoid rocks that were hidden by the full tide, marked only by the flashing light of the miniature lighthouse that was secured to a pinnacle. As we moved smoothly out into the sound, the sea took on the most unreal blue, almost iridescent. When we looked back to Mallaig, the now-setting sun was bathing the hills in a deep rosy glow that reflected in the water, and accentuated the snow on the mountaintops. The street lighting, having come on in Mallaig, looked like two huge wings on the hillside about to carry Mallaig off to its lair.

In the far distance we could see the flash of another lighthouse giving out its warning. Douglas pointed to it and said, very proudly, 'That is Ardnamurchen Point, the most westerly land in Great Britain.'

I looked at him, and I saw a look of peace and absolute contentment.

'I do hope you will love Skye as much as I do. We are nearly home now, just a mile to go when we disembark, and I know one person who will be very pleased: poor old Barley. It's a long journey for her, but she never complains.'

It was only a thirty-minute crossing, and all too soon the voice on the loudhailer was requesting us to return to our cars as we were about to dock.

'Well, here we go,' Douglas said. 'I hope you have enjoyed our trip over the sea to Skye, and that it will be the first of many.'

The ferry quickly disgorged us and we all formed an orderly queue onto the single-track road with passing places. At the end of the pier road, all the traffic was turning right for Broadford. We turned left for Ardvasar.

To our left was the shoreline, with lots of fascinating driftwood lying on the silver sand, and pine trees on both sides of the road swayed in the evening breeze. There were craggy rocks that made interesting shapes, with one just out to sea looking distinctly like a submarine rising out of the water.

On our right hand now were workshops, and opposite was a small boatyard with yachts stored for the winter, their ropes gently slapping the metal masts. We passed the village shop, the village hall, the hotel-cum-village-pub, the post office, and the police station, looming proud as we approached a small hill.

Douglas took a sharp right turn that took us behind the police station and up a very steep road, another right, then swiftly turned left. We came to a stop beside a wooden A-frame house with a cedarwood shingle roof that almost touched the ground. There were wide wooden steps up to the veranda, which Douglas was now taking two at a time to unlock the door.

The air was so pure it was like breathing in pure nectar through a silk scarf that had wound itself around you. I grabbed a bag and followed Barley, who had leapt out of the car. She shook her coat and sneezed, looking pleased to have arrived.

'Welcome,' said Douglas, his arms open wide, 'to my very favourite place. Mary has been in and put the heating on, bless her, so we are all nice and warm.'

It was so small, yet very spacious, the whole height of the building being exposed to the rafters. The small kitchen was complete with fitted cupboards, a breakfast bar, a sink with hot and cold water, cooker, dishwasher, and a decanter of whisky that glowed in the lights Douglas had now put on.

'Right,' Douglas said, once all the bags had been brought in, 'on with the cooker, and we shall soon have a meal. In the meantime, a little whisky to welcome you.'

We sat down on a settee that was strategically placed in front of a picture window that seemed to take up the whole wall. The view was breathtaking, and it took a while to take in all that lay before me.

I had stood up and moved forward to take in the whole vision. Douglas turned off the lights and stood beside me. He handed me a glass of whisky, and with his arm around me raised his glass in a toast. 'Welcome to, I hope, the first of many stays here.'

The full moon had risen above the mountains, and was throwing its silver light down the Sound of Sleat. The water shimmered and reflected its light all around. We stood in silence as we took in the magical scene spread out before us, and sipped our whisky.

The shrill sound of the oven timer telling us the fish pie was ready brought us back to reality. Well, almost, as Douglas next suggested we move the bunk bed mattresses onto the floor and sleep by the light of the moon.

The next morning Douglas was up and about, ready to go.

'Where are we going?' I asked, shielding my eyes against the bright sunshine now rising above the mountains of Knoydart, and wondering if I was ever going to be able to get upright again.

'I always take a trip down to the Point of Sleat when I arrive,' he said, 'as it is such a good walk, and is so remote, yet beautiful. I'll drive down to the old chapel and park there.'

After a quick breakfast, and donning my new walking boots, which Douglas insisted on tying to make sure they would not rub, we set off. Barley was very excited and was first in the car. We retraced our route down the hill and turned right at the bottom to continue along the single-track shore road.

Douglas changed gear as we went up quite a steep hill with no obvious exit, and sounded his horn as we approached its apex. I suddenly gasped as we crested the hill. Laid out before us was a silver glistening sea, out of which rose the Isle of Eigg's dark shape: the most beautiful sight.

Douglas pulled off the road into a small but well-used hard standing where many a traveller had pulled in to take in the view. 'I must just take a picture,' Douglas was saying as he slid out of the car. 'Isn't that the most glorious sight? I never tire of coming round here. It's amazing how many different guises Eigg has.'

We continued almost in silence, passing small croft houses and fields with rockeries. We eventually arrived at a clearing by the old chapel, which also served as a service station for the cattle that were all standing around the gate in the anticipation that we were going to feed them. Barley thought they were fair game for a good barking.

Douglas put her on the lead and made sure she knew it was their field, and no more barking. The cattle very kindly stood back from the gate and let us enter their field with lots of snorts and huffs.

The field had a gentle rise, and I looked forward to seeing what would be around the corner. A steep valley lay ahead, then another and another. Just as I thought I was going to have to suggest that Douglas go on without me, the crest of the next hill opened out onto short soft grass that put a spring in each step, and a gentle slope down to a garden gate.

'Oh, my,' I exclaimed, 'who on earth lives here? And do they have to do that walk each time they want to go out?'

'The lady from the shop on Ardvasar pier lives here with her husband, who is a fisherman. And, yes, unless they go by boat it is the only way out.'

We walked through their lovely vegetable and flower garden, and there before me was the most delightful little port I had ever seen. Sheltered by the wall of high sea rocks was this little inlet with a tiny single-storey house, with lobster pots and ropes coiled up by the front door. There seemed to be a natural harbour wall of rock that wound round the rocks and out to sea. Two small fishing boats were tied up and ready to go. It was absolutely charming; I just couldn't stop staring.

We found a rock and sat to take in the beauty all around us. Douglas produced some cheese sandwiches, which were very welcome.

I don't know how long we sat eating our sandwiches and just drinking in the beauty of our surroundings, but it seemed all too soon Douglas touched my hand and said, 'We must retrace our steps to the car.'

I didn't know it at the time, but it was to be the last time we would do this walk together.

# CHAPTER 51

W e slept well that night after our walk, and had no time to dream, it seemed, so complete was our rest. With a soft stroke of my arm I was awoken to find Douglas sitting on the side of the bed, offering me a steaming mug of tea.

'It's a beautiful day,' he said, with a big smile. 'How would you like a trip to Portree, the capital of this beautiful island?'

'That sounds like fun; how far is it?' I asked.

'Well, depends if we go straight there or take in some of the little diversions along the way,' he said, with that lovely twinkle in his eye. 'Could you be ready in about half an hour? The days are short this time of year, and there is so much I want to show you.'

There was a definite chill in the air as we left the warmth of the house; even Barley shook her duvet-like coat to capture the warmth therein as she did a quick trip around the fence to check who had been there during the night.

As I walked to the car I looked across the sound. I could hear the soft engine of the first ferry of the day leaving Mallaig. She looked like a toy boat on a still pond as she steered her safe course out of harbour. Not many coaches today, I thought, just the people of the area going about their day's tasks.

Barley safely stowed in the back, we set off on our tour. Back through the village to the junction for the ferry; this time we went straight on. The 'last stop for petrol' garage was busy with last minute fill-ups before catching the ferry, which we could now see getting ever nearer through the windbreak of pine trees planted along the water's edge.

The first thing that struck me was the blueness of the sea: quite calm, gently lapping the rocky shoreline that was now running beside the road, which only needed a knee-high wall to keep everyone safe.

We rounded a corner and came to a clearing in the woods and a substantial construction that could have been a coach house for a stately building, but none was in sight. Douglas slowed the car to a stop and pointed to the tops of the trees, where I could now see the ruin of a large house or castle, and a drive with very ornate gates.

'This is the seat of the Clan Macdonald,' Douglas was telling me. 'The island is divided in two, with the MacDonalds in the south and the MacLeods at Dunvegan Castle in the north, and never the twain shall meet.' He laughed.

'Is it still that way today?' I asked.

'I will let you ask our neighbour Gordon that one when he comes in for a drink tonight.' He pulled back onto the road.

After a short while we turned off the single-track road that took coaches and lorries to a smaller variety that I hoped most sincerely was one-way traffic. A sign did try to give me confidence, announcing it as a single-track road with passing places.

The building now on our right was announcing itself as something quite important, I was sure, judging by the number of letters it contained, but utterly unpronounceable to me. 'This is the Gaelic College, which is very popular, to the extent they are building a new one on the sea shore that resembles a lighthouse,' Douglas said, pointing to a clearing in the trees with all the paraphernalia of a building site.

The drive through this ancient woodland was leading us ever further away from habitation with just the occasional croft house in the distance, but always beside or in the road were the whitest, fluffiest sheep I had ever seen, who quite clearly knew who had the right of way.

The scenery suddenly opened out and, with the road following the contours of the land, at some points the car seemed to be almost standing on its front bumper. We rounded another blind corner where the road fell away beneath us, giving no clue as to which way it would go. Then before us lay the sea, with the sun just catching the tips of the small ripples in flashes that looked like precious jewels, glinting their welcome.

The beach, strewn with seaweed, told the story that it wasn't always so calm. But, with the Cuillins as a backdrop and the sun just catching the snow-covered high points of the range, it was a breathtaking sight.

I was aware that Douglas hadn't spoken for a while. He brought the car to a halt on the edge of the sands, switched off the engine, turned to me and, taking my hand, said, 'This to me is the most beautiful place on earth. No matter what time of day you come, Mother Nature is at her best here. Shall we give Barley a run and breathe in the air? It will do you the world of good.'

'Does this place have a name?' I asked.

'Ord,' came the reply.

'Such a small word for such a beautiful place,' I pondered.

'Aye,' came the reply, with a vain attempt at a Scottish accent. 'But when you hear it spoken by a Scotsman it sounds great.'

I can't remember how long we stayed in this beautiful place, but eventually we returned to the car and continued on our way, in silence, before catching up once again with the wider road.

Douglas had learnt all the names of the mountains that we could now see passing on the other side of the Sound of Sleat. There were the twin paps, a mountain that looked like an old-fashioned loaf of bread was Ladhar Bheinn, and they all stood in an area known as Knoydart on mainland Scotland, the last remaining piece of wilderness. No roads crossed it; the small inlets were the only areas inhabited, and only accessed by sea. Today it all looked so inviting with the high spots of the twin Paps, and Ladhar Bheinn looking as if it had been decorated with icing sugar.

As we travelled on we passed Kinloch Lodge, the residence of the MacDonalds that now was run as a hotel by Claire Macdonald, and included her famous cookery school.

As we climbed a slight hill, a large lump of a mountain rose up to our left behind the rise in the land, and with it three red-pointed hills. 'Ah! There she is,' said Douglas. 'Rarely fails to appear, along with the Red Cuillins, and our entry into Broadford.'

We crested the ridge and saw the village curving around Broadford Bay before us.

'Everything you could possibly need on the island can be found here in Broadford,' Douglas said proudly as we drove ever onward.

What was becoming apparent to me was that Skye was quite a large island. There was no sharing of the driving; it was his joy to share the beautiful island that gave him so much pleasure and peace.

We had lunch in the new arts centre on the outskirts of Portree, before driving on around the top of the island, through the breathtaking Quiraing. We had tea at the home of Flora MacDonald, and saw her grave marked with a cross that could be seen from out at sea, with a spectacular view of the Outer Hebrides.

On he drove, past crofts with their plots leading down to the sea, to Dunvegan with its castle and the seat of the MacLeod Clan, and our eventual turn for home. The Cuillin mountains loomed ever larger as we approached Sligachan once again.

'There we are,' said Douglas. 'We have just completed two fingers, and we will now finish the thumb back home.' In response to my mystified glance he explained Skye was in the shape of a hand with four fingers and a thumb. 'So some more treats to look forward to another day,' he said, taking my hand for a moment and giving it a squeeze.

The day had now clouded over, and, it being November, the evening light was disappearing fast. But all around us was this pale blue light that gave a mystical shade to everything.

By the time we were back at Ardvasar it was quite dark, and the car drew to a halt outside the Ardvasar Hotel. 'The car refuses to go any further,' Douglas said, as if she were a horse, 'so we may as well go in for a drink while she gets her breath back.'

The locals were pleased to see Douglas, and there was a bit of leg-pulling about him having me with him, but all in good fun. I saw for the first time how well he was accepted here in a land that had its own language, which was spoken between the locals, but was quickly changed to English to include him.

The drink turned into a supper of fresh fish caught that day; 'Save cooking when we get in,' Douglas said. What a lovely way to end the most enjoyable day, and we had only seen a small portion of this amazing island. *How lucky I am,* I thought.

We arrived back at the house to find the message light flashing on the telephone. 'Better see who wants us before we turn in,' said Douglas.

'I'll make us a cuppa while you are doing that,' I volunteered. The amazing thing was that we were both in the same room but each in our own space, as it were, and both content.

'Well, it's Mark, so I hope all is well. Just says to ring when we get in.' He dialled Mark's number. 'Hello, Dad here, got your message to ring. Is all well? — That's brilliant news; are mother and son doing well? — And how about father and son? — Well, I hope you all have a good night's sleep tonight. — Really good news; we will be home soon to drink to the new arrival. Big hug to Wills, and big kiss to Joanna. See you soon. Bye for now.

'Well, we have another Tom Smith in the family, as Joanna gave birth early this morning,' said Douglas as he sank onto the settee. 'It sounds as if Joanna had a fairly tough time, and the baby came very quickly in the end. But he is fine and healthy, and both are recovering well, which is a blessing.' He took the cup of tea I offered. 'Here's to Tom Smith the second,' he said, raising his mug. 'Must be the first Smith child to be welcomed with a cup of tea!'

'Who is Tom Smith the first?' I asked.

'Oh! My dear, I am so sorry, I have forgotten to tell you all about my dear brother Tom and his unusual wife Honor. My brother and I have always been the best of friends and there for each other, despite the two years' difference in our ages. He and his wife usually come down to stay once a year, so perhaps you will get to meet them before too long. Tom is really into the theory of music and is currently taking a degree in the Open University. He loves Shakespeare as well and often attends summer school at Stratford, so we have a get-together then as well.'

'How did he earn his living?' I asked.

'Well, he was a structural engineer and used to be in charge of all bridges in Northumberland County Council, which he loved. I'm sure when we go to stay with them he will take you on a tour of all the very different bridges he had the care of.'

'What makes Honor unusual?' I asked.

'Well, that is a very good question, but I do not really know the answer. She seems to have a death wish. The most recent incident was when Tom was away at their bridge club, and she jumped out of their bedroom window – she jumped so well she landed in the fishpond Tom had just built for her. Having locked all the doors, she was now soaking wet and couldn't get back into the house, so Tom arrived home to an ambulance which the neighbours had called outside the house, keeping her warm till he got home.'

I could hardly stop myself from laughing, and then gave in as Douglas laughed too.

'Funny, really, if it was not so sad. Poor Tom rarely leaves her alone, so he now feels trapped in their home. I think that is why he gives himself work to do, as with the Open University degree.'

The tea finished, the cups washed, we retired for the night.

# CHAPTER 52

—

A quiet time at home was the order of the day, to enjoy the view, catch up with Gordon and Mary, our neighbours, and check the house for any problems. To the rear of the house was a very smart caravan: 'Extra bedrooms,' explained Douglas, 'if the family or friends descend. It has a very sophisticated and efficient heating system, being made in Sweden, which reminds me I had better drain it down for the winter,' and off he went, closely followed by Barley; the day had begun.

All too soon a trip to Broadford was required to carry out general running repairs. Although the month was November, the day was springlike with clear blue skies; it was easy to hear the shallow waves on the shore, and the chug of the small fishing boat about its business in the sound.

For once Broadford didn't have what was required, so to Kyle of Lochalsh we were now headed, which was exciting as it meant a trip over the Skye Bridge. As we approached I could see the elegant outline now quite clearly, and was surprised by how steep the arch of the bridge seemed to be. 'That's to allow ships like the *Britannia* to pass under safely at high tide, and sometimes in high winds,' said Douglas, 'as the Queen likes to sail through the Sound of Sleat when she is here for her summer break.'

We were now approaching the bridge, and the steep gradient was quite pronounced. But the view from the top was fantastic, being able to see the Torridon mountain range quite clearly, with the Red Cuillins looking quite close and the rest of the Cuillins in the background off to the left.

'We will just call in at the ticket office and get our new book of tickets to cross the bridge at half price,' Douglas said. 'A perk of being a resident of Skye.'

The vital parts found, and some fish fresh from the sound purchased, we were ready to continue on the one-way system around Kyle to get back on the bridge. At the top of the road Douglas stopped outside a furnishing shop. *Fraser's*, it said proudly.

'Golly, they have a House of Fraser all the way up here,' I said with a smile.

'The original, of course,' said Douglas, smiling back. 'Come on, let's see if we can't buy a bed settee and make a little more sitting room at the house.'

Aladdin's cave had nothing on this shop. It had everything you could possibly want, and if it wasn't in stock they would get it and deliver. *Wow, what service,* I thought.

The settee ordered, I spied some blue and green tartan tea towels that would look good in the kitchen and asked the assistant for two.

'You stay in Ardvasar?' she asked.

'Yes,' I replied.

'Then you will be needing these,' she said, handing me two red and blue tartan tea towels.

'But I would like the others,' I said.

'But these are MacDonald, and you stay in the south of Skye – MacDonald country. These are MacLeod,' she said, holding up the blue and green ones, 'from the north of Skye.'

At that moment I realised the kitchen was going to be graced with red and blue tartan tea towels.

The jobs done, I packed my bags with some reluctance for the return trip home. A week had slipped by so quickly. I had realised why Douglas loved coming here; the peace and tranquillity of this beautiful island really did seem to have magical healing powers. So, with batteries recharged, we caught the first ferry next morning back to Mallaig, ready for our journey back to reality.

Douglas thought a stopover in the Lake District would break the journey home, so we made a stop at the Mill at Mungrisdale. It was a rest haven for hill walkers, with wet dogs and clothes everywhere, and meals that equipped you for the day ahead. For once, Barley was on her best behaviour.

An early start the next morning, a Sunday, gave us a hassle-free journey south. On we went, with one more stop. It was a lovely spot, with a lake to walk Barley round and seats to admire the view.

'Let's sit awhile before this time together comes to an end,' Douglas said, 'or could it be a beginning? I have so enjoyed your company. I haven't felt so at ease in a woman's company since my dear Mary, and there have been one or two, as Gordon pointed out, the rascal. I do hope you enjoyed yourself too.'

For once I found myself lost for words, as *lovely, super,* every word I could think of sounded so inadequate to convey how I was really feeling. I took his hands and looked at him directly, and told him I had never been so happy in my life, and that it had been the most enjoyable trip. I thanked him sincerely. We held hands as we walked slowly back to the car in a reflective mood.

Barley settled once more in the back. My offer to drive once more declined, we settled down to complete the journey. Just as Douglas was about to switch on the engine, he turned to me and said, 'Could we get married? Oh, perhaps I should be on one knee; bit difficult in the car. But we seem to be so together whatever we are doing, and to be honest I do not want to be without you ever again, and I am talking too much; what do you think?'

The look on his face was so open and sincere, and almost childlike, I just wanted to take him in my arms.

'Tell me, please, what you are thinking,' he said.

'I want to say yes, as I feel exactly the same, but I am concerned about my daughter, and the fact her father only died in February; aren't we supposed to wait a year? What about your children; how will they take to their father marrying again?'

'Well, those are things to be considered, but my guess is they will be pleased to have the problem of their father taken off their hands,' he said with a smile, 'and I hope your daughter will feel the same. I am sure she and Phil are an item, and perhaps our getting married – as getting married is what I would like to do, none of this "living together" business – will help her feel free to make her choices. What do you say?'

'Yes,' I said, wanting to jump in the air, but the seatbelt restrained me.

He leant across and kissed me, and thanked me most sincerely.

# CHAPTER 53

A s Douglas had guessed, his family were very happy that he
was happy, but Rose was not so happy. On my arrival back
from Skye she had moved out, and left no note or forwarding
address. I was devastated, and was all for calling the whole thing off.
I was desperate to find her and see what could be done to avoid any
more unhappiness. No phone calls.

Douglas was sad to see me so distressed, but reminded me that
I had a right to happiness, and that the hope was that she was with
Philip and happy. She was twenty-eight years old, so she was well
able to make decisions for herself.

He was right, but I just needed to know she was safe and as happy
as could be.

Eventually I decided to call a friend to see if he had any idea
where Rose was. He was able to tell me he had moved her, and gave
me an address.

I persuaded Douglas to take me on a Rose-finding mission one
evening. We arrived at a house where I hoped we would find her.
Douglas decided to stay in the car to give us freedom of conversation,
if any was to be had.

I rang the doorbell, and a very tall young man answered.

'Sorry to bother you, but I am looking for my daughter Rose
Anson; would you know where she is? And would you be Philip?'

He answered yes to both and invited me in.

I was met with a stone-faced Rose, who was not pleased to see
me. The relief at seeing her looking well was overwhelming, but there
was huge sadness in my heart at her loveless welcome.

'I will leave you two to have a talk,' Philip said. 'Is Douglas in
the car? I'll say hello.'

'How are you,' I asked, once Rose and I had been left alone. 'Are you happy?'

'I am not living with Phil, if that's what you're thinking. I rent room in his house.'

'To be honest, the thought hadn't crossed my mind; I was just so relieved to have found you, and see that you are okay.'

'Phil is being very helpful and is teaching me how to manage my money. He's cut up my credit card, so I have to manage on my income.'

'Sounds like good advice.'

'How can you marry for the third time?' Rose asked. 'And Dad only died in February. You'll be marrying before me if you marry in December, and it's November now.'

I felt so sorry I was making her unhappy. I asked if she and Philip had any plans I would be upsetting.

'Not at the moment,' she said.

'So can I suggest we get married – as that is what we would like to do – leaving the new year for you two to make your plans?'

She reluctantly agreed, and we set the date for Christmas Eve. I invited her to give me away; she wriggled her nose in that dismissive way and said she would think about it. Philip and Douglas returned, and invited us all to have a drink.

A truce seemed to have been achieved. I invited Rose and Philip to come to Down Court whenever they felt like it; the door was always open, and I hoped they would join us for the wedding and Christmas Day.

The date of Christmas Eve for the wedding was agreed by all concerned. The vicar came to see us and the choir was booked, along with the organist; Douglas was in charge of music for the occasion. Invitations were made and sent, then came the wait to see if we had any acceptances.

Douglas's daughters and granddaughters in Australia wanted to be there, and the granddaughters wanted to be bridesmaids; flights were booked and accommodation sorted, as we had plenty of room at Down Court. Replies had started to arrive, so far all acceptances.

The final tally was that 148 of the 150 invitees accepted, so we agreed that we would need a marquee. The idea also arose that, if all the family were arriving, we could use the marquee again for a mass Smith and Anson Christmas Day.

I decided that with the help of my team I would cater for both occasions, so a shopping list was drawn up. Freezers were filled, Christmas puddings and cakes made and mince pies prepared by the dozen, alongside a prayer or two that it wouldn't snow!

Rose's wedding outfit was quite a shock, as it was a black costume. She loved hats, so I thought there might be light accessories, but her hat was the biggest black hat I had ever seen. She looked magnificent. She had decided not to give me away, which I quite understood, but I asked if she would like to sign the register along with Cathy, and this she thought she could do.

I was very concerned that my happiness was not making her happy; if anything, I seemed to be driving her away. I was still confused by her comment, when her father had died, that I would never survive without him. I seemed to be doing quite well so far.

As for my outfit, I was struggling. Whether it was the time of year or something else, I could not find something fit for a wedding in white, so I decided to ask a dressmaker if she could rustle something up in time. A quick design with a cloak seemed to be the best choice. The material was chosen, there was just one fitting, and, hey presto, I had a wedding outfit that made me feel very special.

# CHAPTER 54

—

Christmas Eve dawned, and the frost looked like snow under the bright sunlight. I set to work finishing the buffet for the reception; Rose had stayed the night and was busy arranging flowers in the marquee. Then Eileen arrived, my right-hand man, and so the day fell into place.

All too soon 11.30 was here and it was time for me to change. I was amazed by how quickly I managed to transform into a bride.

The commotion downstairs told me the girls had arrived; they looked lovely in their crimson velvet gowns, but I was concerned they were going to be cold. But they said they would be fine, and Joanna assured me she had the boot full of jumpers, scarves and coats for them.

The limousine had arrived; Rose had changed and was looking fabulous, so we all piled into the car and off we went.

The church was freezing, I could feel as I walked behind the vicar to meet Douglas, who looked resplendent in morning dress. The organ was playing a resounding piece that gave me the confidence to make the walk. At last I was holding his hand, and all felt right with the world.

The service over, we walked into beautiful sunshine. Joanna had handed baby Tom to Mark and was waiting with arms full of coats for the girls to put on. A few photos, and back into the car to head to a hopefully warm marquee.

Eileen had done a splendid job on the buffet, champagne was flowing and all seemed to be well with the world. Speeches over, guests slowly began to leave with the comment that it had been a lovely way to start the Christmas celebrations. Mum and her driver left warm and happy; I was so pleased she had been able to come. Then we were on our own. Douglas took me in his arms and said how happy he was, and that he hoped we would have many happy returns of today.

***

On Christmas morning I woke early to get Christmas lunch on the go and lay the tables in the marquee for eighteen. I put the heaters on, plugged in the heated trolley, closed the door to keep the place warm and finished the preparations for lunch, then lit the fire in the inglenook fireplace and waited for everyone to arrive.

Champagne flowed once again and a happy buzz filled the house; with the help of many hands the meal arrived, and all enjoyed it. After watching the Queen we all retired to the drawing room for the giving and receiving of gifts, which proved to be hilarious. All too soon it was William and Tom's bedtime, and so the party slowly came to a close.

Douglas poured us a drink as we sat by the dying embers of the fire and reminisced about the happenings of the weekend.

Boxing Day arrived, a very blowy day, and fears were expressed as to the safety of the marquee, so a quick call to the provider had them rushing over to dismantle it. It proved not to be an easy task; chairs and tables were removed, then came the battle to take the marquee down. Eventually all was safely stowed in the lorries, disaster averted.

Life returned to its normal routine, and all seemed to be well with the world.

# CHAPTER 55

Douglas had put his house on the market, the piano having moved to Down Court when we married, but there were no buyers, so Mark suggested letting it. Douglas needed to go to Skye, so it was decided Mark and Joanna would sort out the house for letting while we were there.

Three young male teachers moved into Douglas's house, and three years of happy tenants followed until one day we popped in to discover they had a car engine in the kitchen, the weight of which had cracked some of the black and white floor tiles. It was pouring with rain, and before long we heard the sound of running water and discovered the skylight on the stairs was letting in the rain; the wall was saturated. We asked the tenants why they had not notified us, and apparently they had thought that, if the problem was too great for us, they would offer us a silly price to take the property off our hands. Needless to say they were given a month's notice, repairs were done and the house went back on the market.

Soon we had a purchaser. Sadly our family thought Douglas would not look after the money and arranged for an advisor to call, who recommended a ten-year bond. Douglas had hoped to buy his little house in Skye back, as it was on the market again, but the family didn't agree, and made their feelings felt. The next thing I knew was that Douglas had slipped away; I heard the car start up and I automatically knew he would drive to Skye.

The wait for him to ring in was intolerable, but wait I had to. Eventually the call came, and by the sound of it he was in a bar.

'Where are you?' I asked.

He didn't know. I suggested he ask someone standing by. The answer came: near Glasgow.

'See if you can stay the night,' I suggest, 'and have something to eat.'

He said he would ring me again in the morning.

The phone rang the next day and I raced down the stairs, only for it to ring off. I redialled the number, and fortunately a man answered the phone, which was in a call box. He had just seen a man with white hair get in his car and drive the wrong way up a one-way street.

'Where are you speaking from?' I asked.

'Kyle of Lochalsh,' was the reply.

I now knew Douglas was in difficulty, as he knew the area well, so I rang the police to try to stop him going back to the motorway. They told me they had just stopped him for driving the wrong way, but had let him go as it was early in the morning. I explained the situation, and they said they would alert the motorway and keep their eyes open, and would stay in touch.

For three days they rang in to say they were still searching, but I had no phone call from Douglas. Then the police rang to say a lady had observed a car with a man in it who was either dead or very tired, as he hadn't moved for twelve hours. They had taken Douglas and his car to the police station in Fort William.

'Where was he?' I asked.

'Arisaig,' they said, which was on the long road to Mallaig; he had obviously forgotten the bridge at Kyle.

They had arranged for Douglas to be assessed by a doctor, who had concluded that he was confused and recommended he not drive. Could I arrange to collect him?

It was going to take me ten hours to drive, then I would have the challenge of how to get Douglas's car back home. Taking the train there or flying would still leave my car in a car park somewhere. I phoned Mark to tell him his father had been found, but he was not free to help me.

I put down the phone and sat there, staring at the mail on my desk, until I saw a letter from the AA. Would they be able to help? I decided to try them.

I explained the situation to the AA, and they said they would ring back. True to their word, ten minutes later they told me a low loader was on its way to the police station, and they would have my husband and car back home around breakfast time. That was exactly what happened.

After a couple of days sleeping and catching up on meals, Douglas woke up and sat upright in bed. 'Cynthia, I have come to a decision about the money from the house sale. I would like to divide the money in four and send a cheque to everyone involved. Will you help me, please?'

After breakfast we sat down and divided the money four ways. I wrote the cheques; Douglas signed them, wrote a short note to explain, and sent them first class. Not another word was said.

Douglas continued to be confused, and he agreed to an appointment with the GP. Douglas could not answer any of the questions the doctor asked, so the doctor recommended an appointment with Mr Fuller, who would arrange further checks. If we were able to go private, he felt it would be of advantage to Douglas, as there was a long waiting list. This we agreed. The appointment came through quickly, along with a date for a CT scan.

The day of the appointment, Douglas was very anxious. When Douglas was taken to another room for a medical check, Mr Fuller had an opportunity to talk to me about the scan results. His scans had proved Alzheimer's was present, but all was not gloom and doom, as there was a new medication called Aricept that he hoped would enable Douglas to live a relatively normal life.

Home with a cup of tea, we planned all the things Douglas would like to do, and he visibly relaxed. The main thing he wanted to achieve was to go to Antarctica. I had great fun trying to work out how we could actually achieve that, but, between cost and the fact the only way to go ashore was in an inflatable, I could not see how we were going to manage it, so I asked for his second wish.

He answered quite quickly that he would like to go to Canada and Alaska to see Mount McKinley. This proved much easier to achieve; there was a package tour. Hotels booked, transport organised, luggage collected and returned at each destination: what could be easier? So we decided to go.

June came quite quickly; bags packed, the taxi arrived, and we were off to Heathrow airport for our flight to Calgary. There we were met by the tour guides and, luggage stowed, we were off to the hotel.

After a good night's sleep, breakfast eaten, luggage packed and outside the door, we made our way down to the reception area. With coaches allocated and luggage stowed, we were off.

A gentle cruise through the Rockies with various stops brought us to Banff, right in the middle of the mountains. Beautiful scenery, just right for Douglas and his cameras.

The next day we were to catch a train, but before we did that we had a stop in a town; its name escapes me, but it had a large pointy mountain as its backdrop. We were both in need of a cup of tea, so we went into a café.

As we were about to leave, Douglas said he wanted the toilet; at the same time I heard the man on the next table say he was going to the bathroom. I asked if he would mind taking my husband and explained why, and off they went together.

The man came back and said my husband was following, but five minutes later Douglas still hadn't arrived, so there was nothing for it; I was going to have to go and find him. No Douglas, and the door at the bottom of the stairs was open, so my guess was that he had gone out that door. Panic; how did I find Douglas in a busy town?

I collected all our things and decided to stand on the corner of the street and hope the mountain would draw his attention.

After what seemed like an eternity I suddenly felt a hand on my shoulder, and there was a very frightened Douglas. After a big hug, I said that would be the last time we went to the toilet alone, and he smiled and agreed.

Safely on the sleeper train, we progressed through the Rockies for another day, eventually arriving in Vancouver. Opposite the station were the docks, where our next mode of transport was waiting: a beautiful big ship that was going to take us up the inside passage to Alaska.

The sea was calm as we set sail. In the sound between the mainland and Vancouver Island, fishermen were fishing from small boats. We suddenly heard the sound of the engines slow down; the captain announced that they were slowing down to avoid a wash to the little boats.

It was different sailing between two land masses instead of through the open ocean. We were following the Klondike trail of the gold rush; it looked very difficult terrain and lasted two whole days of sailing.

Eventually we arrived at a small port that had a very large factory, which we were invited to visit. Douglas was not too keen to do this but valued a walk, so we followed the small canal that led to the factory. To our amazement it was absolutely packed with sockeye salmon all queuing up to go in the factory. There was no one and nothing driving them; it was an amazing sight. We were glad we were not going to see the factory.

The smooth sailing continued, until suddenly we were in a large bay with a huge glacier before us. The ship was sailing ever nearer, and I began to worry that parts of the glacier might fall off. We stopped sailing while a helicopter flew overhead, taking photographs, we were told. Suddenly there was a big bang, like a very big gun going off; cliffs of ice started falling into the sea, and we found the ship riding the wave that was created. That was enough excitement for the day. A drink was required and dinner was formal, so there were glad rags to put on.

Another day at sea, then we were docking in Anchorage, Alaska. We said goodbye to our lovely ship and were escorted to our next mode of transport: four-by-fours to drive us into the hinterland to see Mount McKinley.

Our accommodation was log cabins in a circle around a large hall. In the middle of the hall was a large fire, with a hole in the roof for the smoke to escape. There were low tables and benches at which we were invited to sit for our evening meal, which was delicious.

We were escorted back to our cabins as the wildlife were beginning to come out to graze. Safely in our cabin, with lights off inside and lights on outside, we could see bison and deer quite clearly.

The next morning we woke early, and, my, what a sight awaited us. There before us was Mount McKinley, lit by the light of the rising sun, with the snow on her peaks glistening. Douglas was in his heaven.

A flight to Seattle, then the big flight back to Heathrow. What a trip; fantastic.

# CHAPTER 56

July brought the good news of Rose and Philip's engagement with a wedding in November, so just four months to arrange it. I need not have worried, as they had the whole thing organised. I was anxious about the weather, but even that turned out to be the most glorious springlike day. Everything went according to plan, ending with a lovely fireworks display. Douglas gave Rose away and was so proud walking down the aisle; he managed the whole thing very well. It wasn't until they came to say goodbye that I realised I had also given my daughter away.

After all the excitement of the last four months was over, life returned to its regular routine.

One thing I hadn't realised was that Douglas found practising the piano with an audience difficult, and the B&B guests liked sitting in the drawing room to listen. He asked if I would stop taking B&B bookings until his concert was over. This of course reduced my income, with the cost of heating being the main problem.

The house being too big for the two of us, we decided to sell while we could manage it. Down Court had been my and Rose's home for the last thirty-two years, so it was a big wrench, but looking at houses to move to was quite fun.

We couldn't move with two grand pianos, and selling mine proved harder than I thought. Then, one day, when I was having a conversation with the son of the sister-in-law I had bought the piano from, he said he would like to have it, so another problem was solved.

Eventually we had a buyer for Down Court, and as luck would have it we found a house in Painswick that would accommodate the Steinway and us. The move went well, and the dogs settled into the new routine of a car ride to the golf course for a good stretch. The Steinway fitted perfectly in the entrance hall.

Rose had made her usual Sunday evening call and given us the good news that she was pregnant. She was so happy, the baby due in July.

All went well with the safe arrival of Alexander on the twenty-first. I went in to see Rose; she was very tired, and little Alex began to grizzle. I picked him up and laid him on my chest and covered him with a blanket, and he went back to sleep. It was love at first sight; that bond has stayed with us to this day. He is now twenty-six, and a qualified corporate lawyer.

Then we had the traumatic arrival of George, who with Rose was rushed by air to hospital in Oxford, where he was put on a special programme as he was deaf and blind, with a hole in his heart and a cerebral haemorrhage. This little mite lay like an angel under a lamp with nothing more than a nappy. It was a whole month before they could bring him home for the day.

Douglas played the organ for the Catholic church, and the priest came in with the music for Christmas. When he saw the baby he asked if he could hold him, then he asked us to hold hands while he said a prayer. This we did.

A month later, we took George for a check-up and left him sleeping with the doctors to be tested. When we returned the doctor asked if we were George Walker's family. I could see the blood drain from Rose's face and got her to sit down.

'It's good news,' he said, taking her hand. 'This baby is going to be able to see and hear, which is amazing.'

So George became our little miracle. He is now twenty-four. Both he and his brother are six foot six and something to do with estate agencies; both of them very agreeable young men.

# CHAPTER 57

—

It was ten years after his diagnosis, as Mr Fuller had projected, that Douglas's condition took a steep decline. The mental nurse called on her monthly visit; I had a heavy cold.

'What happens if you are taken ill?' the nurse asked. 'Have you looked at homes?'

'No, I haven't. I hope we are managing okay. What would happen if I became too ill to look after him?' I asked.

'Douglas would be placed in a home that had spare accommodation.'

'Then when I was better he could come home?'

'No, he needs residential care.'

I was horrified.

'I suggest you look for a home for Douglas as soon as possible,' the nurse said. 'I will call again in a month.'

I phoned Mark to tell him the news. He couldn't recommend a home, but he said he was sure I would be fine and he would come with us the day Douglas went in.

I got out the yellow pages and looked up residential homes. There were quite a few, so I decided to select several. Shirley, my daily help, came to stay with Douglas while I went viewing.

I had chosen buildings that looked nice from the outside, but I was not prepared for what happened on the inside, and had quite made up my mind I would get care at home. Just one left to see.

This was a Georgian house of pleasing proportions with a garden and conservatory. Douglas loved to walk, so it looked just right, with high ceilings and big windows. The lady showing me around was very reassuring and everyone looked very happy. I could visit as often as I liked, but not for the first five days to give him time to settle. So it was agreed I would bring Douglas for them to assess his ability and needs.

This we did. Douglas walked quite happily with the lady and seemed to like the garden, so it was agreed with the approval of social services that Douglas would go to them.

The dreaded day arrived; I put his bag in the car early to avoid making it obvious. True to his word, Mark was waiting for us at the home, which was a nice surprise for Douglas, and they walked in together very happily.

We were met by the matron and shown to Douglas's room. Mark kept Douglas entertained while I unpacked his clothes. They brought us tea, then Mark suggested I go and he would stay with him a bit longer. This I did, relieved I was not leaving Douglas alone.

Five days seemed an eternity, but phone calls reassured me that Douglas was settling well. A new routine followed of meeting for a walk in the garden, or a trip to a garden centre or supermarket, or a visit to friends or home for a cup of tea, which was enjoyable for both of us with no worries about taking him back.

Then came the news that the home was going to build a new block, which would involve moving the Alzheimer's residents to the front of the house and locking the door to the garden and conservatory. This caused absolute confusion all round, with queues of people banging and shaking the door all day long.

Douglas refused to sit down for his meals, so he was losing weight fast. I asked if I could come in and feed him, which delighted the home as they didn't have enough staff.

He had also developed a lean. The staff told me he probably had backache. I decided to take him home and give him a nice bath; he was all up for this and started taking off his clothes. To my absolute horror his bottom was red raw. I was alarmed that he was about to get in the bath, but I need not have worried; the relief on his face once he was in the water told me everything was well.

I asked for a nurse when we got back to the home and took her to the bathroom, where I showed her Douglas's bottom. She apologised profusely and applied creams before putting on a clean pad. I asked how often he had a shower. 'On a Monday, if he lets us' was the reply. So I made up my mind; I was going to have Douglas at home with full-time care.

A lady from an agency came and said she would do her best to provide twenty-four-hour care, but she couldn't promise. I thanked her very much.

The telephone rang, and it was a woman from Horsfall House to say they could now offer Douglas a room if he was ready to come in. Horsfall had been one of the first homes I had visited, as it was highly recommended, but they had had twenty-five on the waiting list, so I hadn't considered it. I couldn't believe my ears and related my story.

'We will arrange to visit him,' she said.

'I will bring him to you this afternoon, if that is convenient.'

'Half past two would be fine.'

Douglas had been going to Horsfall on a Wednesday, so he recognised where he was and walked off to the day centre. I started after him, but the nurse said, 'Let's see if he will come with me,' and invited me to have a seat in her office.

She came back with Douglas smiling from ear to ear, pointing at the lovely pictures and the light airy rooms.

'Well,' the nurse said, 'I think Douglas is saying everything is well. What do you think?'

I just asked, 'What happens next?'

Notice given, I moved him within the week. Douglas settled very well without the five-day wait, and so began a very happy time at Horsfall House.

# CHAPTER 58

—

T hree years passed very happily. Then one day, when I went in, the matron told me Douglas was in bed; he had had a fall and was still a bit shaky.

Douglas looked very sorry for himself, and was indeed very shaky. I asked the nurse who had come with me if she thought the shakiness could be shock and asked whether they had checked his hips; she confirmed they had, but she would do it again. Sadly this revealed that Douglas had broken his hip.

An ambulance was called, and a trip to Gloucester Hospital confirmed the break. He was admitted, and they hoped the operation would be within the next twenty-four hours. It was late at night by now, and I could not stay with him, but I was told it would be helpful if I came back at eight o'clock the next morning.

I came back to find absolute pandemonium and the thought that Douglas was having a heart attack, or some kind of seizure. I was not allowed in his cubicle but could hear the fear in Douglas's voice. I asked if I could talk to him and calm him down. At first this was refused, but eventually they were for trying anything.

I held his hand; he opened his eyes. The relief was visible.

The nurses had wanted to change his pad. I confirmed I had done an NVQ in moving and handling, and if they turned him to face me I could hold him and talk to him while they changed the pad. This worked a treat and calm returned to the ward. The other patients asked if I could stay the night so they could get some sleep. I apologised and told them I was not allowed, but I would stay until closing time and hope they could catch up with their sleep.

A whole week passed with no operation, and one day the surgeon came to see me when I arrived. He told me they had thought Douglas would get pneumonia, but I was able to confirm he had had the injection. It was agreed that I would come down to the theatre with him to give him the anaesthetic, and be there for when he came round. This I did, and all went well.

Ten days later the surgeon concluded that Douglas was able to go home. The sister from his unit at Horsfall House came to make sure he was safe to return to them, and an ambulance was duly ordered. Sadly during the move his new hip was dislocated, and all agreed he would not be able to tolerate the realignment, so pain management was the order of the day.

Sadly, Douglas died. It was a great relief that he was no longer in pain, but a very sad day for me and his family. He had shown me such freedom of life, and his music had been beautiful. Life with him had been so good. Thank you, darling.

The funeral was to take place in St Philips and St James in Cheltenham, where Douglas had been organist. The orchestra had wanted to take part. We had the cremation first, privately, so the service became a joyful thanksgiving for his life.

When everyone had gone the house seemed much quieter than usual. I sat where Douglas had normally sat, and in the formation of the lights of the village I saw a lion's head. I had always closed the curtains as the lion gave such fear to Douglas, but I had never seen it before tonight.

I continued to help with activities at Horsfall House for another two years until new legislation came in to say I had to have an NVQ. I decided it was time to move on.

On my way home I called in at the newspaper shop for a *Lady* magazine, if it was still going. There it was, just one left.

A cup of tea, and I settled down with my trusty magazine; was she going to have any work for me this time? Too old for housekeeping; too many stairs. Then there it was: someone requiring a carer companion to go on a cruise. Could I do that? *Well, apply and find out,* I told myself.

The telephone rang a couple of days later, and a gentleman thanked me for my enquiry and confirmed he was the client; would this be a problem for me?

He explained his problems. Having been a Met policeman, he had been beaten up and left for dead with a fractured skull, broken back, and two broken legs. Luckily he had been found and repaired, but he was now in a police retirement home near Chichester. He could get to the bathroom with the aid of sticks, but he needed some help to get dressed. I was to have my own cabin next door to him, and he liked the idea of going on one of the Queens; 'I don't go anywhere from one year's end to another.' What did I think?

My head was buzzing. There were no dressings to do, just helping him to dress and pushing him in a wheelchair. I thought I could do that, so I gave him a positive reply.

You could almost hear the tears in his eyes as he said, 'Thank you, thank you. I can't tell you the pleasure you have given me.'

'Would you like to meet me?' I asked.

'No, my dear lady, your voice tells me all I need to know. We will keep in touch, and as soon as I have made the arrangements, I will let you know. Are there any dates I should avoid?'

'No, my diary is empty.'

He confirmed my telephone number, thanked me once again and was gone. I sat for a while, drinking in what I had just agreed to; was I mad or was I mad?

The phone rang again. 'I forgot to tell you my name. I would be pleased if you called me Bert, and could you tell me how much you will charge?'

'Oh, my goodness, there will be no charge; you will be giving me a lovely cruise, and I am very pleased to be of help.'

The next day I was meeting my friend Jean for lunch and shared with her what I had done.

'Well, that's fortunate,' she said. 'We're going to a funeral near Chichester; we'll call in and check him out.'

I said he sounded very nice and genuine, but there was no changing her mind.

'Well,' Jean told me, after her visit, 'he is very nice, good fun and thought it hilarious we came to suss him out. He is of slight build, so he shouldn't be too heavy to push. He's quite tall, good-looking with lovely white hair, and I'd guess in his seventies.'

'Well, that sounds more like boyfriend material,' I said, 'and it's just a job, but thank you very much.'

The weeks passed, then one cold and frosty morning came the call. 'How does the Med sound for three weeks in June?'

'Fantastic,' I replied. 'Which Queen are we going on?'

'The *Victoria*,' he replied. 'Southampton to Southampton, no flying, and I'll make my own way and get assistance to get on the ship when I arrive, so don't worry about that. I'll send the tickets to you directly, if you wouldn't mind giving me your address.'

'Will you be okay packing?' I asked.

'Oh, yes, I have already asked my daughter-in-law if she will get my dinner jacket and trousers dry cleaned and pressed. She's very pleased you are helping me have this adventure.'

'Oh, golly, does that mean I have to get my glad rags on too?'

'Oh, yes, please! It is required at dinner time; not that I will be able to do any dancing, but it will be fun to watch with a glass of champagne. Please keep in touch if there are any questions any time; I'm not going anywhere until June,' and he laughed a hearty laugh and was gone.

Just four months to lose weight and get a new wardrobe. I wondered if he realised how much pleasure this was giving me as well.

# CHAPTER 59

The weeks just whizzed past, and before I knew it the day arrived. With taxi booked, cases packed and water switched off, the knock at the door told me I was about to set off on a big adventure.

As we approached the docks I wondered how we would find our ship, but I needn't have worried as there she was, big and gleaming in the sunlight. Once the taxi had parked, porters were swiftly at the boot taking my luggage; all I had to look after was my hand luggage and handbag.

Tickets checked, passport control cleared, I climbed the very gentle slope up the gangway to be received by welcoming staff who helped me to the lift for my cabin. Cabin found, I collapsed on the very comfortable bed, took my coat off and prepared to meet Bert.

I knocked on Bert's cabin door and realised it was ajar. 'Come in!' came the call.

I entered, and there was Bert, resplendent as Jean had described, with a big welcoming smile that said everything. 'How are you?' he asked. 'Did you have a good journey?'

'Good,' I said to both. 'Your cabin is very spacious.'

'Yes,' he said. 'It's for a wheelchair passenger, so it gives us plenty of room to manoeuvre.' He ordered tea, and the conversation just flowed.

Soon it was ship sailing time, so out we went onto the balcony for sailaway. His height proved not to be a problem for me, so that was a relief.

'It isn't a formal evening this evening, as everyone is unpacking,' Bert said, 'so no need to change tonight.'

'Oh, my goodness, I must do my job now. I'll unpack for you, then I will leave you to freshen up while I unpack.'

'Thank you,' he said in gratitude.

Lovely roomy wardrobes soon had everything stowed away: a place for everything. I was back in my cabin and just about to freshen up when the phone rang. It was Bert; he had had a fall and he couldn't get up.

Luckily I hadn't fastened his door, so I dashed in to find Bert on the floor by the telephone. He had tripped on the step into his bathroom, lost his balance and landed on his bum, then had to drag himself across the carpet to get to the phone.

Nothing seemed to hurt except the carpet burns on his legs. I asked him to lie flat on the floor with his legs as straight as possible; both heels looked equal, so hopefully no broken hips.

By getting him onto his knees with the help of the bedside table I was able to get him upright, then sitting on the side of the bed. There was still nothing hurting except the burns. I quickly got my first aid bag and applied some medicated cream to the affected areas.

'Can I get you another cup of tea?' I suggested.

He gave me a wicked look and said, 'I think I need something stronger than that!'

He was looking at the complementary bottle of champagne already in an ice bucket, to celebrate our safe arrival on the ship and look forward to a safe and happy journey. I wondered if this was a good idea, but he looked so keen I felt I couldn't say no. I handed him the bottle to open and held the glasses for him to pour; a clink of the glasses, and all was well. If he had fallen when the ship wasn't moving, though, how safe would he be when it was?

I decided to ask. He of course didn't know, so I suggested that, if he promised to be a good boy and I promised to be a good girl, we could ask for the bed to be made into two, then I would be on hand to be of help. I could use my cabin to shower and change and give him a break from me. What did he think?

He looked at me in surprise, but also with a look of relief. 'Would you really do that? I have to say I have been worried.'

'Then that is what we will do.' I rang the bell straight away for our cabin steward, who said it wasn't a problem; he would organise our beds while we were at dinner.

The wheelchair was fine on the moving ship, and dinner was delicious, so all was well.

For the next two days we were at sea crossing the notorious Bay of Biscay, but for us the sun was shining. We docked at Lisbon to refuel and stock up on supplies; people got off, but one look at the steep gangway and Bert decided it was not for him, so we decided to do a tour of the ship while the other passengers were gone.

This we did, and to Bert's delight we found the one-armed bandits, although they were closed while the ship was docked; 'We must have a go at those one evening.' Lovely shops, selling everything from evening dresses to toothpaste. We found a beautiful ballroom which turned into an interesting venue for afternoon tea, with a quintet playing and waiters serving with white gloves. A library, several bars, swimming pools, deck games, gym, everything you could wish for. We decided a cup of tea was required, so we decided to try the all-day top floor restaurant. Fantastic bird's eye view of all around us.

There were coach trips to be booked when the ship docked at beautiful places, but Bert wasn't able to travel by coach. I had noticed taxis, though, so if he wanted to go ashore we could go places by taxi.

Bert seemed very happy just enjoying the ship and people-watching, especially when they went ashore by tender. Then came the day we docked in Rome, and the gangway was relatively shallow, so with the aid of the crew Bert was taken off with me following. We found a taxi that would take us on a trip around the city, which included lunch at our driver's godfather's hotel, which was splendid, and seeing some of ancient Rome. Back to the ship and tea in our room with a nap.

Venice was an exciting trip as the *Queen Victoria* had been built nearby, so she was allowed to dock just off St Mark's Square. When you walked around the promenade deck, you felt as if you were part of the city.

Malta was another destination where we could get off the ship. We got another taxi and had a tour of the island: very interesting, with empty army barracks still rented to the British Army.

One evening, while all dressed up in his white dinner jacket and black shirt with a white bow tie, Bert asked after dinner if I would take him to the champagne bar, park him and sit where I could see him if he got into difficulty. This I did, and I watched as he and ladies in their finery sat and chatted and drank champagne, all having a merry time.

Eventually the other guests slowly moved away to their beds, and Bert gave me a wave. 'Well, I haven't had so much fun for ages; thank you very much. Hope it wasn't too boring for you.'

'Well, I did have one or two offers to dance, but they understood when I explained what I was doing, and had a laugh. Glad you had a good evening.'

All too soon we were docking in Gibraltar, the last port of call before returning to Southampton. We reflected on the adventure and both agreed it had been a lovely experience. Tentatively he asked, 'Could we do it again next year?'

I was agreeably surprised. 'Really? That would be wonderful. Where would you like to go next?'

'Well, I fancy crossing the Atlantic and seeing New York; what do you think?'

'Sounds good to me,' I replied, and so began six years cruising the world.

Sadly the next Christmas I got a card from Bert's daughter to say Bert had died peacefully in his sleep, and thanking me for giving him such pleasure organising and going on the cruises.

# CHAPTER 60

To say I missed Bert was an understatement. Not that he was in touch constantly, but he gave a feeling of excitement in the lonely winter nights.

Then, one day, doing the usual shopping, there it was: the *Lady* magazine. Should I give it another go? Why not; what did I have to lose?

So, home with a cup of tea, I sat down to enjoy my trusty magazine. Eventually I got to the back pages and flicked through the usual *housekeeper, nanny, butler, live-in carer* requests until there it was: companion for formal evenings, Wotton-under-Edge. That was just down the road; should I apply? Why not?

It was about a month before I had a reply. Eventually the phone rang and a very pleasant voice explained he had received many responses, but they all seemed to live in London and places miles away, so it was with some relief he had received my application.

His name was Norman, and he had been married for fifty years to his darling Jane, who had been taken from him by the dreaded cancer. He was a Mason, and that involved quite a few social evenings during the year. Did I enjoy dancing, and did I know Philip Evans, who he knew lived in the same village?

'Yes, very well; he is chairman of one of the trusts in the village, and I am one of the trustees.' This seemed to gain me some brownie points.

After explaining what he was looking for, he eventually asked if I would meet him for lunch at the Hare and Hounds on Tuesday next. I agreed and looked forward to meeting him.

It was a cold, foggy, frosty day when we were due to have our lunch meeting. He was waiting in the car park, so I was pleased I was not late. He was tall and in his seventies, but still had a good head of hair.

He came across to the car, opened the door and asked if I was the lady he was waiting for. 'If your name is Norman,' I said. He confirmed it was, so we walked quickly into the warmth of the hotel.

The connection with Philip was top of the conversation; it transpired that he was Norman's boss, who he liked very much. I explained that two of my husbands had been Masons, so I was used to the social gatherings; this also seemed to go down well. All too soon the lunch was over, and arrangements to meet again were made.

The Christmas season was busy, going to the different Lodges' seasonal get-togethers and meeting Norman's friends. These gatherings usually finished quite late, so Norman would invite me to stay the night, rather than driving home alone on frosty roads. When there wasn't an occasion, Norman asked me to stay the weekend as he was enjoying my company very much, and I enjoyed cooking his favourite meals. Norman enjoyed cooking himself, but it was good some evenings just to take a meal out of the freezer.

One evening Norman suddenly asked if I would enjoy a cruise. I could hardly believe my ears. I related my cruising with Bert and how much I had enjoyed it, but I had not paid for the cruises as I went as his carer; I was afraid I could not afford a cruise.

'Well, when my wife and I used to go I paid for her,' Norman said, so he didn't have a problem with that.

'Well, as long as you wouldn't expect wifely duties I will accept.'

He roared with laughter and agreed.

So continued twenty years of happy friendship. Norman died on 8 October 2023, aged ninety-two.

# CHAPTER 61

—

Through all my eighty-two years, losing friends and family has been the hardest thing, always leaving a hole in my life that is constantly just around the corner in my thoughts.

Today I find myself in a home for elderly people, having spent two months in hospital waiting to be released. According to the powers that be I am no longer able to look after myself. Being told I could no longer drive was a double whammy.

With the help of a social worker I visited home after home in which even the social worker wouldn't have agreed to leave me. Until we came to Millbrook Lodge, just five miles from my daughter in Leckhampton, owned and run by the Orders of St John.

I could bring my desk, bookcase and books, blanket box and ornaments. The biggest bed I have ever seen was installed. All I had to do was ring a bell and someone would come, whether it was for a cup of tea or help to get in or out of bed. Meals served in the dining room, and activities every weekday; what more could I want?

So here I am at the end of my journey.

My apologies to family and friends if I missed bits out, and my eternal thanks to all who have made my life an adventure.

www.ingramcontent.com/pod-product-compliance
Lightning Source LLC
Chambersburg PA
CBHW021222090426
42740CB00006B/327